I'm still
scrambling

I'm still scrambling

RANDALL CUNNINGHAM

and

Steve Wartenberg

DOUBLEDAY
New York   London   Toronto   Sydney   Auckland

PUBLISHED BY DOUBLEDAY
a division of Bantam Doubleday Dell Publishing Group, Inc.
1540 Broadway, New York, New York 10036

DOUBLEDAY and the portrayal of an anchor with a dolphin
are trademarks of Doubleday, a division of Bantam
Doubleday Dell Publishing Group, Inc.

BOOK DESIGN BY CLAIRE NAYLON VACCARO

Library of Congress Cataloging-in-Publication Data

Cunningham, Randall.
    I'm still scrambling / Randall Cunningham and Steve Wartenberg. —1st ed.
        p.   cm.
    1. Cunningham, Randall.   2. Football players—United States—Biography.
3. Philadelphia Eagles (Football team)   I. Wartenberg, Steve.   II. Title.
GV939.C85A3   1993
796.332′092—dc20
    [B]
                                                                    93-8368
                                                                    CIP

ISBN 0-385-47142-4
Copyright © 1993 by Randall Cunningham and Steve Wartenberg
All Rights Reserved
Printed in the United States of America
October 1993

First Edition

10   9   8   7   6   5   4   3   2   1

*This book is dedicated to my family and friends
and to the believers in God and
the nonbelievers who will become believers.*

R.C.

*To Joey Wallace, N. "Woody" Allen
and Michael Hillanbrand. My heroes.*

S.W.

introduction

The Randall Cunningham you'll get to know in this book is the real me. I'm not perfect; I make mistakes. But God didn't create us to be perfect. He created each person to be different and each person has to strive to be the best person they can be and discover the special talents God has given them. That's what I try to do and maybe, from reading this book, some people—especially kids—can use my faith and my strength as an example.

prologue

The Philadelphia Eagles open the 1991 season in Green Bay. On the first play of the second quarter, Packer linebacker Bryce Paup slices through the Eagles' offensive line, stumbles forward on all fours and slams into Randall Cunningham's left knee. It bends backward and Randall falls to the turf clutching his knee.

Before the game, as I was warming up, I remember thinking to myself, "Randall, this is your seventh season in the NFL and you've never really been hurt too bad. You better be careful today, you better not get hurt." In the past, whenever negative thoughts like that came into my mind, my faith in God pushed them out. But this time they lingered for some reason. I guess this was God's way of testing me.

I failed the test. I lost my faith for a few minutes and that's all it takes.

In the first quarter we had some trouble moving the ball. I threw three passes and each time I got hit right after I released the ball. We got the ball again to start the second quarter and I said to Richie

Kotite, our new head coach, "Hey, let's call a regular play—14A." I wanted to hit Keith Byars, our fullback, with something quick out of the backfield and get the offense warmed up and moving down the field. Richie said run it. As I dropped back, I read their defense and saw the Packers had the play covered. But Calvin Williams, our wide receiver lined up on the right side, was one-on-one with their cornerback and had a step on him. I sensed a little pressure coming up the middle as I set to throw and had to release the ball a little quicker than I wanted. I was looking downfield, toward Calvin, when —BAM!—I got hit in the left knee and went down.

I felt something snap inside my knee. I rolled around on the grass, holding my knee and saying over and over, "Who hit me? Who hit me?" Then I heard people on their sideline shouting for the guy who hit me to get off the field.

I just wanted to move around and stretch my leg so it wouldn't get tight. Plus, I wanted to give Jim McMahon time to get warmed up. Then the trainers and doctors got to me and started moving my leg around and poking and prodding it and asking me over and over how I felt. It felt a little loose, but it didn't hurt too bad and I figured I'd be back in the game after a few plays, or, at the worst, it was a sprain or something like that and I'd miss the rest of the game and be back the following week. I wanted to jog off the field by myself, but after I took a step I said, "Nope, I can't do it," and the trainers helped me to the sideline.

I sat down on the bench and Dr. DiStefano, our team doctor, started examining my knee and right away we knew it was serious. When he bent my knee to the outside it kept going out to the left, in a shape like this: >. It didn't hurt when he did it, but we both knew the ligament was blown. He told me it was the medial collateral ligament and that the posterior cruciate ligament might also be torn, but that he couldn't tell for sure without X-rays. At some point, Richie came over and said he wanted me to stand next to him on the sideline to signal in the plays to Jim. I just kind of looked up at him and said, "Richie, I'm gone," and he knew what I meant. He got a sad look in his eyes, patted me on the shoulder and walked away like he was in a daze.

As I was being carted off the field, a lot of the guys on the team came over and hugged me and the fans cheered and I gave them a little wave. The only problem was the truck went the wrong way, to the wrong tunnel, and we had to turn around and drive back the way we came, all the way across to the other side of the stadium. The fans cheered again and I waved again and finally we made it back to the locker room. That's when it really hit me: I'm injured. I can't play. I could be out for the season.

SEPTEMBER 2, 1991

In the morning, Randall goes to Graduate Hospital in Philadelphia, where a magnetic resonance imaging (MRI) test confirms Dr. Di-Stefano's diagnosis: complete tears of both the medial collateral and posterior cruciate ligaments. Randall is out for the season, possibly longer, and some wonder if he will ever be able to come back and be the same player who has electrified the NFL the past six seasons.

From the hospital, Randall drives to Veterans Stadium for a press conference. As he enters the meeting room on crutches and walks slowly to the table set up at the front, a hush falls over the room, which is packed with about 50 reporters and several television crews. "Everyone seemed so serious, like they were at a funeral or something," Randall says later. "When someone asked me about the operation, I tried to lighten things up and joked, 'I'm going to ask them to put in one of those spare parts from the Six Million Dollar Man.'" A couple of reporters laugh at Randall's joke and the tension eases a little. The questions continue and Randall remains upbeat and optimistic as he answers them patiently:

"The worst thing about it is knowing that it's not a dream. I thought I'd wake up this morning and be able to say, 'Nah, I didn't get injured.' But I'm injured and I have to go through what it takes to get back. It's good I have friends like Keith Byars and [Keith and Kenny] Jackson and Ron Solt and the other guys on the team, 'cause they've rallied around me and said, 'Hey, you'll be back.' And they joked around saying, 'You'll be back in six weeks.' That made me feel a lot better.

"Maybe this is a test of my courage or a test that I need to get through. I think I've been through the toughest [tests] already, with my parents passing away, friends passing away, surgery on my right knee right out of high school. And, overall, I've got a lot of people who support me and I'm not going to let them down and I'm going to go out and do whatever I have to do to bounce back.

"I'll come back and play my same style. I've always run and even if I can't run as fast, if I don't have 4.4 speed, it's not the end of the world. But I'm sure dedication can bring the speed back and maybe even get it faster . . . I'm looking forward to getting the operation over with and starting the rehab."

In other words, Randall Cunningham will be back and he'll be back scrambling. That evening, Cunningham flys to Los Angeles, where his knee is examined by Dr. Clarence Shields, who operated on Cunningham's right knee after his senior year in high school.

My senior year in high school, I injured my right knee. I went to a couple of different doctors and finally my brother Sam, who was a star fullback for USC and the New England Patriots, took me to see Dr. Shields. He told me I had a bone disease where my muscle was too strong for my bone and kept contracting and pulling away from the bone. He operated, pinned the muscle down to the bone and everything worked out fine and I established a great relationship with Dr. Shields.

SEPTEMBER 4, 1991

I went under the knife today. Dr. Shields stitched together my medial collateral ligament and later told me it was like sewing together strings of spaghetti. The posterior cruciate ligament was a different story. The day before the operation he laid out my options. Number one was to take the tendon from under my left kneecap and run it back to where the posterior cruciate ligament attaches to the bone and clamp it on with screws. But that messes up another part of my knee and we didn't like that option. The second option was to use a synthetic ligament, but he told me that wasn't 100 percent effective. The third option was to use an Achilles tendon from a cadaver. "What's a cadaver?" I asked. When he told me it was a dead person's body it sent chills up my spine.

I asked if the part from the cadaver would be strong enough and he said it would be even stronger than my original posterior cruciate ligament. Dr. Shields said he would attach it to the bone, bring it up and clamp it to the outside of my knee. "Will I be able to run again?" I asked. He said eventually I would be able to get back most or all of my speed. We decided that was the way to go.

I checked into the hospital that night and the nurses asked me if I wanted some pills to help me sleep. I said no, but I soon wished I had taken them. I woke up every half hour and worried about the operation. Finally morning came and they wheeled me into the recovery area outside the operating room and sedated me. There were all these other people lying there and most of them were just coming out of surgery. Some were looking around the room and looking at me with one eye open and the other closed and some looked like they were dead. I figured everyone was just scared. Then they came in and put in my I.V. and the next thing I knew I had been operated on and was back in the recovery room. I became one of those people with one eye open and one eye closed. I was so tired and my eyes were so heavy, it was all I could do to open one at a time. I felt like

Fred Flintstone when he has to put toothpicks under his eyelids to keep them open.

They wheeled me back to my room and a few minutes later a woman came in and said it was time to start exercising my knee. I just laughed, but she was serious. "I just had surgery," I told her, but she said I had to lift my knee a few inches. I tried to lift my leg and in my mind it was up off the bed a few inches, but when I looked, I saw that it hadn't moved an inch. I kept trying and I started panting like a dog I was so tired. But still I couldn't move it. She came back a couple of hours later and I tried again and this time I lifted my leg an inch. The long road back had begun.

NOVEMBER 15, 1991

After a week of rehab in Los Angeles, Randall flew back to Philadel-phia and began working out under the watchful eye of Eagles' trainer Otho Davis and his assistant Dave Price.

Otho Davis: I think he's gonna test my fortitude. Randall is such a competitor, so I hope that doesn't end up being a fault because he'll want to work too hard and get ahead of himself. The thing about tissue is that there are only two things that will do it any good—rest and the good Lord. From my experience I've learned that it takes patience and before it's over, we'll have to put a halter on him and pull in the reins and he'll get irritated and disgusted.

Today is a typical day for Randall. He arrives at Veterans Sta-dium in the morning for the start of his three-hour rehab session. The locker room is long and narrow and, as you enter, the first lockers on the left belong to the quarterbacks. A door midway down the left side of the locker room leads to the team weight room and a door midway down the right side leads to "Otho's Wildlife Preserve" —the training room. Behind the training room—and separated by

Otho Davis's office and a glass partition—is the rehab room, which contains the various devices of torture that injured players use to strengthen their damaged parts.

Randall changes at his locker and heads to the weight room, where he usually starts off his day by lifting for half an hour. "I'm so skinny, probably the skinniest player in the NFL," Randall jokes. "I have to build up my upper body." Jerome Brown is lifting and sweating and listening to a 2 Live Crew tape. The music is loud and nasty.

"Hey turn that down," Randall shouts over the music.

"Shut up," Brown answers with a smile. "I'm not in here that often so I get to listen to whatever I want to."

"I know better than to argue with Jerome even though his bark is louder than his bite," Randall says. "Jerome's a big puppy dog and he just likes to hear himself bark. Jerome is the 2 Live Crew of the NFL. He's loud, he's fun loving, he's outgoing. A lot of people just see this side of Jerome, but the guys on the team know the real Jerome. Jerome has a big heart and is lovable and would do anything for you."

After he finishes lifting, Randall heads into the training room where the mark of Otho Davis (a Texan through and through) is everywhere. The walls are lined with various western motif momentos, including photos, horse collars, saddles, and an old wooden toilet seat. Lift up the seat and underneath is a photo of a very obese and naked women. Hanging in the center of the room is an impressive collection of football helmets that date back to the start of the sport. Otho makes a wicked-hot chili and often makes up a big pot for the players. "Otho is the best trainer in the league," Randall says. "And he's more than a trainer—he's everyone's psychiatrist. My first year here he grabbed me and pulled me aside one day and said, 'You have to be strong mentally and keep your confidence.' We developed a rapport and now I can come in here and talk to him about everything."

Randall walks into the back room and assistant athletic trainer Dave Price hooks him up to the Biodex machine, a computerized *apparatus that measures and develops leg strength. Randall sits down with his left knee bent at a 90 degree angle and his leg strapped to a metal rod. He then begins the first of several sets of leg raises. At first Randall lifts the weight easily, but his leg quickly becomes tired and starts shaking. Sweat pours down his face and Randall grunts louder and louder with every repetition and his entire leg and then his body begin shaking more and more violently. Finally he finishes and smiles, takes a brief rest and does another repetition.*

While Randall works on the Biodex, injured offensive lineman Ben Tamburello rides the stationary bike.

"Say hello to everyone reading my book," Randall says.

"Hello," Tamburello answers.

"See, offensive linemen always listen to their quarterback," Randall says with a smile. "Ben has been a consistent lineman for us since he came here in 1987. But early in training camp this year he tore up his knee pretty bad. What was it you did?"

"I tore the interior cruciate and have some bone spurs," Tamburello answers as he pedals.

"Anyway, Ben has been my inspiration," Randall continues. "He hasn't missed a day since July and he's in great shape now, much better than me. When I first started rehabbing, Ben pushed me and encouraged me. Now, I'll try and do the same thing for Ben Smith, our great young cornerback. A couple weeks ago, Ben tore up his knee in a game against Cleveland. He got operated on last week and has a long recovery ahead of him. Ben's a young player and has never been through anything like this, so he'll need to get a little guidance from Ben and me. It's kind of like we're our own team back here and this is our practice field and we have to stick together."

Tamburello: I got hurt the first week of training camp and was put on preseason injured reserve. The first month I was in here by myself every day. You'd never wish an injury on anyone, but since Randall's been here, he's really picked things up and made this a very positive place. I see how enthusiastic and positive he is and it's contagious.

While the two players work, Price sits at his desk doing paperwork and eating a bowl of cereal.

Antone Davis, the Eagles' 1991 first round draft choice and a 300-pound plus right offensive tackle, walks into the training room singing a song.

"Hey Antone, you can't be singing in here, we're trying to record on this tape recorder for my book," Randall says.

Davis looks at Randall, smiles and keeps singing.

"We call Antone 'Burger' and all you have to do is look at his butt and you'll know why," Randall says, loud enough for Davis to hear. "But enough about Antone; he gets too much press already. Let's get back to my workout.

"Basically, Otho and Dave set up my program, but Dave is the one I work with every day. When I first came back after the operation, we sat down to talk and Dave asked me if I was willing to go through what it would take to get back. I said yes. Now, Dave pushes me and gets me to work hard and he rewards me with an apple every day."

"But only if you say please," Price retorts.

"Please," Randall says and Price tosses him an apple. "See, he's making me a more humble person. Dave knows me and knows that I like to be pushed, but he also knows when it's time to back off."

Dave Price: When Randall first got back here, we told him you either do what we tell you or you won't play again; listen to us, we've been through this before. He realized we were right. Randall never had to depend on anyone else before, and now, all of a sudden, he has to depend on other people, even though it's him doing all the work.

We approach every individual differently. There is no such thing as a cookbook approach to rehab. The first phase is a protective *phase and that's the most important phase. You have to make sure the surgery heals properly and you don't do anything to damage it. The second phase, which we're in now, is a moderate phase where Randall can return to certain activities, but not full bore. This lasts about three or four months. Then he can return to activities that are specific to playing football: running, dropping back, agility drills. But we don't have any set dates for anything. We take it one day at a time. So far, there haven't been any setbacks, such as swelling or pain from breaking down scar tissue too soon, which is a little unusual. But I credit this to Randall following everything the doctors and Otho and I have told him.*

Safety Rich Miano enters the rehab room.

"Hey dude," Randall calls to Miano, "Can you pick up that trash can over there so I can throw away this apple?"

Miano holds up the trash can. "Let's see if you can make a shot," he says. Randall hits the side of the can.

"Hey, make sure you tell everyone in your book how I picked you off in college," says Miano, who played for the University of Hawaii, while Randall played for the University of Nevada-Las Vegas (UNLV).

"That's what you tell me every chance you get, but I don't remember you picking me off," Randall shoots back.

"He won't admit it, but I picked him off," Miano says. "We used to go down to Vegas every year, whip 'em on the field, win money in the casinos, steal their girls and then go home."

With that, Miano quickly leaves before Randall can get in another shot. Randall begins another set on the Biodex machine, and while he's grunting and sweating and straining, McMahon, who is in the training room and separated from the rehab room by a glass partition, begins making obscene gestures toward Randall, who tries hard not to laugh.

"That's just Jim; he's crazy," Randall says after he finishes his set. "Listen to what he told me the other day. When you get a knee

injury one of the things you have to do is break down the scar tissue by bending your knee back a little further each day. And every time you break up a little scar tissue it hurts—a lot. But Jim, who's proba- bly been hurt more than any player in the history of the NFL and is an expert on the subject, told me what he does to break it up. He says he just bends his knees and drops his butt to the floor and breaks it all up at once. Jim's nuts."

At first my knee was swollen up like a softball. And not a regular softball, but one of those extra-big softballs they use for little kids that don't go very far and can't hurt anyone. Gradually the swelling has gone down and I'm getting some strength back in my knee and I can bend it further and further. Right now, I can bend it 140 de- grees if I really push. All the way back is 160 degrees and that's where you can touch your heel to your butt.

Last week I went back to Los Angeles to have Dr. Shields check my knee. He tested my range of motion and it was about 120 de- grees and he said that was great for three months and I told him it had only been two months and a week. He said I was ahead of schedule and could start riding the stationary bike and walking in the swimming pool. But Dr. Shields told me not to do any hamstring work yet because that could pull the bone graft apart. Then they ran some tests to see how much the posterior cruciate had moved and it hadn't moved at all, which was a great sign. It means that the ca- daver's ligament is holding in place. He also said I could start run- ning at the end of January and I told him I'd be ready to run in a week. Dr. Shields just laughed and said not to rush it.

When I got back to Philly last week, I rode the stationary bike for the first time. I started off doing 10 minutes and my leg got real tired. I made it up to 15 minutes after a couple of days and yesterday I tried to go 20, but my leg got so tired and started shaking so much I had to stop.

One thing I've learned is that I have to be patient and listen to what the doctors and trainers tell me. Patience was never something I had much of, but now I'm learning that patience is a virtue.

JANUARY 9, 1992

We finished up the season at home against the Washington Redskins (who would go on to win the Super Bowl). The week before, at home, the Dallas Cowboys beat us 25-13 to knock us out of the playoffs. That was a killer.

Against Washington, we were pumped up to play, but got behind early. At halftime Seth Joyner, our Pro Bowl linebacker, got pretty upset and he started hollering at the offensive line, saying they had to block better for the quarterback—who was Jeff Kemp. McMahon, who had already come back from a knee injury during the season, cracked four ribs in Game 14 and was out for the season. Seth was very serious and upset and was saying if people didn't want to do their job, they should pick a new job. Seth and Ron Heller, our left tackle, started hollering at each other and Jerome Brown just stepped in and said, "Enough, we win together and we lose together." That's all we needed to hear and we went out and dominated the second half and won 24-22 to finish the season 10-6.

After the game ends, Joyner grabs Randall and the two embrace in front of the Eagles' bench. "I can't wait till he comes back scrambling," Joyner says. "God, I can't wait."

The week before the Dallas game, after Jim got hurt but we still had a chance to make the playoffs, I went in and talked to Richie and told him I could be ready if we made it to the Super Bowl. He looked at me like I was crazy or kidding, but I was serious. I knew I wouldn't be 100 percent by the end of January, but I figured I could play with a brace and still have enough speed to drop back and get rid of the ball and take the hits when they came. I would risk getting hurt again for the chance to play in the Super Bowl. You don't get many chances to play for the championship and I figured if Jim was hurt, I could go in and get the job done.

But Richie told me to forget it.

MARCH 3, 1992

Randall is at the stadium rehabbing and while he lifts weights to strengthen his knee, Ben Smith, the injured cornerback, slowly pedals the stationary bike. As usual, the two trade insults, which helps to pass the time.

"I'm telling you, when I get back I'm going to geek you," Randall says. "You know what a geek is?"

"Yeah, you're a geek," Smith answers.

"No man, a geek is where I hit you so hard you go GEEEEEEEEK! And I'm gonna geek you. What do you weigh—a buck 80?"

"If that."

"With full pads on, I'll be coming at you with 225 pounds," Randall says. "I'm telling you that now."

"Some of those big running backs are 230 pounds and I take them down no problem," Smith fires back.

"You just jump on their back and hold on till Seth and some of the other guys get over there. I'm telling you, I'm coming around that corner and I'm gonna lay some wood into you."

"You ain't getting around no corner with a knee brace on and running a 4.8," Smith says.

"I'll be lucky to run 4.8," Randall says.

"You better run at least 4.8 or you'll be in trouble," Smith says. "And I'm telling you, if you run around my corner, you'll get up looking out your earhole."

Speaking of running, I finally got the go-ahead to begin. To be honest, I had cheated a bit and did a little jogging in mid-January, but not too much.

Right before the Super Bowl, I went back to Los Angeles and Dr. Shields checked my knee. He said the strength in my hamstring was 85 percent and the strength in my quadracep was 84 percent—which was pretty good—and he gave me the go-ahead to start some light running. My first run was the next day in Las Vegas, where I spend a lot of my time in the off-season. I worked out at Gold's Gym and after I lifted, I went three minutes—slowly—on the treadmill. That gave me a lot of confidence and the next day I went out on the track and did some real jogging—three minutes—and then ran a nice easy little sprint at the end just to prove to myself that I could do it. I could. I couldn't go very fast, but at least I was running. Gradually I started running more and more and now, a little more than a month later, I can run a few laps around the track and my speed is improving.

After he finishes working his legs, Randall heads into the training room to get his knee iced and massaged. Jerome Brown is on the training table next to Randall. A few weeks ago Brown had his knee scoped and he's back in Philly to have the trainers give him the once-over.

"You're writing a book?" Brown asks. "Make sure you tell everyone the truth."

"I will," Randall says.

"Tell them how you used to party and drink all the time in college," Brown says.

"I will," Randall insists. "But I wasn't any different than any other college student. I went to beer bashes and once I remember drinking almost a case of beer with a couple of friends and then I puked for half an hour. But now I don't drink at all."

"Doesn't matter," Brown continues. "You got to tell the kids that

you overcame something. That you used to party and gave it up for football and God."

"That's your book," Randall says. "You guys at the University of Miami were known for partying. With a capital P."

"No way," Brown says. "We were known for winning. With a capital W."

There's not another defensive tackle in the league as good as Jerome. This past season, standing and watching from the sidelines, I got a chance to really appreciate Jerome's talent. We rotate our defensive tackles to keep them fresh and one time Jerome came out and told me he was a little frustrated. "I'm trying the over-arm technique [on the offensive lineman], but it's not working," Jerome said. "I keep thinking it's going to be a pass play and it's a run. I have to read the guard's technique better."

So Jerome stood there and studied the offensive guard's technique that series. The next time the defense went out, Jerome was back in and for the rest of the game he dominated his man. That's an example of how smart Jerome is.

MARCH 28, 1992

I just got back from Las Vegas and Camp Cunningham, where everything went great.

Camp Cunningham—which is what the media started calling it —was something I came up with at the end of the season. People kept asking me what I would do to get ready for training camp and, when I started thinking about it, I came up with the idea of taking the guys who I'll be throwing the ball to—Keith Byars, Keith Jackson, Fred Barnett and Calvin Williams—to Las Vegas for a week of training camp. Their time is valuable, so I decided to pay them and the whole thing—including airfare, hotels, food and salaries—cost something like $30,000. It was money well spent. It might even be a tax deduction, I'll have to ask my accountant to check up on that. Eric Dickerson, who is one of my best friends, spent the week working out with us, but since he isn't on our team, he had to pay his own way. Mike McDade, who played wide receiver for me at UNLV, was also there. Roger Craig was supposed to show, but never did.

Everyone took the week very seriously. We got up early, ate breakfast, went over to Gold's Gym to work out for about an hour and then over to Rebel Field at UNLV and ran pass patterns. Even though I still don't have my speed back, my leg feels fine and the main thing is for me to get used to playing with a brace on. The first day out I had the receivers run basic 14-yard patterns, but my throws were all five yards short. So basically, all I was doing was killing worms, which showed me that I was rusty and needed a lot of work.

When we worked, we worked hard, but in the evenings we had fun. We saw a few shows and checked out a couple casinos. That week showed me my arm was fine and my knee was coming along right on schedule, but I had to keep working hard. Even more important, it was great to be with the guys again and feel like I was part of the team. I was especially grateful to Keith Byars for coming. His wife, Margaret Bell (who is a very talented gospel singer), was about eight-and-a-half months pregnant. I don't think she wanted him to go, but "Tank," who is probably my closest friend on the team, knew how important it was to me, so he showed up.

Keith Byars: I'm going to get Randall back when he gets married and his wife gets pregnant. I'm going to come up with something for him to do and we'll see how much of a sacrifice he's willing to make for me. My wife and baby [Taylor Renay, who was born on April 19] were very much on my mind and I carried around a beeper with me and was ready to hop on the next plane back to Philly. My wife was pretty mad and she said, "I'll never forgive you if you miss this baby. I'll tell the baby your Daddy was in Vegas when you were born." But luckily I made it back in plenty of time and I won't have to face her wrath.

I did it for Randall. He's a good friend and he's at a very important time, where he wants to get back his confidence and know he can come back. I've been through it before after an operation on my foot, and I know it's not easy.

We had a lot of fun and joked around, but once we stepped on the field it was serious. Randall looked good. He's not in football shape yet, but he's getting there. He hasn't lost anything from his arm—it's as deadly as ever. But the first day he was using all arm to throw the ball, which I guess is natural after a knee injury. It's hard to just go out there on Day One after an injury like that and do it like you did it before. You have to retrain those muscles and that's what he's starting to do.

Fred Barnett: Randall is back further than I thought he'd be. His leg seemed pretty strong and his arm is definitely strong—maybe even stronger than before. A couple of us were complaining that he was throwing it too hard. It was nice not only to work out and get the timing on certain patterns down, but it was also good to be together and get some team unity. I wish the whole team could have been there. Randall could afford it.

JUNE 25, 1992

I was out somewhere today, I think it was a shopping mall or something, and a guy, a stranger, came up to me and asked, "Did you hear about Jerome?" I said no and he said Jerome Brown died in a car crash. My first thought was, "Don't be joking around like that, that's not even close to being funny." Then someone else told me the same thing, but I still didn't want to believe it. Then I got home and Eric Allen, our cornerback, called and told me the same thing and it finally hit me and I had to accept that Jerome was dead.

One of the first things I thought about was how lucky I was to have known Jerome. Just a month ago, I was down in Brooksville, Florida, Jerome's hometown, with a bunch of the guys from the team, for his football camp. Jerome held this camp every year, free-of-charge, for all the kids in Brooksville. It was great to see how much everyone in that town—black and white—loved Jerome and how close he was to his family.

JULY 1, 1992

I got back the other day from Jerome's funeral and it was an incredible experience. Everyone in Brooksville attended, plus Jerome's friends and teammates from all over the country. The church was filled and there were probably three hundred people outside who couldn't get in. At first it was sad, but then people started rejoicing that Jerome was going to a better place and then his parents got up and everyone started singing and dancing. Alonzo Highsmith, Jerome's teammate at the University of Miami, got up and told some funny and touching stories about Jerome and that made everyone feel better. At one point I felt like I couldn't breathe and was starting to hyperventilate. I was sitting next to Keith Byars and he gave me his handkerchief and I tried to be strong, but the tears started to flow.

It was amazing to see how strong Seth Joyner and Clyde Simmons were. They are probably Jerome's closest friends on the team, along with Reggie White and some of the other guys on the defensive line. But they were there for Jerome's family. I guess they knew that's what Jerome would have wanted them to do.

JULY 24, 1992

It's the first day of training camp and all the Eagles and want-to-be Eagles are gathered at West Chester University, located about 30 miles west of Philadelphia. All eyes (and cameras) are focused on Randall. It rained the day before and the grass is still a little slippery. At one corner of the field, the quarterbacks work on taking snaps from center and dropping back. Randall, wearing a brace on his left knee, squats behind Dave Alexander, takes the snap, drops back and promptly slips and falls on his butt. With everyone watching, Randall, a small smile on his face, picks himself up and sets up under Alexander again. He takes the snap, drops back and this time he doesn't slip.

Later in the practice, Kotite calls for a passing drill where there are no linemen—only receivers and defensive backs. This will be Randall's first time throwing the ball, but Jeff Kemp, who started the last two games of the 1991 season after McMahon went down, steps in for the first several plays. McMahon is absent, embroiled in a contract dispute that won't be settled until two weeks before the season begins.

After Kemp finishes throwing, Randall steps in. Barnett runs down the sideline, with a step on the defender, but Randall's pass sails over his head. On Randall's next pass attempt, the receiver slips as he makes his cut and the ball slams into the turf, digging up a few worms. Next comes a sideline route and this time Randall overthrows his receiver, followed by a deep pass that is broken up by the defender. Finally, Randall connects. Barnett runs a long fly and Randall's perfect spiral lands in Barnett's fingertips for a touchdown. "Way to go Randall!" several players shout.

Rich Kotite: I didn't want him to do too much; I just wanted him to get acclimated to things, but the man does everything, the man wants to do everything. He's a great competitor and he wants to go and that's what makes him what he is, but you always have to use good judgment.

I'm back. I made it through training camp and preseason without a problem. I got a minor groin pull in our next-to-last preseason game against Atlanta, and Richie held me out against the Jets the following week, but it's fine now and has nothing to do with my knee. Right now, I'm just anxious for the season to start. In fact, I keep having this dream where I'm so pumped to play that I run out on the field and forget to put on my uniform. I'm out on the field, in front of 70,000 people, look down and realize I'm in my underwear—a black G-string. So now, before our first game, I'm going to double-check and make sure I have my uniform on before I head out onto the field.

CHAPTER

1

SEPTEMBER 6, 1992

God is everywhere. Sometimes you can even find him at Burger
King.

I realized this today, a big day for me—my first regular season
NFL game since my knee injury. On the way to the stadium, I
stopped for breakfast at the Burger King near my house. I don't
want this to sound like an endorsement for Burger King; I also eat at
McDonald's. After ordering my breakfast at the drive-in window, I
pulled my car up a little and stopped behind the car ahead of me. I
thought I was on level ground so I put the car in neutral, but for
some reason it started rolling backwards and then it suddenly
stopped. I said to myself, "Why is this car rolling backwards? There
must be a reason." So I looked around and there, to my left, I saw a
church in the distance. I'd been to this Burger King maybe a hundred times before but I'd never noticed this church. It was as if God
was speaking to me, saying, "I'm with you, go out and play and have
some fun."

Maybe some of you reading this have had a similar experience
and will get tears in your eyes when you think about it. I know it's

that way for me now as I think about it all over again. I had such a warm feeling in my heart knowing the Lord was with me. After being injured in the first game of the previous season and missing the entire season, spending nine months rehabilitating my knee, after my whole outlook on playing football had changed, I felt like the luckiest man on earth. My faith had pulled me through and I was back, more confident and positive about myself than ever.

Before the game we had a tribute for Jerome Brown. Jerome was someone who had as much talent and ability as anyone in the NFL, but to tell the truth, we'll all miss Jerome more as a friend than as a player. Jerome was loud and outgoing and fun-loving and had the biggest heart of anyone I've ever known. He was one of the greatest people you could ever meet, and to have him as a teammate and friend for five seasons was something very special.

Normally, before a game, we would warm up out on the field and then go back into the locker room. But today we all stayed out on the field for Jerome's tribute. His parents came out and then the team announced that they would be retiring Jerome's number and nobody would ever wear number 99 again. None of us knew about this and when they made the announcement, I just lost it. It hurt to know that Jerome wasn't with us and I cried like a baby. A lot of guys did.

After the tribute, we went back into the locker room. It was quiet, real quiet. Too quiet considering we were about to play a football game against the New Orleans Saints. Seth Joyner sensed this and screamed, "HEY, WE HAVE TO GO OUT AND PLAY BALL. COME ON, FORGET THIS QUIET STUFF." Seth has taken over as the most vocal leader on the team, especially for the defense. Seth was right and what he said was exactly what we needed to hear. We snapped out of it and started getting back some of our intensity. We knew Jerome was still with us in our hearts, but we couldn't afford to mope around. We had to go out and play some football. I know Jerome would have told us, "Stop feeling sorry for me. Go out and kick their ass."

While we were getting ready, Byron Evans, our middle line-backer, came up to me real serious and said, "Zookie, two is all we need." He held up two fingers and that meant that if the offense scored two touchdowns the defense would do the rest. Zookie is his nickname for me and comes from those Godzilla movies. Although I've never seen one, Byron tells me that Godzookie is Godzilla's son or nephew or something and that I look just like him. I think middle linebackers watch a lot of Godzilla movies. It must get them psyched up to destroy a few running backs. I sometimes call Byron "Bob Hope" because he has the facial features of Bob Hope—especially the long nose—but on a black person.

We got the ball to start the game and began on our own 20. On first down Herschel Walker, who we picked up in the off-season after he was released by Minnesota, ran for eight yards over the right side. The idea was to get Herschel and the running game established early and pound out the yardage all day. Herschel ran over a guy, broke a tackle and sent a message. On second down Herschel lost a yard, setting up a third-and-three. I was ready and knew what to expect from the New Orleans defense.

I had studied the game plan Richie gave us—it was over 100 plays—and I knew it cold. Plus, I also had my own little game plan of how I wanted to attack the Saints' defense. When I study films, I'm probably the only quarterback in the NFL who starts with the defensive line. Everyone else concentrates on the defensive backs and coverages, but I want to know where the rush is coming from, how much time I'll have, what lanes I can use when they blitz, and what stunts they might run so I know who'll be in the backfield first. For example, whenever we play the Washington Redskins, I know that Charles Mann, their great defensive end, will bull rush to the inside and they'll loop the inside guy around his end. So the pressure from the Redskins comes up the middle.

From watching films I knew that on passing downs, the Saints almost always rush two defensive linemen up the middle and their outside linebackers—Pat Swilling and Ricky Jackson—come around the outside. I knew they'd be coming hard, so I knew I'd have to set up about seven yards deep in the pocket, which is a little shorter than I normally like to drop back. That would enable my offensive tackles—Antone Davis on the right side and Ron Heller on the left, to push Swilling and Jackson past me. We were going to double-team the two linemen coming up the middle and that meant my escape route was through the gaps between the linebackers and defensive linemen. I also knew from studying their coverages where their two middle linebackers cover in the zone and that their cornerbacks give receivers a lot of room. I knew I could hit the tight end over the middle or go to the short stuff to the wide-outs. And I knew, once we got inside their 20, that the corners would have to close up on Fred Barnett and Calvin Williams and that we could beat them for a score.

I was ready. All week I studied and prepared and knew what to expect. My only worry was that I would go into the game too nervous, too fired up. In previous years I was so fired up at times I made little mistakes. So I kept telling myself to be patient, relax, play like you do in practice. What I've been doing in practice will carry over into the game. I knew my passing efficiency had improved and I needed to let it flow, let the offensive line do their thing, let Herschel establish the run, get the ball to Freddie and Calvin and hit Tank over the middle and move the team up and down the field. Keith Jackson was still holding out and was in the midst of a bitter contract dispute. We switched Keith Byars to tight end and Heath Sherman took over Tank's spot at fullback.

So, on third-and-three on that opening drive, I took what they gave me. We had Floyd Dixon in as a third receiver and the defensive back was playing 10 yards off him. Floyd ran a quick out and I hit him for four yards and a first down at the 31. Herschel picked up three yards on the next play and then I hit Freddie for six more on a quick out to make it third-and-one. I knew eventually the corners would have to tighten up on Freddie and Calvin and I kept that in the back of my mind for later, when we'd fake an out and send Freddie or Calvin deep.

Herschel bulled his way for the first down, then Heath ran for five yards over the left side. On second-and-five I dropped back, but they had the play covered. The pressure was coming up the middle, like I expected, and I saw a big lane open up. Antone Davis contained his man, I beat a big lineman around the corner and picked up 10 yards to the Saints' 43. On the next play, Herschel followed a great block by our left guard, Mike Schad, broke into the secondary, terrorized a few defensive backs and picked up 33 yards to the Saints' 10. Everything was working—the run and the pass—and the Saints didn't know what was coming next.

From the 10, Richie called a rollout pass to the left. I faked the handoff to Herschel, rolled left, but they had everybody covered. So I took off. I thought I could score, but as I crossed the five their free safety, Gene Atkins, closed on me. I hurdled at the four, but he hit me real solid on the hip and I went down at the two. It was a good, hard hit—I have to give him credit. That was my welcome back to the NFL, but despite the pain, I couldn't help smiling. My knee was fine and I was back scrambling.

From the two I called a play where Herschel is supposed to go out into the left flat, and when the defense goes to cover him, Pat Beach, our second tight end, was supposed to delay and slip into the open space for the easy score. The only problem was that Pat, who had only signed with us about a week before the game, still didn't know all the plays and he stayed in to block. It didn't matter. The defense was slow to cover Herschel and I flipped him the ball for the score.

Later in the game, we were driving and had the ball at the Saints' 20. The play Richie called was a slant 38M, which was Herschel running to the right side. But the Saints were lined up in their 34-plus defense, which is where they overshift to the tight-end side, which was exactly where Herschel was supposed to run. So I called a new play—37 blunt—which is Herschel running to the left between the tackle and guard. But right before I was about to call for the snap, their safety came all the way into the gap where Herschel was going to run. So I called another audible, Zero 80, Zero 80, which for this game meant a hitch pass, but depending on where the defense was, Freddie and Calvin had to make adjustments. Calvin went up the left side, but the safety came over to double him. I kept dropping back, saw Freddie put a move on his man and run a fade into the corner of the end zone. He had his man beat so I just threw it to him and he went up and got it.

I was very emotional after Freddie's touchdown. The first score had seemed easy, but this one we had to work for. I hugged Freddie and said, "I don't know how you made that catch," but later when I watched the films I saw that he beat his man and went up high and got the ball.

Freddie's touchdown put us up 15-6 and we went on to win 15-13. (Roger Ruzek added a field goal after the first touchdown, but missed both extra points.) I guess Bob Hope was right; all the offense had to do was score two touchdowns.

It was such a great feeling to be back and to be with the guys and for us to play so well as a team against a great team and win. The offensive line came together and Herschel ran for 114 yards, Heath added 50 and I had time to complete 18 of 25 passes for 165 yards. Afterwards, Herschel said that he should have run for even more yards, that the holes were there all day and he missed a couple. That's the kind of person he is—a humble, honest person who always gives a lot of credit to his teammates and always works hard to improve. I made mistakes too. In fact, I fumbled the ball four times and we lost three of them. I think the reason for all the fumbles was that I wasn't used to getting hit. That's not something you can work on in practice. That's where the rust from my year off hurt the team. Plus, Pat Swilling, who stripped me three times, is such a great player he can make any quarterback look foolish. Still, throughout the game, and despite the fumbles and other mistakes we made, there was this amazing feeling that was going through the entire offense. We all knew what we were doing wrong and yet, at the same time, we were confident that we could go out and get the job done. No one made excuses and no one pointed any fingers at anyone else. We just went out and got the job done and overcame our mistakes. That's the most maturity I've ever seen out of this team.

Before the game, Zeke Bratkowski, our quarterback coach, read me something from the Bible. He told me the message was that I was one of only a few people who had this gift from God, so I should appreciate it and concentrate on it and go out and do something great. After the game he came up and said, "See, that pass to Freddie, off the wrong foot, off an audible, was right on target. That's exactly what I was talking about before the game." He said nobody else could have done that.

CHAPTER

2

I was born on March 27, 1963, in Santa Barbara, California. My father, Samuel, worked for the railroad company and later as a janitor before hypertension forced him to stop working when I was about 10. He was a big man, about six-feet tall and 300-plus pounds, which I think was one of the reasons he got sick. His nickname was "Heavy." Pops was mostly a quiet, easygoing man, but you definitely didn't want to get him angry. When he got mad, he had this gangster look, a Humphrey Bogart look, that came into his eyes. He had this hat that he would tilt down and he'd grit his teeth and we all would say, "Leave Pop alone."

My mother, Mabel, was a nurse. She was a very beautiful and a very strong woman who really controlled the family, especially after Pop got sick. Mom didn't let us get away with anything. If she said, "Get in here and wash the dishes," that meant now—not in five minutes. If you didn't, she'd sneak up from behind and whack you in the butt with a belt. Mom made sure we went to church every Sunday and she made sure we dressed right. That's part of the reason I appreciate fashion and enjoy dressing up today.

One of my first memories was going to Disneyland when I was two or three. All I really remember was that when the day was done,

I was so tired and Mom just picked me up and I fell asleep in her arms. A lot of people who knew my Mom tell me I look just like her and that makes me feel very happy. Aunt Nettie, Mom's sister, visited us a lot and even lived with us for a time and was like a second momma to us.

I was fortunate to grow up with three older brothers—Sam Jr., who is 12 years older than me, Anthony, who is seven years older, and Bruce, who is two years older. All three of my brothers were football stars, so it was only natural that I grew up playing football. You probably heard of Sam "Bam" (we called him Junior), who was a star fullback for the University of Southern California and the New England Patriots.

When I was three or four my parents split up for about a year or so. My father moved into a house right across the road and Sam and Anthony lived with him, while Bruce and I lived with Momma. I didn't understand what being separated was back then, and later, after they got back together, it wasn't something we ever really talked about. But I do remember that almost every morning Bruce and I would cross the highway to Pop's house and ask him for a dime for lunch and he'd give it to us and then we'd continue on to school.

Santa Barbara was a great place to grow up then and still is today. It was a racially-mixed town, with whites and blacks, Hispanics and Asians. Everyone got along and later, when I got out into the world, I was kind of shocked and surprised by the prejudice I saw. One of my first days at college in Las Vegas, I was walking across the street and this car roared by and the driver yelled, "Get out of the street, nigger." I was shocked and hurt. Nothing like that had ever happened to me before. I grew up thinking people just got along.

We didn't have a lot of money, but we weren't poor. Until I was in junior high, we lived on 222 Santa Barbara Street. It was a small house with a big dirt yard. Next to our house was a hardware store and next to that was a place where they fixed up boats and across the street were a few other houses. A block away was the Pacific Coast Highway. The ocean was a 10-minute walk. Later, when Sam was in the NFL and making a nice living, he bought the family a house up on the mesa—4550 Murrell Road.

My mother made sure she taught us the value of a dollar. She didn't hand us money, we had to go out and earn it. On Murrell Road, there were about 75 houses within a few blocks of our house and I would go around asking the neighbors if I could wash their cars or cut their grass. Even then, and probably because of my mother, I was a perfectionist. When I washed a car it was clean when I was finished. I figured if I did a good job, they'd hire me back the next week to wash it again. I'm still like that today. When I do something, I do it right and I'm a fanatic when it comes to keeping my house and cars clean.

When I was a little kid, probably five or six, my parents took Bruce and me to Sears to get our first football uniforms, complete with pads and helmets. The jerseys didn't have team logos on them, but my uniform had New England Patriots' colors and Bruce's was green and yellow—just like the Green Bay Packers.

When we got home we put on our uniforms and went out into the yard to play one-on-one football. We had a big yard but it was all dirt—no grass. When we played our one-on-one games, Sam was always my coach and Anthony always coached Bruce. Basically, what they told us to do was clobber each other. I would kick off to Bruce or he would kick off to me and then we would try and tackle each other. Then Anthony would hike the ball to Bruce or Sam would hike it to me and we would try to score. Bruce was always faster than me and he would try to use his speed and moves to get around me. But I was rougher and more hard core and would try to run right over him. When you got tackled you would wind up with a face full of dirt. The end zone was our driveway, so you didn't want to get tackled there, or you'd wind up with a face full of cement.

Sam "Bam" Cunningham: Anthony and I had played one-on-one games against each other when we were little, so the tradition was passed on to Bruce and Randall. It wasn't that we had any dreams to grow up and be football stars, it was just what we did to have fun. In Santa Barbara everyone played sports—football in the fall, basketball in the winter and track and baseball in the spring. On Friday nights, before I was even in high school, Pops used to take us to Santa Barbara High to watch the football games. We'd wind up playing tackle the man with the ball or the tin can underneath the stands and never really watch the game, but it was a natural thing that one day we would play football for the high school. It was the same for Anthony, Bruce and Randall.

When Randall was a little kid, he was real slow and awkward and gangly and had a long, skinny body that he didn't grow into until much later. But he had a lot of heart and even then he was tough. Bruce was faster and quicker, but I don't think he had as much heart as Randall did back then. I don't know who won those games; we didn't keep score. But we did urge them to hit each other and lay some pops on each other. Eventually they would squabble and get ready to fight, but we would never let them come to blows.

Randall was a pretty intense little kid. He was hyper, full of energy and always getting into something he shouldn't be getting into. One time I had this stereo system—a Marantz stereo. In retrospect, it probably wasn't a very good stereo, but to me, at the time, it was a great system. One day he was messing around with me, being his usual pain-in-the-butt self about things and I was lying on the couch trying to rest. He kept bugging me and bugging me and wouldn't leave me alone. Finally, I just picked up my shoe and threw it at him. He might have ducked or I might have just missed him, but anyway, the shoe smashed into my stereo and just destroyed it. I looked at the stereo and looked at Randall and he understood what the problem was and just disappeared. I don't think I saw him for a week.

The way I grew up and the way Randall grew up was different. You would think it was the same since we grew up in the same family, but there was so much time between us and things changed. First off, Randall and I are only half brothers. My mother died right *after I was born and Pops remarried a little while after that. But Moms [Mabel Cunningham] raised me and I still think of her as my own mother. Anthony and I had a much stricter upbringing than Bruce and Randall and couldn't get away with any of the stuff they got away with. Since our parents were busy working Anthony and I raised them. I was responsible for Anthony, Bruce and Randall; Anthony was responsible for Bruce and Randall; Bruce was responsible for Randall; and Randall, well, he wasn't responsible for anyone. He was the youngest, the baby, and he did whatever he wanted to do. When Randall was acting up and destroying stuff like my stereo and you wanted to smack him, Mom would tell us to leave Randall alone. He was her baby.*

Sam said what, that I was spoiled. He's crazy.

Actually, I have to admit, he's right. Momma did spoil me pretty bad, but my brothers made up for it by beating up on me when she wasn't looking. Still, I was fortunate to have three older brothers. I studied and watched them and learned a little from each one, especially Sam, who I have to admit, was my role model.

Sam was the man in high school. He was so big and strong he ran over people and all I remember about his games was Sam scoring on long runs every time he got the football. His getting a scholarship to USC was an inspiration to the rest of us that we could make it too if we worked hard and did well in school. We used to make the two-hour drive to the Coliseum for the USC Trojans' home games and they were something. Sam's roommate was Lynn Swann and we used to go to their apartment to visit. The two of them were always carrying on and wrestling and fighting with each other and one day they were fighting on the bed and it broke. Sam got to USC right after O.J. Simpson graduated, but I met him at a game once and got my picture taken with him, which was the first time I ever had my picture taken with a celebrity.

There were so many great players at USC when Sam was there—

Lynn Swann, Anthony Davis, Charles Young and on and on. I used to go into the locker room afterwards to see Sam and that's where I really began to appreciate football and dream of playing in college or maybe even the NFL. It was just so great to be in there with all those big guys and smell the grass and all the smells of the locker room, and look at the shiny helmets with the Trojan on the side and dream that I would be there one day too. I got a bunch of autographs on a yellow USC elbow pad that was way too big for my skinny, little arm, but I taped it on and wore it when I played in my youth football games. I was in the locker room after they won the Rose Bowl and Sam had just scored four touchdowns to set a record and USC won the national championship. I was so proud to be Sam "Bam" Cunningham's brother. So now, when I see kids come into our locker room after a game, I make it a point to be nice to them. I'll give them a wrist band or something like that because I remember what it was like to be in the USC locker room when I was a little kid.

It got to the point where Bruce and I expected to go into the locker room after Sam's games. When he was a rookie with the Patriots, they played at San Diego and we all piled into the car and drove down for the game. Afterwards, they wouldn't let us in the locker room, even though we told them who we were. I was kind of shocked.

Sam "Bam" Cunningham: By the time Randall was in high school, I could start to see his potential. He was still pretty skinny, but I could see him blossoming. I used to tell him that it wasn't so much the football—he had that part down—but the studying and doing well in school that was most important. If you weren't a good student, you couldn't go anywhere.

In the off-season, after I was with the Patriots, I used to come home and would work out. I needed a quarterback to throw balls to me and that was Randall. But it was hard to get Randall to practice with me for as long as I wanted to practice. He had his own agenda and after a while wanted to leave to go and be with his friends or do his thing. My thing was I still have a half hour or 40 minutes to go and I need you to throw me 20 or 30 more passes. He said he had to go and we'd argue for a while and then he'd go. This would happen every once in a while.

Later, when Randall was at Vegas, he came up to me one day and apologized. He said he didn't realize it at the time, but I was right and now that he was in college and playing football he realized how hard you had to work to make it. This is when I realized that he was maturing and on the right track. If you're the quarterback, the trigger man for a football team, you can't just rely on your talent. You have to work hard and study and be a leader and he understood those parts of the game too.

When Sam came home during the off-season, he would put me through pro workouts. He would run a pattern and say put the ball here, right over my shoulder so I can catch it on the run without making any adjustments. One day he told me I had a good enough arm to make it in the NFL. At the time, the Patriots' quarterbacks were Steve Grogan and Jim Plunkett, who were great quarterbacks. Sam said my arm was every bit as strong as theirs. But, he said I had to work hard in school and mature and be a leader if I wanted to make it. At the time I didn't fully understand what Sam was saying, but I looked up to him and wanted to be like him, so some of it sunk in.

So Sam would run 25 patterns to the right and say put it over my left shoulder and then run 25 patterns to the left and say put it over my right shoulder. I would get competitive about it and try to put the ball exactly where he wanted and he made me realize if I didn't do my job, he couldn't do his job.

Still, after an hour or so, I was ready to go. But Sam worked hard and long and wanted me to stay. I would get mad about it and we'd argue and I'd stick my lip out and leave. Even though I wouldn't admit it at first, I learned from working out with Sam that you couldn't just go out and play football. If you wanted to be better than another player, you had to work harder than that player. In high school, in the summer, I used to get a few guys to work out with me and before you knew it, 10 or 12 guys would show up every day. In college, I would stay in Vegas over the summer and work during the day. In the evenings, when it was still 102 degrees, I would get Mike McDade and sometimes Tony Gladden, two receivers on the team, and we'd go down to the field. First we would run gassers, which are sprints across the field four times without stopping in 36 seconds or less. We did that twice and then I would throw passes to Mike so we could get our timing down and then I would have Mike throw passes to me so he could know what it was like to be the quarterback.

Even now, after all these years in the NFL, I still work out hard in the off-season and that goes back to what Sam taught me when I was 11 or 12 years old.

Anthony might have been an even better athlete than Sam. In fact, he might have been the best athlete in the family. Anthony was a lot like our father, in that he was a quiet, easy going guy, but when you pissed him off—look out! Since Anthony came right after Sam, everyone was comparing him to Sam and wanting him to be like Sam. Anthony had a lot of pride and he rebelled against this and tried to be his own man. He could have been a great running back too, but Anthony decided to play linebacker instead, probably because he didn't want to play the same position as Sam. Anthony played at Santa Barbara Community College and then received a scholarship to Boise State, where he did real well at linebacker. I think he could have gone to the NFL, but he cut the end of his big toe off mowing a lawn and that really finished him as a player. Anthony still lives in Santa Barbara and works as a landscaper. He's married and has a son named Louis who's going to be a great football player one day. Louis is only 12, but he's a tall, slender left-handed quarterback. Can you imagine that: another Cunningham, left-handed, playing quarterback in the NFL. That would be something.

Since Bruce and I were the closest in age, we were always together when we were growing up. In fact, as we got a little older and Bruce was in high school and I was still in junior high, Momma used to make Bruce take me wherever he went. "He would say, 'Oh man, I don't want him coming along,' but there was no lip about it and if he wanted to go out, I went with him. I remember Bruce's best friend, Tony Gilbert, would pull up to the house in his old Camaro and away we'd go, usually with Donnell Dixon, another of Bruce's best friends. It was pretty exciting for me to be out with the older guys, and Tony Gilbert, who was a great athlete, became my idol. He went on to Michigan State, where he was a star in football and track. Since I was a quarterback and Tony was a receiver, we worked out together and developed that special understanding that quarterbacks and receivers sometimes have. When we worked out, I'd throw and Tony would play receiver and Bruce, who played cornerback, would cover him.

Things were pretty equal with Bruce and me. One day he would beat me in some sport or game and the next day I would beat him. We hung out together and looked out for each other, played on the same teams and wound up going to the same college and rooming together for a year. If I would get a girlfriend he would get a little jealous, like someone was getting in the middle of our relationship. To this day, he still feels that nobody should be closer to me than him.

When both Mom and Dad were working, they would send Bruce and me to the Santa Barbara Boys Club every day after school and then pick us up for dinner. The boys club was where I started to develop my athletic skills. I'll always remember this one game we played all the time on the basketball court—Warball. We played it with these small red rubber balls and the object was to hit someone with the ball and then they were out of the game. We weren't happy just to hit someone, you had to hit them hard. Warball was rough—real rough. I was one of the youngest kids playing and some of the older guys were pretty good athletes. This one guy was a great baseball pitcher and he could really throw that rubber ball. After the game, we would have little red marks all over our bodies. But it was a great way to learn to compete and handle anger and frustration.

If you got out of line at the boys club, they would send you to the library as a punishment. But I didn't mind. There were books and puzzles and games there and I learned a lot. There was also pool, ping pong, arts and crafts, ceramics and woodworking. In the summer it was packed with kids and you had to wait an hour just to play ping pong or pool.

I started playing Pop Warner football when I was nine. I had to play with Bruce's team because Mom didn't want to drive us to two separate practices. So, of course, I was the youngest and skinniest kid on the team. But that helped me mature quicker and made me a lot tougher. I hadn't developed enough to be a quarterback at the time, so I played mostly defensive back. But when I would fool around with friends my own age in the park, I was always the quarterback. I played on the same team as Bruce for two years and then, finally, I got to play with kids my own age and play quarterback.

One of the guys I was always bumping heads with in Pop Warner football was a quarterback named David Ritchie. He was a little shorter than me, but he was a very talented player. We both wound up at Santa Barbara High School and as a sophomore, I beat him out for the starting job on the varsity. I think one of the reasons our coach, Mike Moropoulos, favored me was that he knew and had coached my brothers. He remembered Sam gaining 50 yards a carry and Anthony, who was just as good. And by the time I was a sophomore Bruce was starting at defensive back. Everyone used to say, "If you think they're good, just wait until you see the youngest one." That was a lot of pressure on me, but I didn't mind. I learned how to handle it by studying my brothers' talents. Sam set the tone and showed us what we could achieve. Anthony was his own man and showed me you have to be a little bit stubborn to get what you want. Bruce was the fastest and quickest, so when I ran, I decided I'd be like Bruce.

Randall became an outstanding high school quarterback. In 1980, his senior year, he led Santa Barbara to the championship game of the California Interscholastic Federation Championship where they lost to Long Beach Poly. He passed for 2,344 yards and 24 touchdowns and averaged 48 yards per punt. Grainy, black-and-white films of Randall's high school games show an extraordinary athlete who could win games with his arm or legs and improvisational skills.

In the spring of Randall's senior year of high school he underwent an operation on his right knee, which left two long, parallel scars on either side of his knee cap.

This cut short Randall's final track season. Already he had set a school record in the high jump (6-10) and was a very talented pole vaulter. In fact, if Randall had picked track over football, he could have become a world-class decathlete.

Living that close to the beach meant that life wasn't all football. In fact, when I was about 11 years old, I got into surfing and boogie boarding for a few years until I finally started concentrating on football. You don't see too many brothers out there on a surfboard, but there I was, just about every day. At first, I had to learn the rules of the beach. The first few times I went, I just kind of showed up—no towel, no suntan lotion, no boogie board, no surf board. I went home and searched all over for a beach towel, but we didn't have one. I wound up using a raggedy old white towel that had holes in it. Next I got an inner tube; I couldn't afford a surf board. I would paddle way out and ride it in on a wave and it was like, wow, that was fun, but it was so tiring to paddle that thing that I'd have to come in and rest after one or two rides.

Then I got smart. I would go to my friends' houses and ask, "Are you going to the beach today?" If they said no, I'd ask to borrow their boogie board. Then another friend of mine got a brand-new wet suit and gave me his old one. Little by little, I was starting to look like I belonged out there. I even bought suntan lotion. So instead of looking all gray and ashy, I started getting darker and darker.

Finally, I got a used surfboard. Another friend got a brand-new one and gave me his old one—a big, heavy, hand-made board we called "the log." He tried to teach me how to put Sex Wax on it (don't get excited, that's the brand name of the wax), and then he showed me how to paddle out and jump up on the board at just the right time to catch the wave and then ride it in. He said, "Good luck," and there I was—out in the ocean sitting on my surfboard waiting for that first good wave. Here it comes. I jumped up on my board just like he showed me and the next thing I knew I was underwater.

I also started getting into girls about this time, but being so skinny—a toothpick—they weren't as interested in me as I was in them.

After I went through my surfing phase, I got heavily into bike riding, which led me into one of the few bad phases of my life. I had this friend, Judd, who had just moved to Santa Barbara from Manhattan. He was cool and we hung out together and I even got him to go down to the beach with me. You should have seen this brother from Manhattan trying to ride a boogie board. It was hilarious.

We used to ride our bikes to school every day and race the bus. We usually beat it because we didn't stop for red lights or stop signs. We both had beat-up old bikes with bent frames and rims and we were always patching our blown tires back together. One day, we were out riding and sure enough, my tire popped. We decided, what better place to get a new tire than the beach, where everyone left their bikes while they fooled around in the water. We looked around and found a tire that looked like it would fit my bike and hid in the bushes. Judd said I had to go get it because it was my bike. When the coast was clear, I ran out and snatched it off the bike and we raced back to my house to put it on my bike.

Then like idiots we returned to the scene of the crime. There was a police car there and they were talking to some people gathered around the tireless bike. You never saw two guys panic like we did. All of a sudden people started yelling, "There they are," and we took off. I was really scared because I was known around the neighborhood. I was Sam Cunningham's little brother. Everyone knew the Cunninghams.

We thought we got away, but then the cops pulled up behind us. Judd wanted to take off and lose them, but I said no way, they know who I am. We tried to lie our way out of it, but people had ratted us out and the cops knew we were the ones. Finally I just admitted it. "We did it. Please don't put us in jail."

They took me back to my house and Pops was there. He got kind of quiet and said, "Wait until your mother gets home." When she did get home I was scared and for good reason—I got a good whipping. Plus, Judd and I had to go to this program called Crossroads. We met with a counselor and a group of kids who got in trouble like us and we had to talk about why we had done what we did. We spent four hours a day for two weeks there and we felt out of place, especially when they took us to visit a juvenile detention center. I learned a lot from that trip, including the fact that I didn't want to end up there. They showed us around and that's all it took for Judd and me to realize that tiny cells with no windows weren't for us. I remember the counselor saying if we kept getting in trouble, this was where we'd be living for the next few years. The whole time I was thinking, "No way, I can't handle this. I'm not going to end up here."

I never stole another bike tire.

CHAPTER 3

The first *Dallas week* of the season is over. Thank God. As far as I'm concerned, this has been one of the longest weeks in the history of the NFL. Actually, it's been two weeks since we were off last weekend and had 14 days of hype before we finally played the Cowboys tonight.

Dallas week is always something special in Philadelphia, a town that takes its sports teams very seriously—especially the Eagles— and hates the Cowboys almost as much as it loves the Eagles. This week, with both teams undefeated and playing on ABC's Monday Night Football at the Vet, Dallas week is extra special. The Eagles are currently 3-0 and coming off two very impressive wins: 31-14 over Phoenix in Week Two and 30-0 over Denver in Week Three. The Denver game was a masterpiece throughout, as the Eagles controlled the ball for 39 minutes and 18 seconds and racked up 388 yards of offense. A cool, calm and collected Randall completed 18-of-25 passes for 270 yards and three touchdowns and ran for another 46 yards on eight carries—including a 29-yard scamper through traffic that was vintage Randall. On a third-and-10 play, Randall dropped back to pass. The two defensive ends rushed too far upfield, Randall stepped up into the pocket and was gone, winding his way through linebackers and defensive backs before he was finally tripped up by a diving, shoestring tackle at the Broncos' 31. This was Randall's first long scramble of the season and after he got up he shook his clenched fist in triumph.

Before the game, Richie came up to me, got real close to my face and said, "When you see a hole—run. Take off." All during the preseason and the first two games of the regular season, the coaches had been trying to make me into Mr. Pocket Passer, but now Richie was telling me to run. So I did and it was fun, especially the 29-yard run. When I run, I try to play a mind game on the defensive players. Sometimes they call me the "Rubberband Man" because my hips and legs and head keep swiveling back and forth. When I run, I know where I'm going, so when I make my cut and change directions, the defensive player doesn't know where I'm going or what I'm going to do until after I make my cut. If I explode when I make my cut and if I come out of it real quick, they might get an arm on me, but I'll usually be able to get separation and keep running downfield.

The praise for Randall after the Denver game is effusive. A column in the Philadelphia Inquirer *states: "At this point in time, in fact, he is the best quarterback in the game. No longer does he need that asterisk, that begrudging, hem-hawing, damn-with-faint-praise qualifier about being 'the best athlete at the position.' No, he is, at this moment, the best all-around QB, period."*

The Cowboys are just as hot as the Eagles and are coming off a 31-20 win over Phoenix. The Cowboys' Emmitt Smith is the top rusher in the league after three games and Herschel is just a few yards behind. Plus, there's the whole Herschel versus the Cowboys sidebar. The Cowboys traded Herschel to Minnesota during the 1989 season for eight draft choices—choices the Cowboys have wisely used to stockpile talented young players and rebuild from a dreadful 1-15 finish in 1989.

The Cowboys' Michael Irvin has the most receiving yards in the league and Fred Barnett is just a few yards behind. Randall is the top-rated quarterback in the entire NFL and Dallas's Troy Aikman is also having an outstanding season. "I didn't realize all the great individual matchups," Randall said before the game. "That should get everyone even more pumped up."

About seven seconds after the Denver game, the hype for the Dallas game began and that's all anyone wanted to talk about for two straight weeks. It was crazy. For me, *Dallas week* began on the Monday night a week before the game. I was asked to appear on halftime of the Monday night game to start hyping up our game the following week—as if it needed any more publicity. The only problem was Keith Jackson came on right before me. Keith had been holding out all season and a few days earlier Judge David Doty ruled that Keith and New England's Garin Veris, Cleveland's Webster Slaughter and Detroit's D.J. Dozier were all temporary free agents and had a week to sign with whoever they could make the best deal with before their rights reverted back to their original teams.

All along I had been positive that Keith—who is the best tight end in football—would be coming back to the Eagles. So, while I was watching the halftime show while I waited to go on camera live, Keith came on and announced he was signing with the Miami Dolphins. I was shocked. The next thing I knew I was on live television being asked questions about Keith leaving. "I'm very upset," I remember telling Al Michaels. "I'm going to miss my boy. Of course he was my main target and we've had to restructure our offense. Congratulations, Keith."

I meant what I said. Keith is my boy, my friend and a great player. I knew I was going to miss him on and off the field. But there wasn't any resentment about Keith leaving. He had to do what was best for himself and his family and the fact is, he got a better deal from the Dolphins. Keith had a once-in-a-lifetime opportunity to be an unrestricted free agent and sell his talents to the highest bidder. From what I understand about the deal, the two offers weren't that far apart, but the Dolphins offered a bigger signing bonus and guaranteed the entire contract, which the Eagles weren't willing to do. So, a week before the Dallas game, we lost the best tight end in football and got nothing in return. Or, you could look at it and say we lost Keith, but used the money we saved from his salary to sign Herschel. Or, you could look at it and say we should have put out the money to sign both of them. But that's not my decision to make. Now it's time for us to find a tight end.

The Eagles always seem to have more holdouts and contract problems than any other team in the league and it's not hard to figure out why. This summer there were statistics released in conjunction with a court case between the NFL and the players that showed the Eagles made more money than any other team over the last few years, yet it seems like management won't give players what they want or deserve. Management says players are holding out, but in essence players don't hold out, they're held out by the team. They want to sign, but the negotiations aren't going on. The Eagles say, "This is our best offer—take it or leave it—" and there doesn't ever seem to be any real negotiating.

I don't know if this has had a negative effect on the team. Before the 1991 season, Seth Joyner, Clyde Simmons and Jerome Brown all had bitter contract disputes and didn't get signed until the first week of the season, yet all three went on to have Pro Bowl seasons. So, the negative of three great players holding out and missing training camp was turned into a positive for management and the team. This year it was the same thing with Eric Allen, Calvin Williams and Keith Jackson. Eric and Calvin finally signed and we all know what happened to Keith.

Some of my teammates say I have to get more involved in these contract negotiations and talk to management, but I have no pull.

It's no secret that this summer I told management I needed Keith and Calvin. They basically told me to shut up and play football—only they said it nicer. I'm just a player on this team like everyone else. Norman Braman owns this team, Harry Gamble is the president and Richie Kotite is the head coach. As far as controlling things, don't kid yourself, I'm way down the line with the parking attendants.

We didn't let Keith's leaving get us down or affect our preparation for Dallas. After all, we were already 3-0 without him and the offense was clicking. I was completing 73.6 percent of my passes for 704 yards, eight touchdowns and no interceptions through three games. Freddie and Calvin were both coming up with big plays, Keith Byars moved from fullback to tight end and then back to fullback after Pat Beach got acclimated to our system and took over at tight end. Tank did a great job wherever he played. Herschel was doing everything we asked of him and more and was on pace to gain well over 1,000 yards, and Heath Sherman was doing a super job backing up Herschel and Keith.

Everything that has been going good on offense for us starts with the line. In the past, we've had a lot of problems in this area and could never settle on a set group of five players who had a chance to develop some consistency. This year, so far, everything seems to be falling into place. During training camp someone asked me about the offensive line and I said that they needed to develop a nasty attitude like the Hogs in Washington. Not dirty—nasty. I meant they had to be overly aggressive and do whatever it took to get the job done. That's exactly what has happened. It started with left tackle Ron Heller and left guard Mike Schad and then spread to center Dave Alexander, right guard Eric Floyd and right tackle Antone Davis. They're starting to get nasty and cocky and that's exactly the kind of attitude it takes to become an effective offensive line.

Heller has a reputation as a dirty player, but Ron is someone who will do anything to get the job done. He'll push and grab and fight to block his man. Ron usually pisses off the guy across from him and that's why he seems to get into so many fights. That's the kind of guy you want at left tackle—a right-handed quarterback's blind side. Ron sets the tone for the entire line and gets everyone pumped before games.

I'm close with Schad—or Schadillac as he likes to be called. In fact, he's been renting an apartment from me for the past couple of years. He calls me his slumlord. I keep telling Mike if his man gets by him and sacks me I'm going to raise his rent.

Mike injured his back before the 1991 season and spent the year on injured reserve. Most people didn't think he would make it back, but Mike worked incredibly hard and was ready to go when training camp started in August. At one of the first practices, Mike's back was stiff and sore from sleeping on one of the terrible mattresses we have to sleep on in the dorms during training camp. I saw Otho Davis go over and talk to him and there were tears in Schad's eyes. He had worked so hard and cared so much about playing football and now he was afraid his career was over. But Otho got his back loosened up and as soon as practice ended Schad went out and bought a brand-new mattress. The next day he was OK. Still, Mike's back is tricky and he has to sleep in a certain position every night, with a pillow between his legs, to keep it from getting stiff. But he does it—that's how much he loves football. I respect Schad a lot and would do anything for him—except lower his rent.

Dave Alexander is the nice guy on the line. He's a real family man and doesn't curse or carry around. He's a scratch golfer who claims to have a five handicap and then he goes out and wins everyone's money. So be careful if you ever play golf with Dave.

I would describe Dave as a very consistent golfer and that's exactly the way he is on the football field. Dave calls all the blocking assignments for the line and controls everything. The play doesn't get going until Dave's ready. Sometimes, when I miss something he'll yell, "Get out of it, get out of it," because he sees a guy who he knows we can't block. I always listen and change the play. Dave makes my job a lot easier.

Eric Floyd was a Plan B pickup during the off-season and we had no idea how he'd fit in or if he would play for us. But Bill Muir, our new offensive line coach, put him into the lineup during the preseason and Eric's been doing a great job ever since.

Eric and Antone Davis are like a team within the team. They're a couple of big puppies who are always slapping each other and high-fiving each other when they make a good block. They kind of feed off of each other and give each other confidence. They're both way over 300 pounds and when you have close to 700 pounds on the right side of the line drive blocking, something has to give. Of course, everyone is always making fat jokes on them. We call them "Cheeseburger" or "Lambchop" and things like that. We also call Alexander the Pillsbury Doughboy, because if you poke him in the stomach, he'll start giggling.

Antone was our first-round draft choice in 1991 and was the starting right tackle from day one. That's a lot of pressure for any rookie and Antone struggled at first. Everyone does. My rookie year I threw eight interceptions and had only one touchdown pass. But Antone has worked hard and now he's starting to show his potential. I think, if he keeps working hard, Antone will be the best right tackle in the NFL.

Now we have a talented offensive line and there's not going to be any more changes and switches and confusion. Heller, Schad, Alexander, Floyd and Davis are it—period. They're big and talented and starting to get downright nasty.

We went into the Dallas game very confident and played that way. The Cowboys got the ball to start the game and right off the bat the defense came up with a big play. John Booty picked off Troy and we took over on the Dallas 14. On first down I dropped back, saw my receivers were covered and took off up the middle to the three-yard line. On third-and-goal from the two, I rolled right, got past the linebacker and scored—my first rushing touchdown of the season. I wanted to do a special celebration, the "shoot-em-down" where you pull out your pistols and start firing, but just as I was about to do it, I saw Keith Byars running toward me to give me a hug. I figured it would look stupid if we ran into each other and fell down, so I jumped into the air and Keith caught me and we celebrated.

Dallas came right back to tie the score at 7-7 and on our next possession I threw my first interception of the season. Actually, I should have had three in the game, so I was lucky. After the interception, the defense stopped Dallas and the Cowboys had to punt the ball right back to us. It's a comforting feeling knowing we have such a great defense that can make up for any mistakes the offense commits.

We got the ball back on our own 40. Herschel ran for seven and then Freddie caught a short out for the first down. Herschel ran for four more and then I took off on a scramble up the left sideline. I ran out of bounds after gaining 12 yards, but one of their linebackers hit me late and the penalty moved the ball all the way down to the Cowboys' 13. We got called for a motion penalty, and after three incompletions, Roger Ruzek kicked a field goal and we led 10-7 at the half.

On the sidelines, the offensive line was pumped up. They were in one of those zones where they felt they could do anything they wanted. At halftime, Richie didn't really say much—he didn't have to. He said we were going to run straight at them.

We got the ball to start the second half and I almost got knocked out of the game. On a third-and-long play, Antone and Eric both missed the snap count and their men blew right past them. I tried to put a move on to escape, but Jimmie Jones dove at my right knee and hung on and Jim Jeffcoat came over the top and landed right on me. I grabbed my right knee, but it was OK and I jogged it off. Floyd ran over and apologized and said it would never happen again, but I said, "Don't worry about it, man."

After we punted, Seth Joyner blitzed and hit Troy's arm just as he released the ball. It bounced straight up into the air and Byron Evans grabbed it. We took over on the Dallas 45 and quickly drove down to the 23. On second-and-10, I got chased out of the pocket. I put a few moves on some linemen and was about to take off downfield. Then I heard Keith Byars hollering, "Whooo! Whooo!" which is his signal to me that he's open. Sometimes he yells, "Randall, Randall," but because I'm wearing a helmet, all I hear is "Rann-el, Rann-el." Keith and I know each other very well and he knows exactly what to do when I get into trouble and start scrambling. If he's open, Keith will start hollering and I'll throw him the ball. If he's not open and I start running, Keith will usually level some guy and allow me to escape for another five or 10 yards. On this play, when I heard Keith go "Whooo!" I sidearmed the ball to him at the last instant, he caught it and ran down to the nine. On the next play, Herschel took it in for the score. He stopped in the end zone and it looked like Herschel was going to do a monster spike, but then he stopped in mid-spike and just let the ball drop to the ground. The fans went crazy and we were up 17-7.

On Dallas's next possession the defense came up with another turnover and we got the ball on our own 48. I hooked up with Freddie on two straight passes to give us a first down on the 16 and Herschel took it the rest of the way to give us a 24-7 lead. With about five minutes to play, Byars scored on a 12-yard run and we wound up winning 31-7.

I had an average game. I completed 11-of-19 passes for 124 yards and ran for another 43. Herschel ran for 86 yards and Freddie caught five passes for 76 yards. The defense did a great job, as they came up with three interceptions and a fumble recovery. The thing is, in the past, the pressure was always on the so-called "star" players to win the game for us. Buddy Ryan, our coach before Richie, used to put the pressure on me and say it was up to me to make the offense work and that I had to come up with five big plays a game—throwing or running. So far, this season has been different; I don't have the same pressure I did back then. I can hand the ball to Herschel or throw it to Freddie or Calvin or Keith and let them do their thing. The offensive line does its thing and we've become a machine. I like it much better this way.

One of the best moments of the entire day came after the game when I saw my girlfriend—Felicity de Jager. Felicity is from South Africa—she's my African princess—and is a ballet dancer with the Dance Theatre of Harlem. Felicity had been on tour for about six weeks and got back the day before the Dallas game. We met as friends three-and-a-half years ago in New York during "The Night of 100 Stars," a charity function. We were friends for three years and then started dating seriously a few months ago. I truly believe God brought me this lady. Felicity is the nicest, most down-to-earth, intelligent, beautiful, caring and respectful lady I have ever met and I look upon her as a gift from God.

Felicity: Like Randall said, we met at "The Night of 100 Stars." The producers of the show selected two dancers from the New York City Ballet, the American Ballet Theatre and the Dance Theatre of Harlem. I was one of the two from the Dance Theatre of Harlem. During the evening, someone came up to me and said that Randall Cunningham wanted to meet me. I didn't know anything about football or who Randall Cunningham was.

Right before I went onto the stage, someone introduced us and we spoke very briefly. Randall asked me about my accent and I told him I was from South Africa. We talked for a little while, but then I had to go out on stage. We said we would talk more at the reception after the show, but we never saw each other there. I wasn't even sure if Randall knew my name.

A few days later I got a call from the director of the show and he said Randall had called him, asked for my number and was it all right for him to give it to Randall. Then he made a joke saying, "You better let him call you; he just signed a three million dollar contract." That didn't matter to me and I told him it was OK if he gave Randall my number. Even though we had only spoken for a minute or two, Randall seemed like a gentleman, someone with a lot of class. Randall called a few days later and we got together the next time he came to New York and for the next two-and-a-half years we were friends.

From the beginning I was very impressed with Randall. He's the sweetest person in the world and he has so much class. He treats a lady like a lady, which is very important to me. I'm very old fashioned. Plus, Randall's tall, which is also important to me. I'm six-feet tall and Randall is so tall and has so much style and looks so good.

I think it was good that we were just friends at first. We learned to like each other and trust each other and respect each other. Randall takes the time to get to know you as a person. He's so down-to-earth and caring. He could get all caught up in being a celebrity, but he doesn't. He's just so normal and nice and patient with everyone. We'll be out at a restaurant and people will keep coming up and asking for his autograph. He'll sign them, or if he's eating, he'll very politely say he's eating and could they come back after he's finished. Or, we'll be shopping or walking down the street and people will come up and want to talk to him and ask for autographs and Randall is always polite and signs or poses for pictures. I've seen other celebrities who aren't so patient and are rude with people.

When Felicity and I first met, we were both dating other people. So we were just friends and learned to appreciate each other. Felicity didn't want anything from me; she had her own life and career. One of the first times we were together we went to the mall. I'm a very generous person and I like to buy my friends things—especially beautiful clothes. I saw this beautiful orange outfit and I asked Felicity to try it on. She looked so fine in it; she had it going ON! I just enjoyed seeing her in it and wanted to buy it for her. But Felicity said, "No, I don't know you that well; I can't let you buy it for me." I was sort of hurt by that. It was like she was thinking I was buying the dress so she would be with me or owe me something. That wasn't it at all. That's just the way I am. I like to buy things for my friends.

I got over being hurt and liked her even more for not letting me buy the dress. I thought to myself, "This is a very honest, beautiful, respectful person. She is a dancer, doing her own thing, and she doesn't need me or my money."

I've never been one to run around with a lot of different women.

I enjoy having one girlfriend and I've been blessed to have had some special ladies in my life. I was engaged once, only things didn't work out. I met Lisa while I was in college and we started dating and got very close. We broke up for a while when I came to Philadelphia in 1985 and then Lisa moved here and we got back together and eventually got engaged and were supposed to be married on June 4, 1988, but things didn't work out. I was truly in love with Lisa at the time, but I think what happened was I got cold feet. And I think the reason I had such cold feet was that deep down I knew I wasn't ready to get married. There were times afterwards when I wanted to call her up and say, "I love you," and "Let's forget about all the problems and get married," but I didn't. I was too young; I wasn't ready for marriage, and Lisa, if you read this book, I want you to know it was all my fault.

Right after Lisa and I broke up, I started dating a woman named Rose and we were together for about four years. She taught me a lot and helped make me an even stronger person. But eventually, in early 1992, we broke up.

Of course, everyone always wants to know about Whitney Houston and me. After all, according to the tabloids, we were all set to be married. But remember, you can't believe everything you read about Randall Cunningham—unless it's in this book. I first met Whitney in Las Vegas at a reception after the Mike Tyson-Frank Bruno fight. I was with Carl King, Don King's son, and Whitney was sitting at a table near us. There was a policeman right there, and a bodyguard or two, and her table was roped off. I wanted to meet her, but I was afraid to go over to her table. Then someone came over and asked if I would like to meet Whitney. I said yes. I went over and we talked briefly and had our picture taken. She seemed very nice and down-to-earth and I thought it would be nice to get to know her better.

I met Whitney again at a small dinner party after a BeBe and CeCe Winans concert. After that, I received an invitation to her birthday party and was asked to bring along a few guys from the team. I think this is where all the rumors about Whitney and me began. We had a preseason game the same day as the party, and in order to make the party, we had to leave the game at halftime. The other guys were all afraid to ask Buddy, figuring he'd just get mad and say no. I figured this was a once-in-a-lifetime opportunity so I'd ask Buddy. Even though I knew I was only supposed to play the first quarter of the game, I still figured Buddy would say no and that would be that. I went into Buddy's office and asked and he shocked me. He said sure, we could all go. He said we should make sure not to take off our gear at halftime and that we should trot out for the start of the second half in uniform and then sort of disappear. However, there was one condition. Buddy said I had to get him a tape of one of Whitney's songs that he really liked. I couldn't believe Buddy said yes. We did what Buddy said and snuck off right after the second half started. Of course the media found out and made a big deal about it for weeks. All along I think Buddy knew that would happen, but he let us go anyway just to show people that he ran his team his way and wasn't like other coaches. I still owe Buddy that tape.

We got to the party late and Whitney and I spoke briefly before we left. About a year or so later I got invited to a party Whitney's record company was throwing for her and that's when we got our first real chance to talk and we had some pictures taken—Whitney, Lawrence Taylor and me all together. The tabloids somehow got hold of the pictures, cut out L.T. and made it look like Whitney and I were together. So, not only can't you believe everything you read, you also can't believe everything you see.

As I got to know Whitney a little bit better, I realized she was a very beautiful, caring person. While we were talking I asked her if she would like to take a vacation to Antigua and she told me how beautiful it was and suggested we meet there. We did, but it's not like we went together or stayed in the same room or anything. We were both down there at the same time and spent some time together and got to know each other better and became friends. I was in Antigua for two days and then had to fly to the Super Bowl for some appearances and Whitney had to get back and start putting her concert tour together. Somehow, the tabloids got photos of us together—Whitney rubbing suntan lotion on my back—and ran them with big headlines saying we were engaged.

I'm just glad I've had a chance to get to know Whitney. She's married to Bobby Brown now (I attended their wedding reception) and I think they'll be very happy together and have great kids: dancers with great voices.

You have to be careful when you're somewhat of a celebrity. People always want something from you and you never know who you can trust. Including women. I get letters from ladies saying they saw me on television and think I'm handsome and so on and would like to meet me. Some even send pictures and some of the pictures reveal a lot more than they should. Early in my career, when I went out a lot more than I do now, I had women come up to me all the time in clubs. If they were drunk or loose or loud, I didn't want anything to do with them. But if they seemed nice and classy, I would talk to them and take the time to get to know them and sometimes we would exchange numbers. My thing was, I liked to go out and have a nice dinner, but I didn't have anyone to go out with since I wasn't dating Lisa at the time and was new in town and didn't know that many people. My line would be, "Let's go out and have dinner."

Most of the ladies I met were very nice and we would end up becoming friends. I hate rejection, so I would rather not ask than ask and get shot down. I also got this a lot: because I'm a football player and a celebrity, women would think I was jumping into bed with a different girl every night and could get anyone I wanted. They believed the image and wouldn't want to be with me before they even got to know me. That's not the way I am. I was brought up to be humble and treat people with respect and to be a gentleman. I'm Mr. Nice Guy when it comes to women.

I've only had one real problem with a lady. A friend of mine (I won't say who, but he was once the MVP of the Super Bowl) introduced me to this woman. She was from down south and flew up just to meet me. She was cool, very nice and intelligent and we hit it off and saw each other every few months. One time, she came for a visit and I took her to the airport to catch her flight home. We pulled up to the airport and she didn't want to get out of the car. I started to get worried. I told her I had a meeting and had to leave, but she still wouldn't get out of the car. I said you'll miss your flight and she said she didn't care, she just wanted to stay with me. I got out and walked around to her side of the car and opened the door and offered her my hand, but she still wouldn't get out. I was starting to get scared, like it was some sort of "Fatal Attraction" or something. She wouldn't say why she wouldn't get out or what she wanted—she just wouldn't get out. I was trying to be polite and nice, but I was starting to get angry. Finally, she got out of the car and walked around to my side and got between the car door and me so I couldn't close it or pull away. People were starting to stare, but luckily it was early in my career and not too many people knew who I was. I begged her to let me close the door, but she wouldn't. I didn't know what to do; I couldn't just pull away. Finally, she moved away from the door and I shut it and drove away.

She called later and apologized. She said she didn't know why she did what she did and apologized over and over again. I think she was just lonely. We talked a few more times, but we never saw each other after that day at the airport.

Now I'm with Felicity, which I know is a blessing from God. Don't tell her, but deep down in my heart I know we'll be engaged soon and spend the rest of our lives together and be very happy. I think finally, after all I've been through in my life, I've matured and settled down and am ready to get married. Luckily, I found the perfect lady at the right time.

I've learned a lot about relationships and marriage from watching Keith Byars and his wife. Keith is my roommate during training camp, which is great because Tank is a good Christian brother. I may not be his best friend, but he's my best friend and I appreciate him totally. However, there is one problem with rooming with Keith. He snores like a train. I don't know how Margaret can stand it. It's like someone is cutting down trees—make that entire forests—in our room every night. When Keith inhales, the closet doors come off their hinges. I've had to develop this whole strategy just to fall asleep before Keith does, and then, if I wake up during the night, it's all over and I know I'll never get back to sleep.

I've learned from Keith that to make a relationship last, you have to work on it, just like you work to become a better football player. From watching Keith, it's easy to see that he loves Margaret very much and his marriage is very important to him. He spends the time it takes to make his marriage work and that's what I plan to do.

CHAPTER

4

Because of Sam, everyone assumed I would accept a scholarship from USC. The three top senior quarterbacks in California in the fall of 1980 were Stefan Derrick, who played for Long Beach Poly, the team that beat us in the CIF championship game my senior year, Sean Salisbury, who is currently playing for the Minnesota Vikings, and myself.

My top three choices were USC, the University of Washington and UNLV. A lot of people think the reason I didn't go to USC was because they wanted to convert me into a receiver or defensive back. That's not true. USC wanted me as a quarterback and there was never any talk about moving me to another position. The problem was, I didn't think they spent enough time recruiting me. I got jealous of all the time they spent trying to sign all the other top players in the state, especially big offensive linemen. I guess the coaches at USC assumed I was coming there, so they didn't think they had to spend too much time recruiting me.

Still, I was leaning toward USC and the coaches invited me to watch them play Washington. The Huskies wound up winning. More and more, I began thinking seriously about UNLV. They already had a black quarterback—Sam King, who would be a senior my freshman year. I figured the coach, Tony Knapp, who everyone called the "Silver Fox," didn't have any problems with playing a black quarterback. Plus, at UNLV, they treated me real nice and made me feel like I was their top recruiting priority that year. I enjoyed my visit and got to meet a lot of the players, see the school and Las Vegas. I was impressed that UNLV had a great business department and I wound up majoring in recreation, with a minor in business. Coach Knapp told me I would play for the junior varsity my first year and then take over as his starting quarterback my sophomore year. I believed him and signed with UNLV.

Bruce was also at UNLV during my freshman year (the fall of 1981), which was another reason I picked the school. We wound up rooming together in a dingy little apartment off campus. On the football field, things went well. My knee was still a little weak from my operation, but it held up. When I first got to training camp, I was full of confidence. Growing up, I had always been the tallest guy out there and one of the better athletes on the field. Now, all of a sudden, I was surrounded by great athletes at every position and it was intimidating at first. It took me a while to rebuild my confidence and realize I belonged.

We won our first four junior varsity games of the season and our final game was against the BYU [Brigham Young University] junior varsity. The game was played the day before the two varsity teams squared off and all our varsity players came out to watch us play. The game went back and forth, with both offenses moving the ball up and down the field and scoring points. In the last two minutes, we marched down and scored and could have tied it with an extra point or won it with a two-point conversion. We went for two and didn't get it, but at least we had proved our point, that we were every bit as good as BYU. The next day the varsity went out and beat BYU—at BYU—which was a big upset and a huge boost for our program.

For the season, I completed 42-of-81 passes for 658 yards, three touchdowns and five interceptions and ran for three more scores.

For the last varsity game of the regular season—at Texas-El Paso—I got to travel with the team and suited up. This was the first away game I was able to attend as part of the team. We were behind late in the game and a lot of players and even a few coaches were saying, "Give Randall a chance." I didn't get to play, but it made me feel good that the players and some of the coaches had so much confidence in me. I couldn't wait for my sophomore season and the chance to start.

Off the field, things didn't go so well. Right before I left for college, my mom was diagnosed with cancer. At the time, I didn't understand what cancer was or how bad it was or that she could die. Cancer hit Mom hard. She fought it as best she could, but it was a losing battle and she got worse and worse. I didn't want to go away to school, but Mom told me I had to go. She said this was what I had worked so hard for and I had to work even harder to make something of myself on and off the field. So I went off to Las Vegas, but my thoughts and prayers were with my mother and Bruce and I called home almost every day.

In November, I got a call from Sam saying Bruce and I had to come home right away. When we got to the hospital, Mom was in bad shape. She was drifting in and out of consciousness and was hooked up to all sorts of machines and was in an oxygen tent. All we could do was hold her hand and tell her we loved her. I'm not even sure if she understood what we were saying. It was such a helpless feeling. At one point, I had to take one of my little cousins to the bathroom and when I got back to Mom's room, she was gone. Bruce ran out of the room crying and I was right behind him in tears.

It hit me hard that she was gone and wouldn't be there for me any more. My mother was a very strong woman and taught me so much. At the funeral everyone said she was going to a better place and that made me feel better. I decided to go back to school; I know that's what Momma would have wanted.

Pop took Mom's death hard. It was like all the life went out of him when she died. Bruce moved back home to be with him, but Pop just sort of gave up. One night in November the next year—1982—I called Pop and he was angry when he answered the phone. He said Bruce was out, he was all alone in the house and why did I have to call him up and bother him when he was in the bathroom. I told him I just wanted to call and see how he was doing and tell him I loved him. He calmed down and we had a nice talk. The next day Bruce called and said Pop was dead from a heart attack.

A little while before my mom died, Tony Gilbert, our friend from Santa Barbara, was also diagnosed with cancer and he passed away too. Tony was someone I looked up to and was a big influence on my life and football career. He gave me confidence and style and was a role model. Tony was away in college, doing great in football and track, and had his whole life ahead of him when he died. Tony was like a brother to Bruce and me and we took his death hard.

I had never had anyone close to me die before, and now, in a year, my mother and father and Tony had all passed away. At first I kept saying to myself, "Why does all this have to happen to me? Why did my parents have to die? Why did Tony have to die?" Finally, I decided I had to dedicate myself even more to school and football and make something out of myself. This is what Mom and Pop taught me. They paved the way for all four of us to have a better life than they had and I wasn't about to let them down. I was lucky to have my brothers and a lot of people in Las Vegas who were there for me and helped me get through all the hard times.

For a while, it looked like even football wasn't going to work out. My sophomore season a new coach—Harvey Hyde—took over for Coach Knapp. Coach Hyde came from Pasadena Community College and had a real gung-ho attitude and was determined to build up the program. UNLV was known for basketball at the time, and a lot of people didn't even know we had a football team or that we were in the Pacific Coast Athletic Conference. Coach Hyde was determined to change all that. He was enthusiastic and was all for his players. The only problem was he wanted me to red-shirt my sopho-more season. He had brought in a quarterback with him, plus there were two backups returning for the varsity. He wanted me to sit out the year and then still have three years left to play. I was in a hurry to play and told him, "You may think I'm red-shirting, but I'm not." I said I'd transfer to USC before I sat out the year. I even told him I'd play receiver or defensive back, anything, just so I could play. He told me I was staying at quarterback and that he was red-shirting me. I was ready to leave right away, but an assistant coach talked me into staying for the time being.

Our first game that year was against BYU and they were out for revenge. They beat us 27-0 and none of the three quarterbacks ahead of me did much of anything. Late in the game, guys were saying, "Put Randall in." But the coaches wouldn't. They knew if I played even one play, they couldn't red-shirt me for the year. I was pretty frustrated and was set to leave. School still hadn't started, so, if I left before classes started and enrolled somewhere else, then I could sit out the year and still have three years left to play.

After the BYU game, I read in the paper where Coach Hyde said, the quarterback position was wide open and "even Randall Cunningham has a chance." I read it over and over: "Even Randall Cunningham has a chance." I got so excited and was determined to do whatever it took to win the job. That week in practice, you never saw four guys work so hard. It was like, if you were off on one pass, your chances of starting were gone. I didn't miss too many passes. Toward the end of the week, we had a scrimmage and I threw a couple of touchdown passes and played real well.

The next day quarterback coach Randy Whitsitt called the four of us into his office. He said he had decided who would be the starting quarterback and I remember thinking to myself, "Hurry up and say who it is," and "I'm going to USC if he doesn't call my name." Then he said, "Randall Cunningham is our quarterback." I was kind of stunned. It seemed like all the air went out of me and I slumped down in my chair. Then I saw the faces of the other three guys and how upset they were and I felt bad for them. One of the guys just got up and left and never came back to the team.

In Randall's first college start, the Running Rebels lost to New Mexico, but Randall gave a glimpse of the good things to come as he completed 19-of-44 passes for 246 yards and two touchdowns. The offense continued to improve and in UNLV's fifth game, the Running Rebels beat Texas-El Paso 28-21 as Randall hit on 17-of-34 passes for 251 yards and two touchdowns. Randall saved his best for last, as he completed 23-of-37 passes for 413 yards and four touchdowns and ran for 53 yards as UNLV beat Cal State-Fullerton 42-23 in the last game of the season.

UNLV finished the season 3-8, but Randall established himself as a rising star. He completed 200-of-381 passes for 2,847 yards and 16 touchdowns and was fourth in the nation in total offense (290.8 yards per game) and the Running Rebels had the seventh best passing attack in the nation. If all that wasn't enough, Randall averaged 45.7 yards on 27 punts.

Heading into my sophomore year I was very frustrated. I was the fourth string quarterback and the coaches wanted to red-shirt me. I think the mental strain of my mother not being there affected my thinking and at one point, early in the season, I was ready to switch positions—to wide receiver or defensive back—just to get into the lineup. Back in high school, when people said I would have to play another position in college—the typical stereotypical thinking about a black high school quarterback—I refused to buy into that and it only made me more determined to play quarterback in college. But now, because of what was going on around me and all the confusion in my life, I almost gave in. I wanted to be a football player so bad so that one day I could make it to the NFL and say, "Mom, I made it."

I let my mother's death affect me in a negative way and was ready to accept less than what I wanted out of life. Eventually I got my faith back and my mind back and realized I couldn't change the situation. I couldn't bring my mother back. I decided to push and push and work to become the starting quarterback and began to realize if I was going to do something positive with my life, I would have to do it for my mother.

Obviously, my mother never got to see me play college football. But my father did—once. My sophomore year we played at Long Beach State on November 13, 1982. I saw Pop in the stands during the game, but he wasn't feeling well and left right after the game and I didn't get to talk with him. But Anthony was there afterwards and told me that Pop told him to tell me he loved me and I told Anthony to tell him the same thing. Pop died a few weeks later. It hit me hard, but because I had already gone through this when my mother died, I was afraid to let myself be hurt so bad again. I tried to hold all my feelings in and was afraid to cry. I may have shed one or two tears, but I didn't really let them out like I had after my mother passed away. I also decided I wasn't going to fail and was going to do whatever it took to make it in the NFL.

After the 1988 season, I went to visit my parents' gravesite in Santa Barbara. I had just come back from the Pro Bowl, where I was fortunate to win the MVP award. I brought along the button they give all the players in the Pro Bowl and placed it on my mother's grave. Tears came to my eyes because I knew I had made it and I knew they knew it and were proud of me.

In 1983, UNLV was 7-4 and Randall was even more efficient as he completed 189-of-316 passes for 2,545 yards and 18 touchdowns and averaged 43.5 yards a punt. Randall was named the PCAA's most valuable offensive player and made the all-league team as a quarterback and punter. He was also named to the Kodak All-American team as a punter. Sam Cunningham was a Kodak All-American his senior year at USC and little Randall used to try on the bright yellow sweater awarded to all the members of the team. "I remember it had a big patch on it that says, 'Kodak All-America, First-Team,'"

Randall said at the time. "I'd put it on and it was so big on me. Now I have one of my own to hang next to his. I feel like I'm fulfilling my dreams and expectations."

The Running Rebels continued to build and improve under the leadership of Hyde and the brilliant play of Randall. In 1984 they won their first three games, lost 16-12 at Hawaii, and then reeled off seven straight wins. The sixth game of the streak, a 36-20 win at Utah State, clinched the PCAA title and earned the Running Rebels a berth in the California Bowl. In the game, Randall completed 15-of-25 passes for 242 yards and three touchdowns. In their last regular-season game, the 10-1 Running Rebels hosted tenth-ranked Southern Methodist University.

We had a chance at cracking the Top 20 if we could beat SMU, which was a big-time football school. Before the game, Coach Hyde pulled all the seniors together for a meeting. We were his guys, the ones who had helped him build up the program and put UNLV on the football map. He told us this could be our last home game together and that all the seniors would be captains. We all got emotional and were pumped up and ready to play. I wish I could tell you we won and got ranked and invited to a New Year's Day bowl game. But we didn't. SMU was huge. They had guys 6-5 and 290 pounds. We had never played against a team so big and strong. Still, we were able to move the ball on offense. Late in the first half, I hit Byron Brown with a long pass all the way down to the SMU one. With time running out, I tried a sneak and they stopped me just short of the end zone and held me down. They wouldn't let me get up to run another play and the clock ran out. If we had scored, we would have gone into the locker room behind 17-14 and with a lot of momentum. Instead, we trailed 17-7. That was the turning point and they began wearing us down in the second half and won 38-21.

In the game, Randall completed 23-of-37 passes for 314 yards and a touchdown and also became only the third quarterback in

NCAA history to throw for 2,500 yards three straight seasons. The first two were John Elway and Doug Flutie. At halftime, Randall became the first UNLV player to have his jersey retired.

On December 15, Randall's illustrious college career came to an end at the California Bowl as UNLV smashed the University of Toledo 30-13. Randall completed 18-of-28 passes for 270 yards and two touchdowns. For the season, Randall completed 207-of-332 passes for 2,628 yards and 24 touchdowns and averaged 47.5 yards per punt. Randall was the PCAA's offensive player of the year for the second straight year and was also the all-league quarterback and punter.

When I look back on my senior year in college, it brings back a lot of fond memories. We really came together as a team and developed a lot of love and respect for each other and played about as well as we could. A few of the guys went on to play in the NFL or Canadian Football League, but for most of my teammates, that was their last football game. I've kept in touch with a few of the guys, but the sad thing about college football is once your senior season is over, everyone goes their separate ways and you lose touch with all the guys you were once so close to. Tom Polley, our middle linebacker, was drafted by the Eagles and we played together in 1985. He got cut the following year. Kenny Rose, a linebacker, graduated a year ahead of me and is with us on the Eagles. Kenny didn't get a chance to get a California Bowl ring, but maybe we can win a Super Bowl ring together.

After Bruce left, I roomed with Ray Taylor, who we all called "Chief," for the next two years and then Ronnie Scoggins my senior year. Mike McDade, one of my receivers, was one of my best friends. He still is and we always get together when I go back to Las Vegas.

Most of the guys on the team were from California and we all got along great, which is a little surprising when you consider all the different backgrounds and personalities that make up a college football team. We did have a problem my junior year. Two guys—one black and one white—got into a fight during practice and neither one of them would let it end. For the next two weeks they kept battling and a couple other guys got into it and it started getting pretty nasty. Finally, Coach Hyde called the guys involved together and told them we're all a team and that we have to come together. Nothing like that ever happened again.

I think what happens in team sports is that everyone forgets their differences and prejudices and pulls together to help the team win. There's no room for racial discrimination in sports. Color shouldn't matter, only ability. And ability is a gift from God.

I enjoyed my four years at UNLV, but I was anxious to get on with my life and take my shot at the NFL.

Mike McDade: We had a lot of fun together at UNLV and I had a chance to watch Randall mature and develop into a great quarterback. His first year he might have gotten by on his athletic ability, but by the end of his junior year, Randall was reading defenses and calling audibles and making all the big plays. And you should have seen him punt. He practiced one day a week—Fridays—and would kick the ball about three times. Then the next day he would go out and BOOM!—a 60-yard punt.

My junior year, after three games, I was leading the nation in catches and yards and I was walking around campus like a big man, saying, "You need me, Randall." He said, "I need you?" Then he started audibling out my stuff, and not passing to me. I kept saying he needed me and he kept throwing to the other guys and I kept dropping down in the rankings and wasn't even leading the team in receptions. I stopped talking and started apologizing. We were on an away trip and I bought "Hook" a chili dog with onions and made it up to him and that game he started audibling plays to me. See, I screwed myself out of catches. We called Randall "Hook" because of his nose. Take a close look and you'll see why.

Randall and I started the Wings Club, which was for the best receivers and quarterbacks. We would make our wings out of new socks. We would cut off the ends and put them on like wrist bands, but they went all the way up our arms to our elbows. In order to get your wings, you had to perform and you had to be tough. You had to catch passes, block and run. I got my wings, but then, I got them stripped away because I didn't block or something like that. Randall was the president of the Wings Club and he was the one who stripped me. So I had no socks, no wings. I was just a naked guy out there. Losing your wings was like losing your best girlfriend. Our next game was against Oregon State and I was determined to get my wings back. I caught five passes for 72 yards, but I was diving for balls and got big cherries on my elbows from the new turf at Oregon State because I didn't have any wings on. I got my wings back and never had them taken away again.

C H A P T E R

5

OCTOBER 18, 1992

For the second straight week the Eagles lose and their record drops to 4-2. The first loss is 24-17 at Kansas City, followed by a dismal 16-12 loss to Washington today that is worse than the score would indicate.

Immediately after the loss to the Redskins, Seth Joyner speaks out as only he can: "Our special teams look like garbage. Our defense is giving up too many big plays. Our offense, it seems like you say 'Washington Redskins' and they fall to pieces. Ain't none of us playing worth a (#*&), and until we get our act together, we're going to continue to get our butts beat."

To make matters worse, safety Andre Waters suffers a broken leg in the game and will probably miss the remainder of the regular season. This now means the Eagles have lost Jerome Brown, Ben Smith (still out from his 1991 knee injury), Keith Jackson (free agency) and Andre Waters—four Pro Bowl-level players. Sooner or later, and perhaps already, these loses will start to catch up with the Eagles. Plus, Ron Heller didn't play due to a strained arch and An-

tone Davis limped off the field late in the third quarter with a pulled muscle after struggling most of the afternoon trying to stop the Redskins' Charles Mann. The Eagles, who looked unbeatable two weeks ago, are struggling.

Losing Andre was a big blow to the team. I'd say that in the last eight years, Andre has intimidated more players than anyone else in the NFL. Receivers don't want to go over the middle against the Eagles and it's because they know Andre is back there waiting to lay them out. Even when they do go over the middle, they keep one eye on the ball and the other on Andre.

Andre has a reputation for being a dirty player and sometimes people call him "Dirty Waters." But Andre has cleaned up his act the past couple of years and I've watched him grow from being a rookie free agent into a Pro Bowl-level player. The only problem is, because of his reputation, Andre never gets voted to the Pro Bowl even though he deserves to be there. People say Andre goes for the knees a lot, but he has to. Andre weighs 190 pounds and in our defense, he's asked to play like a linebacker, which means he has to take on 290-pound linemen, shed them and then tackle running backs who almost all weigh over 200 pounds. The best way to tackle them is to go for their legs, get leverage and send the guy flying. Andre does that better than anyone else in the league and he's delivered some monster hits that inspire the entire defense. Wes Hopkins, our other safety, is the same way and the two of them are the best safety combination in the NFL.

Andre's a great guy off the field, but still he's Andre, which means he's a little nuts. I remember once he was driving around after practice in the parking lot, swerving around and pretending like he was going to hit everyone's car. By accident, I think, he nicked someone's car. I think it was Chris Carter's car. Chris was pretty upset, but it was Andre so there wasn't much he could do. I'm sure Andre took care of the damages.

That reminds me. Jimmie Giles, who used to play tight end for us, hit my car in the parking lot once and put a scratch in it and knocked off the side mirror. Jimmy never paid me back. So Jimmy, if you're reading this book, you still owe me $1,500.

We'll miss Andre. He sets the tone for the entire team and is one of the key players on our defense. There's a chance he could be back for the playoffs and that would give us a big lift.

Randall, who went into the Washington game with an incredible 111.4 quarterback rating—easily the best in the NFL—has a very mediocre game by his standards, completing 22-of-40 passes for 207 yards, with one touchdown and one interception. The Redskins' rush is fierce from the opening whistle and at times the Eagles' offensive line barely seems to slow down the Redskins on their way to Randall, who was sacked five times, hurried 10 more times, had four balls knocked down and two others tipped at the line of scrimmage. After the game Randall sports a nasty cut on his throwing hand, an ugly welt on his shoulder and a slightly sprained ankle.

"We had some problems," an understated Kotite says after the game. "[Randall] had to run for his life a great deal of the time . . . They had a 'spy' on him early. When we ran left, toward our bench, you could see them sliding along the line that way."

"You have to give them credit," Randall says after the game. "They are a very well coached team. Joe Gibbs might be the best coach in the NFL. They have great players and a great scheme and they are very tough to beat in Washington. They've played me for eight years, they know my style. They have a couple of schemes maybe other teams won't try because they don't have the personnel."

Although his accomplishment is diminished by the loss, late in the game Randall scrambles for six yards on a quarterback draw to break Fran Tarkenton's all-time quarterback career rushing total of 3,674 yards. Randall finished the day with 39 yards on five carries and a career total of 3,683. What took Tarkenton 16 seasons to accomplish, Randall does in seven.

The rushing record was a milestone for me, but since we lost, I didn't really get too excited about it. I thought they were going to stop the game when I broke the record—they did the week before when Art Monk broke the record for the most career receptions—but they didn't and I wasn't even aware I broke it until after the game. I know I couldn't have done it without my teammates. There have been plenty of times when I'd be running downfield and was about to slide or go out of bounds, but I'd see a guy make a great block and I'd run for another five or 10 yards. I thank God for the ability to run like I do and I hope I can rush for 5,000 yards before I'm finished. That would be something, to be the first quarterback to run for 5,000 yards.

I watched a lot of football games on television when I was a kid and the quarterbacks I enjoyed were the scramblers, like Fran Tarkenton, Roger Staubach, Vince Evans and James Harris. They added another dimension to the game and were exciting to watch; I wanted to play like they did.

But I don't consider myself a scrambling quarterback: I'm a running quarterback. As a quarterback, your first weapon is your ability to throw the ball. Your second weapon is the ability to scramble around and create some time to allow your receivers to get open. That's what Tarkenton and Staubach did so well. I think I've added a third weapon—a new dimension—to the game by running the ball. I consider myself a dual player—a quarterback and a running back. I've passed for over 3,000 yards three straight years (1988-90) and in 1990 I ran for 942 yards. I'm not trying to sound cocky, that's just how I like to play. I'll do whatever it takes to win, and if that means taking off and running downfield and jumping over people or diving into the end zone or flying through the air and getting crunched or landing on my head, I'll do it if it will help us win. If a guy is open, I'll hit him with a pass. If everyone's covered and I can run for five or 10 yards, I'll do that.

People always said I would get killed scrambling and running and I should be like every other quarterback and stay in the pocket

—where it is safe. Well, guess where I was when I got hurt? That's right, in the pocket. The pocket is where big, sloppy, nasty 300-pound guys hit you at full speed, then land on top of you, knocking out all your wind and sometimes dislocating your shoulder or cracking some ribs and all sorts of stuff like that. I'm not just going to stand there and let them hit me.

When it comes down to either staying in the pocket and letting a 300-pound guy drop you for a five-yard loss, or running and maybe picking up five or six yards, I'll run every time. When I see or feel pressure coming up the middle, I can buy some time by stepping one way and then stepping back the other way. This helps my offensive linemen set up their blocks because their man will be coming right back at them and the defensive player is usually so intent on sacking me that he forgets where the offensive linemen are. He won't see my lineman hit him right in the middle of his chest. Or, if a guy is coming at me fast and out of control, I'll sucker him with a move and take off through the gap he just left. Normally, our offensive linemen's technique is to grab the inside of their defender's shoulder pads and tie up his arms. That means I can run right by a guy and even though he's a foot away, he can't reach out and grab me.

Once I'm past the line of scrimmage, instead of getting hit by a 300-pound lineman, I'll be facing 240-pound linebackers. Hopefully, I can put a move on the linebacker and gain some more yards and get hit by a 190-pound cornerback or safety or run out of bounds or slide.

They say reading the secondary is the most important thing for a quarterback. As you may have already learned, I'm different from other quarterbacks. To me, the important thing is reading the defensive line first. I study their fronts and stunts and how they rush and make sure I know where the rush is coming from so I know where I can run to escape. Plus, I'll tell the guys on the line if they are tired or having trouble with their man, "Hey, Antone, if your guy is rushing hard to the inside, let him go to the inside and I'll roll to the right around him and you can just keep pushing him to the inside." That makes things easier for Antone and gets me away from the rush. Then I can roll out and hit the receiver or keep running.

Sometimes I decide at the line of scrimmage, before the snap, if I'm going to run. If I see the linebackers are going to blitz, I'll drop back and throw it to the hot man—Keith Byars or another running back coming out of the backfield or Freddie or Calvin who also have to read the blitz and adjust their routes. If the defense isn't blitzing and it's only a few yards for the first down and I know the linebackers are going to take a seven- or eight-yard drop into coverage, I can run straight up the middle for the first down. Or, if I see the defense is playing man-to-man on my receivers, I'll send them all long and then I'll take off, knowing all the defensive backs will be dropping back into coverage and can't get to me until after I get the first down.

I love to roll out because that gives me a lot of options and puts a lot of pressure on the defense. If I roll out and I see only one or two guys in front of me and I have a blocker, I usually run. If there are three or more defensive guys there, I usually pass. When I roll out, or when I'm scrambling, and looking for an open receiver, I always look deep to short. Here's why: when a quarterback runs out of the pocket, the defensive backs have a tendency to leave the receivers they're covering and rush up to the line of scrimmage to try and get the quarterback. I always tell my receivers, when something happens and I'm running around, just go deep. If it's Freddie and his defender is still on him, I'll throw the ball deep to Freddie anyway because I have confidence he can go up and grab it or outrun the defender to the ball.

A perfect example of this was a play against Buffalo in the 1990 season when I scrambled around and around in the end zone and then threw it as far as I could to Freddie, who outjumped the defender and went 95 yards for the touchdown. I saw the defensive back covering Freddie, but I had confidence I could get the ball to him high, where he had a chance to go up and get it.

Keith Jackson and I used to do something special when I scrambled. Normally, the tight end is supposed to run toward the quarterback when he's scrambling, so the quarterback can see the receiver easier and it's also a shorter throw. But Keith used to run the opposite way I scrambled. It's a tougher throw because I have to throw away from where I'm running, across my body. Although it's a tougher throw, it's easier to get open that way and Keith and I hooked up on a lot of big plays doing that. Keith Byars also knows what to do when I start scrambling and has a knack for getting open. Keith has incredibly soft hands and catches everything close to him and runs with the ball after he catches it as well as anyone in the league. If I don't see Keith or if there's a defender on him, Keith just turns around, finds someone to block and lays him out.

When you run with the football, you get hit. That's rule number one in the NFL. And defensive players always seem to save their best licks for quarterbacks. Believe me, I've taken my share of hard hits over the years. It's kind of ironic that I set the rushing record against the Redskins. I've rushed for more yards against Washington (473) than any other team, and I've also taken more hard hits from the Redskins than any other team.

We used to have this play where I would drop back and then dash right and throw to the outside receiver on the right side, who was running a 25-yard come-back route. If the receiver was covered, I had the option to run. The first time we ran it in a game against the Redskins, Monte Coleman, their outside linebacker on that side, came up and jerked me up under the chin right after I threw the ball. I went to the sidelines and said, "Don't call that play again, they got it covered," and then I forgot about it. Later, the coaches called it again and this time Coleman hit me even harder. There was stuff coming out of my nose, my helmet was turned halfway around, I was looking out the ear hole and my head was ringing.

In another game against the Redskins, on a third-and-long play, I dropped back from inside our own 10. Nobody was open and I started running downfield. A guy was coming on me—I think it was

Coleman again—and I jumped up and over him, but while I was in the air, their safety Alvin Walton came up and knocked the snot out of me. Since I was so high up in the air, it was like getting hit a second time, even harder, when I hit the ground. I felt a BOOM! when Walton hit me and a BAM! when I hit the ground. I got right up, trying to be tough, but all my wind was gone and my back was killing me. I didn't want to give them the satisfaction of knowing they'd got me with a good one, so I walked back to the huddle like nothing happened. I got about halfway there and had to signal for McMahon to come in. I just sat down right in the middle of the field and said, "Man, I don't care how much it costs, I'll give my whole salary right now just for a couple of breaths of air." But I wound up coming back into the game the next time we had the ball and we won the game.

Since I know I'm going to be running and taking some hits, I take precautions. First of all, I don't wear quarterback shoulder pads. They aren't solid enough. Some guys like the lightest possible pads, especially receivers. Mike Quick used to wear these shoulder pads that looked like he got them from a kid playing in the Pop Warner League. I want protection so I wear linebacker or defensive back shoulder pads. I found I was getting hit in the thigh a lot, and, when someone hits you with a helmet in the thigh, that hurts like you wouldn't believe. So I wear inch-thick thigh pads. I wear the normal knee pads, but under them I wear a foam rubber sleeve. I cut the middle out of the sleeve, right where it covers my knee cap, so I don't lose any mobility. This year, of course, I have my brace on my left knee. It's an Orthotec Performer and gives me a lot of mobility and protection.

You can take all the precautions you want and wear every pad in the locker room, but still, you're going to take some shots and get hurt. My rookie year I sprained my ankle pretty bad. In 1987, against the Cardinals, my thumb got hit and swelled up so much I couldn't grip the football and I had to come out of the game. But overall, I've been blessed by God not to have had more injuries. I know you must be saying, what about your knee, but like I said, I believe the reason I got hurt at the start of the 1991 season was because for a few minutes, I lost my faith in God's protection. Now, I have my faith back stronger than ever and I'll never lose it, not even for a second.

I took a good shot in our game today against the Redskins. Late in the fourth quarter, I ran out of the pocket and was heading up the sideline. A guy hit me hard and I went down and I think my head hit the ground. Things went black for about a second or two. I got up a little dingy and was thinking to myself, "Should I stay in or come out for a play or two to let my head clear?" But you have to be tough out there—mentally and physically—and I decided to stay in the game. I knew I had about 25 seconds to let the dinginess clear up before I had to call the play, so I stood there and tried to shake it off. I got to the huddle and our guys were still arguing with the Redskins' defense. "Chill out," I said. I couldn't really see the 25-second clock and was having trouble seeing the play that Zeke was signalling in from the sideline. Finally, I got it, called the play in the huddle, walked up to the line, took the snap and hit a guy with a short pass for a first down. I was getting my bearings back and figured everything was OK, but all of a sudden things got worse and I had a bad case of tunnel vision. This happens to me once or twice a year. When you get tunnel vision, it's like you're looking through the tube from a roll of toilet paper. Things in the middle are clear, but outside of that small, center circle, everything else is blurry. Your peripheral vision is gone. Only time—about 30 minutes—can clear it up, but you don't have the luxury of time in the middle of a game.

When you get tunnel vision, you have to focus even more on everything around you to compensate for the fog in your head. First, I yelled to the sideline that I couldn't see the signals and for Zeke to shout them to me. Then I kept saying the play over and over in my head to memorize it and make sure I said it the right way in the huddle. One little mistake could throw the whole play off. We were running our two-minute offense. I concentrated on my receivers, connected on a few passes and began to get my confidence back. I hit Calvin with a 20-yard pass and a few plays later hit him for six yards and a score to cut the lead to 16-12 with only 25 seconds left to play. My head didn't clear up for another 20 minutes.

CHAPTER

6

The 1985 draft wasn't considered a strong one for quarterbacks. Doug Flutie, the Heisman Trophy winner from Boston College, was considered too short for the NFL and wound up signing with the United States Football League (USFL) before the draft. The University of Miami's Bernie Kosar, who left school early, was picked by Cleveland in a special supplemental draft held after the regular draft. Of the quarterbacks eligible for the draft, the top players were: Randall Cunningham, Steve Bono from UCLA, Frank Reich from Maryland, Steve Calabria from Colgate, Rusty Hilger from Oklahoma State and Gale Gilbert from the University of California. Randall helped his cause when he was selected the most valuable player in the East-West Shrine Bowl. Randall showed all his skills as he threw a touchdown pass and caught a touchdown pass. That's right. Randall caught a touchdown pass. On the play, he handed off to wide receiver Vance Johnson, who was faking an end-around. Randall then ran down the sideline and Johnson threw him the ball for the score.

The Shrine Bowl marked the end of an extremely successful and prolific college career for Randall, who set every UNLV career passing record, including completion percentage (57.9), completions

(614), yards (8,290) and touchdowns (60) and was chosen All-PCAA three straight years and was named the league's offensive player of the year after his junior and senior years. Randall was also an all-league punter three straight years, posting a career 45.2 average.

Despite these credentials, there were some question marks about Randall. A couple days before the draft, in the Philadelphia Daily News, *a so-called expert was quoted as saying Randall was, "a Walter Lewis, Reggie Collier type. Probably will be a better Canadian [Football League] guy as a quarterback. You draft him and let him punt and then try and bring him along as a quarterback."*

I was kind of the unknown guy in the draft because I played at UNLV. We weren't a well known program and didn't play on national television every week. Plus, I was known as a scrambler and NFL teams like pocket passers. Then there was the "black" thing. The one guy compared me to Walter Lewis and Reggie Collier, even though our styles are completely different. The only thing we have in common is all three of us are black and quarterbacks and I guess, to some people, that makes us similar.

Even though I tried not to think about it, I guess there were still a lot of people in the NFL who didn't think blacks had what it took to play quarterback. I grew up watching James Harris and Doug Williams play in the NFL and they inspired me and were my football role models. Over the years, I've learned that there are going to be people out there who won't like me because of my color. That's something I can't control, so I don't let it bother me. I'm just going to be myself and not get involved in the whole race thing. I know who I am, where I came from and what color I am. I respect people for who they are and don't worry about what color, religion or nationality they are.

Before the draft, all the teams come to visit you on campus or invite you to camps where they time you and test you on all sorts of drills. In a lot of the camps, I was there with Vance Johnson, a wide receiver who wound up being taken in the second round by the

Denver Broncos. Vance and I tore those drills up and impressed the scouts. On the vertical jump test, Vance outjumped me by an inch— 37 inches to 36 inches. But he cheated. Well, he didn't really cheat, but he took advantage of the rules. When they measured us, Vance took off his shoes so he would be an inch shorter. Then, when we jumped, he put them back on so he gained an inch. I still say we tied.

Daman Allen, who played quarterback for Cal-State Fullerton and is the younger brother of Marcus Allen, was also at a couple of the camps with me. Both of our teams were in the PCAA, so Daman and I knew each other and were always competing against each other for all-league honors. I was worried he might be picked ahead of me. Daman threw a great long ball—a better long ball than I did —even though I was known for having a strong arm. Daman was about 6-2 and thin, about 170 pounds. But he was tough and could take a hit. They timed us in the 40-yard dash and Daman ran a 4.58 and I ran a 4.59. As far as we knew, these were by far the two fastest times turned in by any quarterbacks in the country that year. I couldn't believe it when Daman wasn't drafted. Daman went up to Canada and is still playing and doing well in the CFL, where he helped his team win a Grey Cup (the Canadian equivalent of the Super Bowl) one year and was the MVP of the game.

I wasn't sure where I would be drafted or by who, but from what I heard, I could be picked anywhere from the first round to the fifth round.

According to Len Stiles, the Eagles director of player personnel in 1985: "In our opinion there were two quarterbacks worth considering—Bono and Cunningham. There was very mixed opinion relative to our scouts and coaching staff. In fact, the majority of our scouts favored Bono . . . There were two big controversies about Randall. One, maybe there was too much sandlot in him, that you couldn't depend on him to stay in the pocket. Two, there was concern that he had a windup motion in his delivery. Well, Ted [Marchibroda, the Eagles' offensive coordinator in 1985 and a big Randall fan] came up with the idea of using one of those old Bell & Howell projectors to evaluate Randall's delivery frame-by-frame. We measured [Dan] Marino, [Ron] Jaworski and Randall. Marino had the quickest delivery, about eight frames. Jaworski released the ball in 10 or 12 frames. Randall was in the same vicinity. Maybe one or two frames slower. So, even though it looked like a windup, Randall's delivery was very close in time to Jaworski's."

A week before the draft, the Eagles worked out Randall and Bono one final time.

"Randall had an outstanding workout," Stiles said. "He had touch on the long ball and the short ball. I felt he had comparable downfield velocity to Elway. I told our coaches, 'Don't look at Randall's style. Just watch the ball.' He could really throw that thing, and he could throw on the run . . . There was a uniqueness about Randall as a competitor. Not that he had the best arm or was the best at reading defenses. He was just a unique competitor. If he threw an interception, he'd hit the guy like a strong safety. I'd never seen a quarterback make a stick like that. He could punt too. I got a hang time of 5.4 seconds over 55 yards. Anything above 4.5 is what you're looking for. He was just a take-charge guy. Still, we knew it would take some time."

On draft day, the Eagles knew they wanted Randall. They just weren't sure what round to select him. On the first round the Eagles drafted offensive lineman Kevin Allen. The Eagles didn't want to use a second-round pick to take Randall, but they didn't have a third-round pick and were afraid to wait until the fourth round for fear that Randall would already be snatched up. When it came time for the Eagles to make their second pick, they chose Randall, who wound up being the thirty-seventh player and first quarterback taken in the draft. Bono was the second quarterback selected and went to Minnesota in the sixth round. The Eagles had their heir to

Ron Jaworski, who was still a very effective quarterback but was 34 and closing in on the end of his great career, which included leading the Eagles to the Super Bowl in the 1980 season.

"I figured I'd sit behind Ron for a year or two and then take over," Randall said. "It seemed like the perfect situation for me."

The day after the April 30 draft, Randall flew to Philadelphia with Jim Steiner, his agent. Eagles' owner Norman Braman was effusive in praise of his team's number two pick. "We no longer have to worry about what we're going to do when Ron Jaworski retires," Braman said. "Randall Cunningham is the Eagles' quarterback of the future. He is a fine young man and an exceptional athlete and we expect him to lead this football team for many, many years."

A day later, Braman wasn't so complimentary. "I really question his character," Braman fumed. "What he did was totally unethical. It showed a lack of honesty and good faith. To think this was a kid that we were talking about leading our team in the future for years to come. As far as I'm concerned, Randall Cunningham doesn't exist. He's not going to play for the Philadelphia Eagles."

What could have caused such a turnaround? The answer is simple. Before the draft, and secretly, Randall signed a conditional contract with John F. Bassett, the owner of the Tampa Bay Bandits of the United States Football League. According to the four-year, approximately $3 million contract, Cunningham would be free to negotiate with the Eagles, but the Bandits would have the right to match any offer made by Philadelphia. Tampa Bay had a few weeks to exercise its option and guarantee the contract. If they didn't, the Bandits would give up any claim they had on Randall, but would still owe him a $650,000 breach-of-contract penalty.

At the time, there wasn't even a USFL. The league had disbanded for a year after the previous season and announced that it would start up again in the spring of 1986. In the meantime, the USFL was in the midst of a nasty court battle with the NFL, which it was suing for violating anti-trust regulations. There was debate as to how binding the contract was that Randall—and several other NFL draft *picks—signed with Bassett, who had cancer and was in very poor health at the time. The USFL eventually lost its case and folded.*

"We just found out today [about Randall's contract with Tampa Bay]," Eagles' general manager (and now president) Harry Gamble said on May 2. "But as far as real facts, we don't have any. I don't have anything to go on. Until we get some information, it's a little difficult to even comment on." Nobody knew exactly what was going on, including Randall.

I had no guarantee where I would get drafted or how much I could sign for. So when John F. Bassett came along and offered me $3 million over four years, I was very interested. That's a lot of money and definitely a lot more than a second-round NFL quarterback could ever get. I figured I couldn't lose. I could go to the Bandits for about $3 million, or, if they were willing to pay, I could go to the Eagles for the same amount. Plus, the contract said I would get a lump sum payment of $650,000 if Tampa Bay breached the contract.

I really wanted to play in the NFL—that had been my goal since I was a little kid playing one-on-one football with Bruce in our backyard—but I'd have to be crazy to sign a contract for less than $1 million with the Eagles when I could get two or three times that from John Bassett.

Now that I look back on it, I realize it was a negotiating ploy by my agent, Jim Steiner, to get me more money from the Eagles. All along, Jim never thought I would actually play for the Bandits. Jim, who is still with me, is an excellent agent and takes care of all his clients and gets us the best deal possible, which is what he was trying to do for me in 1985. Eventually, Tampa Bay did breach the contract and I did receive a portion of the $650,000. John F. Bassett died about a year later, owing a lot of people a lot of money and I was just one more name on the list of people trying to get paid.

Eventually I signed with the Eagles—for a lot less than $3 million—and went to West Chester University for my first NFL training camp. I got to camp a week late and it took me a little while to fit in and be accepted by my new teammates. First of all, I had a Jerri-curl hairstyle. I enjoyed Michael Jackson and his music and liked his Jerri-curl and wanted to have some fun with my hair. I also thought it would improve my looks, which needed some work. Everyone was always telling me to get a nose job once I signed my contract and had some money. After I signed, I threatened to do it, but everyone said, "Don't do it, don't do it." I was never going to get a nose job; I was just joking with them. But, after I signed, I did buy a 944 Porsche and a long leather coat. I came to training camp wearing a tee-shirt that read, "Any Questions, Call My Agent." Jim Steiner gave that to all his clients as a publicity thing. It didn't mean anything.

I guess people who didn't know me started judging me from my hair, my tee-shirt and so on, and they decided I was a cocky rookie who needed to be taught a lesson. At dinner one night, some of the veterans told me I had to get up and sing my college song. I asked Kenny Jackson, who was the Eagles' number one choice in 1984 (and quickly became one of my best friends), if he had to sing a song the year before and he said, "I didn't sing no songs." I figured if Kenny didn't have to sing, I didn't have to sing either. I didn't realize I was going against the norm and this really pissed off a few of the guys. Eventually I did sing, but I didn't know any UNLV songs so I did my version of "We Are The World." I don't think it went over too well, mostly because I can't sing.

A day or two later, a couple of guys—including Ray Ellis and Mark Dennard—put some hot stuff in my jock before practice. Sure enough, when I put it on, it burned like hot sauce on the tongue. I was pretty mad and asked Dennard why he did it. He was a big offensive lineman and he kind of looked at me and said, "What you going to do about it, punk?" Then he pushed me. I wasn't scared; I give people three chances and then I lose it. I said don't push me, but he pushed me again and I got so mad tears were coming out of my eyes. I told him do it one more time and I would have him jacked up and taken care of by some of my friends. I walked off and he never messed with me again. Ray Ellis and I eventually became friends, but Dennard and I never were friends, and he was gone after the 1985 season.

Things got better after I started practice and showed what I could do and the guys got to know me a little better and realized I wasn't the cocky jerk they may have thought I was. There's always going to be some resentment toward rookies, especially a high draft choice who gets a nice contract, a lot of publicity and is perceived as being cocky. But all that stuff was over with in a week and I got to be one of the guys. I did learn a lesson and now I go out of my way to be friendly to rookies.

Randall's new teammates quickly got a first-hand look at his talents. In a 37-17 preseason win against the New York Jets on August 10, Randall made his professional debut and completed 3-of-6 passes and scrambled for 86 yards on five carries.

Veteran tight end John Spagnola sarcastically summed up Randall's performance: "He's really got quarterbacking down. He took a very sophisticated position and narrowed it down to one receiver. If the receiver is covered, he just takes off and runs 50 yards. Maybe we shouldn't worry so much about strong and weak zones and everything else."

Asked to rate his performance by a reporter, Randall gives himself a 75 out of 100. "That's all I deserve because I didn't get the ball and throw it, and that was nobody's fault but my own," Randall said. "When I dropped back and the linebackers were blitzing, I didn't necessarily read the coverage. I'm learning. Once I start picking it up, I'll see exactly what I need to do."

Despite his scrambling start and growing confidence, Randall knew his place once the regular season started—on the bench. Jaworski was the number one man in town. "Ron is the quarterback,"

Randall said after his first preseason game. "He's the number one quarterback and is going to be the number one quarterback. He's the best quarterback on the team and is going to be the starter. I know that. I'm just here to learn right now."

It turned out to be a cram course. In the Eagles' first regular season game of 1985, a 21-0 loss to the Giants, Randall replaced Jaworski late in the game. A couple of days later, coach Marion Campbell shocked everyone on the team and in the city—including and especially Randall—when he named the rookie as his starter for the Eagles' second game—at home against the Los Angeles Rams on September 15, 1985.

I'll always remember that first game against the Giants at Giants Stadium. It was raining and windy and neither team could get much going on offense. In fact, I'm sure that Bill Parcells, the Giants' coach at the time, opened up the tunnels at the end of the field whenever we had the ball just so it would be windier for our offense.

The past few years the Giants had always beat up on the Eagles, and it was like, "Here we go again." I didn't expect to play, but still I was all pumped up. I got my Jerri curls processed for the trip to New York; I wanted to look sharp. The guys had prepared me. They said when we get to Giants Stadium it won't be like a preseason game, it would be loud—real loud. I kind of said, "yeah," but let it go in one ear and out the other. Then we got there and it was loud. They introduced the starting lineups and I couldn't even hear the announcer's voice. That made a big impression on me and I wondered to myself if I was ready for this. I found out sooner than I expected.

In the fourth quarter, they said, "Cunningham, go in." I don't know who said it or if I even had time to warm up. I was in shock. I almost pooped on myself I was so nervous. I went to the huddle and called the play right, which surprised me as well as the rest of the guys in the huddle. Then I walked up to the line of scrimmage and it hit me—I was playing in the NFL. There was Lawrence Taylor—

L.T.—the greatest linebacker ever to play the game, a couple of feet away, glaring at me like he wanted to kill me. Next to him was Harry Carson at middle linebacker and over on the right side was Carl Banks. That made three Pro Bowl linebackers. Plus, they had Jim Burt at nose guard and Leonard Marshall at tackle. That was a serious defense. Those guys just glared at me, like a bunch of sharks who smelled blood. My blood. It felt like L.T.'s eyes were burning holes through me. I dropped back and started scrambling and picked up a few yards.

Guys had been talking all week about how fierce the rivalry was between the Giants and the Eagles and now I was getting a first-hand look at it. I was getting hit from every which way and when I tried to get up, guys were pushing me back down and saying, "We'll be back!"

I completed one pass and ran for a few yards. We did get things going on one drive and crossed the 50 for the first time in the game and that gave me a little confidence. I was just glad to get it over with and get out of there alive.

A day or two later, Marion Campbell told me I would be starting the next week against the Rams. To say I was shocked was an understatement. Looking back on it, I realize I wasn't ready. Right after he told me I would be starting, I started worrying about how Ron would take the news. We were just starting to become good friends and now, all of a sudden, this rookie was taking his place. I was sitting by my locker and finally Ron walked in. He came over and put his arm around me and said, "Hey, big guy, this isn't right what they're doing to you, but I'm behind you 100 percent." Ron shook my hand and said he'd be there to help me and answer any questions I had. Ron showed a lot of class and made the whole situation a lot easier for me. I gained a lot of respect for Ron and we ended up becoming very good friends. I learned a lot from Ron. He taught me to study game film for what it is, to look at it as a game and not be awed because it was the NFL. He taught me to look at playing football as a job and to be prepared and go out and be competitive. Plus, Ron told me I wouldn't always be playing football, so I had to take care of myself financially while I was playing, do my endorsements and take care of my money and be ready for life after football.

The week before the Rams' game, I watched more film than I had in my whole life up to that point. Ted Marchibroda, our offensive coordinator, gave me six reels of film every night and I took them home and watched until I fell asleep in front of the television. When the game came, I was prepared. We ran a basic offense and the Rams showed that they were only going to rush three people and drop everyone else back into coverage. Being a rookie, I figured I'd revert back to what I did in college, which was to just drop back and throw quick, on rhythm. But in the NFL, all the guys are much faster and better athletes and my college style wasn't quite ready for the NFL.

The Eagles lost 17-6 and Randall completed 14-of-34 passes for 211 yards, threw four interceptions and ran for 90 yards on 10 carries. The following week against Washington, the Eagles won 19-6 and Randall completed 8-of-15 passes for 187 yards, rushed for 60 yards and threw his first NFL touchdown pass—17 yards to Earnest Jackson.

I didn't play great, but the main thing was, I made the plays I had to make to keep some drives going and help us move down the field. But, for the most part, the key to the game was the defense stopping the Redskins.

The following week, against the Giants, the Eagles lost 16-10 in overtime. Randall's next and last start came the following week in New Orleans. Randall struggled and was replaced by Jaworski, who got hot, but the Eagles still lost 23-21. Randall got into one more game in 1985—November 17 at St. Louis against the Cardinals.

My mother, Mabel, was the strongest woman I have ever met. (FAMILY PHOTO)

My father, Samuel, was a quiet, easygoing man, but you didn't want to get him angry. (FAMILY PHOTO)

I came into the world on March 27, 1963, at 10:50 P.M. (FAMILY PHOTO)

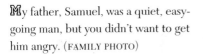

Our Baby
Name Randall Wade Cunningham
Born at Cottage Hospital, Santa Barbara, Calif.
On March 27th Time 10:50 p.m.
Weight 9 lbs. ½ oz.

Parents
Samuel Lewis
Mabel Zudell

1963

Here are the Cunningham brothers. (From upper left clockwise: Anthony, Sam, Bruce, and Randall.) (FAMILY PHOTO)

Here I am in the third grade, taking the snap from center. (FAMILY PHOTO)

Here I am sharing my high school
graduation with my
parents and Bruce.
Next stop: UNLV. (FAMILY PHOTO)

Although I was a passer in college, I still managed to do a little
scrambling now and then. (UNLV PHOTO)

After my junior year at UNLV, I was named to the Kodak All-American team as a punter. (UNLV PHOTO)

Having my jersey retired during halftime of my last home game at UNLV was a great honor. (From left to right: UNLV Athletic Director Dr. Brad Rothermel, coach Harvey Hyde, Randall, UNLV President Dr. Robert Maxson.) (UNLV PHOTO)

My brother Sam was my role model and inspired me to dream of making it in the NFL. (DICK MARTIN PHOTOGRAPHY)

This is the hit that ended my 1991 season and started the long route back. (PHOTO BY MICHAEL MERCANTI / PHILADELPHIA DAILY NEWS)

Here I am being carted off the field in Green Bay. To make matters worse the truck went to the wrong exit and we had to drive across the field a second time. (PHOTO BY MICHAEL MERCANTI / PHILADELPHIA DAILY NEWS)

@n Monday Night Football I showed the country I'm still scrambling. (PHOTO BY MICHAEL MERCANTI / PHILADELPHIA DAILY NEWS)

Early in the third period, Freddie Joe Nunn slammed Jaworski to the turf and he bruised his shoulder and had to come out of the game with the score tied 14-14. Randall played with more confidence and control and led the Eagles to a 24-14 win to raise their record to 6-5 and keep alive their slim playoff hopes. The Birds finished the season 7-9 and missed the playoffs. For the season, Randall completed 34-of-81 passes for 548 yards, one touchdown and eight interceptions and ran for 205 yards on 29 carries—an average of 7.1 per carry.

I got hurt in the second Giants game; I twisted my ankle real bad. I was hobbling around in practice all week and didn't think I was going to play against New Orleans, but I started. I struggled, threw three interceptions and was pulled. After the game, Earl Campbell, who had been such a great running back with the Houston Oilers and was now finishing up his career with the Saints, came up to me and said, "You're going to be one of the best quarterbacks in the league, keep your head up and don't let this bother you. You're young and you have a lot of potential." That was the only thing that enabled me to keep my confidence. To sum it up, 1985 was the worst year of my career. I went out there mentally prepared for games, but found out that wasn't enough. The players were physically and mentally better than the ones I had played against in college and I realized I had a lot to learn and Ron should be the starting quarterback. I realized that in the NFL, football wasn't a game—it was a job and I would have to spend more time learning what I thought I already knew, which was *Professional Football.*

Following the 1985 season, Marion Campbell was fired and replaced by Buddy Ryan, who was one of the hottest assistant coaches in the NFL. Before coming to the Eagles, Buddy was the defensive coordinator for the Chicago Bears and ended the 1985 season being carried off the field by his players after the Bears whipped the New England Patriots in the Super Bowl.

When Buddy first came to town, he was very verbal and open to the media about how he was going to come in and change things and get rid of anyone who he didn't think could fit in with his style of football. It was intimidating and we didn't know what to make of Buddy. We soon learned that Buddy was a coach who was determined to win. Buddy had a lot of confidence in himself and his coaching ability and he was determined to do things his way, no matter who he pissed off or offended. You have to understand, Buddy gives orders, Buddy doesn't take orders.

Jaworski held out during the early part of training camp and the Eagles brought in Matt Cavanaugh from the San Francisco 49ers, where he had been a backup to Joe Montana. They gave up a third-round pick in 1986 and a second-round pick in 1987 for Matt, and everybody was saying Ron and Matt were going to battle it out for the number one job. That left me as the third-string quarterback and I wasn't sure Buddy was going to keep three quarterbacks.

Buddy announced to the media that anyone who held out would lose their job and Ron was one of the guys he was directing his remarks toward. I played well in the first couple of preseason games and was starting to think that I had a chance to be the starter. Then Ron signed his contract, came to camp and was named the number two quarterback and a few days later regained the number one position. Matt was number two and I was dropped to third string, which I wasn't too pleased about. I was doing a good job in practice and thought I had a chance to be a starter. Now, all of a sudden, I'm third string. I figured I was going to be cut, so I started pouting. I got mad and developed this attitude that it doesn't make sense to work hard if I was going to get dogged out by Buddy like that. I moped around in practice the next morning. Before the afternoon practice, Mike Quick talked to me and told me to keep working hard, that I would eventually get my chance. In the afternoon practice I was zipping the ball and hitting guys right on the numbers. The next day in the paper, Buddy was quoted as saying that Randall Cunningham's shadow practiced for him in the morning, but that he was back in the afternoon practice. Buddy was playing a game with me, testing my mental capacity and toughness. I think I earned his respect when I came back strong after being dropped to third string.

In the first two exhibition games, I completed 6-of-13 passes for 106 yards, a touchdown and no interceptions. I also ran for 144 yards and three touchdowns. I think these two games planted a seed in Buddy's mind about how to use me during the regular season and a little later he shocked the NFL by making me his third-and-long or "nickle" quarterback. This meant that when it was third-and-six or more, Buddy would take Ron out of the game and put me in to make something happen and try and get the first down. If I was successful, Ron came back in. This was something that had never been done before in the history of the NFL.

Doing this during preseason games was one thing, but nobody believed Buddy when he said he was going to keep doing it in the regular season. Right before our first game in 1986, Buddy came up to me and told me to stand next to him when we had the ball and be ready to go in. I was like, "yeah right," still not believing he was going to do it. But sure enough, early in the game, it was third-and-six and he said, "Go in." The fans couldn't believe it either and they cheered. I scrambled and got the first down and came off the field and Buddy said, "Be ready to do it again." At this point, I started to believe I was the second-string quarterback and Buddy was trying to utilize my abilities and develop me as a quarterback.

The Eagles lost 41-14 to the Redskins and Randall completed 1-of-3 passes for eight yards and rushed for 31 yards on two carries. The Eagles' second game was against the Chicago Bears, the defending Super Bowl champions and Buddy's former team. Buddy had the Eagles fired up and late in the game the score was 10-10. With just over a minute to play, Jaworski was buried by William "The Refrigerator" Perry and had to leave the game with the Eagles facing a third-and-nine on their own 33. It looked like the perfect situation to bring in Randall, who had already completed 1-of-3 passes for 13 yards and run for 16 yards on one carry. But Ryan decided to go with the more-experienced Cavanaugh, who came in and threw an interception on his first play. Cavanaugh threw another interception in overtime and the Eagles lost 13-10.

"That was my fault," Buddy says after the game about his decision to go with Cavanaugh instead of Randall. "Because Jaws was down and [Bears' linebacker Mike Singletary] was down on the field at the same time. Both of them are great players and I was concerned about both of them. I should have been paying attention to business. But [offensive coordinator Ted Plumb] told me he just felt like the way the situation was that Cavanaugh was ready to roll in there, and [quarterback coach Doug Scovil said] the same thing."

Buddy stuck with his revolving quarterback strategy and Randall began to play more and more as the season wore on. Against the Giants on October 12, Randall converted on three third-and-long situations. The following week, during a controversial 17-14 loss to Dallas, Randall saw considerable playing time. With Jaworski out with a bad passing hand, Cavanaugh, who was still officially the number two quarterback, started and played the first half, but he completed only 3-of-10 passes and was pulled in favor of Randall at the start of the second half. Randall immediately brought some life to the Eagles' offense and they began moving the ball down the field and scored twice—on a 14-yard run in which Randall eluded three would-be tacklers and on a 15-yard pass to Mike Quick.

Late in the game, with the score tied 14-14, Randall dropped back to pass on third down. He was chased out of the pocket and started to stumble and fall. Just before he hit the ground, Randall threw a pass that landed in front of Quick. Referee Red Cashion called intentional grounding and the Eagles had to punt. "I thought it was a horsebleep call," Ryan says after the game. "The kid is running, he's stumbling, and he throws."

Dallas took over and drove for the winning field goal. Still, Randall's performance (8-of-15 passing for 127 yards and 58 yards rushing) electrified the Veterans Stadium crowd and already there were calls to make Randall the number one quarterback. Buddy did his best to feed the growing quarterback controversy. "I don't know," Buddy responded when asked if Randall would start the following week. "He might be the first [quarterback]. Who knows? We'll have to take a look. We've got three of them. I'm not worried about who's one or two or three."

Later in the week, a healthy Jaworski moved back into the starting lineup and Randall was officially elevated to the number two position. Against the Giants on November 9, Jaworski tore a tendon in his throwing hand and was out for the remainder of the season. In the game, a 17-14 loss, Randall threw for one touchdown and ran for another to bring the Eagles back from a 17-0 deficit in the final nine minutes of the game.

With Jaworski out for the season, the starting job was now Randall's. "We've been hoping we could bring him along at a little slower pace," Buddy said after the Giants game. "But right now, we're going to have to put him in there. I think he's further along right now than [John Elway] was in his second year. He puts points on the board."

Randall is up and down in his five starts (he missed one game with a thumb injury). The highlight of the season came on November 30 during a 33-27 win over the Los Angeles Raiders. In the game, Randall completed 22-of-39 passes for 298 yards and three touchdowns and ran for 60 yards and a touchdown. Even the Raiders were raving.

"Randall Cunningham is unbelievable," cornerback Lester Hayes said. "He must shower in Vaseline. There's only one Randall Cunningham in the entire NFL and he really gives the Eagles' offense life."

"Randall Cunningham is a phenomenal athlete," defensive end Howie Long said. "Given time, he could be better than John Elway."

For the season, Randall completed 111-of-209 passes (53.0 per-

cent) for 1,391 yards, eight touchdowns and seven interceptions. Randall rushed for 540 yards on 66 carries (8.2 yards per carry), which was second on the team to Keith Byars's 577 yards.

The weird thing was, right before Ron got injured, Buddy told both of us that Ron had one more series and then I was going in. The significance of that was to show we were rebuilding the team with young players and I was going to be the quarterback of the future. The fans knew we were rebuilding and getting better and they wanted to have some fun and I added a little excitement to the game by scrambling and running. I think this is when Philadelphia accepted me as a quarterback. By the end of the season, I had my confidence back and thought I had a chance to start in 1987. I was ready.

1987

In March of 1987, the Eagles allowed Jaworski's contract to expire. He became a free agent, free to make a deal with any team in the NFL. Buddy Ryan made it clear that he was no longer interested in Jaworski's services, effectively ending the veteran's 10-year reign as the Eagles' starting quarterback. (Eventually he signed with the Miami Dolphins where he was the backup to Dan Marino.) No longer was Randall the Eagles' quarterback of the future; Randall was the quarterback of today.

"We all agreed that Randall would never mature as long as Ron was here," Buddy explained at the time. "That was really the reason we let Ron go. We were building a young team, and Randall was going to be our guy. Ron had been here so long, and as long as he was here, players were going to look to the old quarterback."

I was shocked when Buddy let Ron go. I think Buddy figured it would be better for me, if I was going to be the starter, if Ron was gone, so there wouldn't be as much pressure on me to produce or on Buddy to put Ron in if I had a bad game or two. It was like, when he let Ron go, he said "Randall, this is your team now." I really appreciated that. Buddy's confidence in me gave me a lot of confidence in myself.

Another thing that helped me was the addition of Doug Scovil as our quarterback coach before the 1986 season. I was on vacation in Las Vegas the day Doug was hired and I got the word from the Eagles that I had to come back to Philadelphia to meet with Doug and work out with him. I said, "Are you crazy? It's snowing in Philadelphia. I'm in Vegas, where it's sunny and warm." But they insisted I come and I did. Doug was hired to work with me and develop me from a raw rookie into an NFL quarterback.

I already knew Doug. He was the head coach at San Diego State when I was at Nevada-Las Vegas. My senior year, they were favored to beat us, but we wound up winning 30-14 at their stadium. When I got back to Philadelphia, it was freezing cold and there was snow on the ground. I went to the stadium and Doug had me throw some passes in the hallway. Right away, he noticed that my delivery was too high—too straight up over my head and he had me do drills to correct it. First, he had me get on my knees and throw from there and then he said, "Let's go outside." I looked at him like he was crazy, but we went outside and worked on some things. The snow was up to my calf, but I was thinking, "This guy is going to work with me and make me a better quarterback." We hit it off right from the start and I knew if I listened to Doug I would get better.

We watched hours and hours of films together and Doug started teaching me the little things, the finer points of the game. He built up my confidence and kept telling me I could be a great quarterback and could complete 60 percent of my passes and throw for 30 touchdowns every season. He helped me improve my drop and throwing motion, he taught me how to recognize different coverages and blitzes and what to do when I saw them and how to improve my timing with my receivers. And Doug didn't jump on my back when I did something wrong, even when I was being immature and hardheaded. Doug was always patient and always encouraged me and was willing to listen to what I had to say.

In 1987, I know Doug told Buddy I was ready and pushed me for the starting job, and once I got it, he was there for me every step of the way. We prepared for every game together. Doug always said that what you do in practice is what you'll do in a game and that stuck with me and now I always work as hard as I can in practice and study films and come to games prepared.

Doug and I got closer and closer over the years and our relationship developed into a father-and-son-type thing. Doug was someone who cared about you and didn't care what color you were. He recognized my talents and wanted to help me bring them out and become the best quarterback I could be. He always told me, "I want you to become the best quarterback in history and you have the tools to do it, all you have to do is work hard." Doug was like a father who pushes his son hard because he loves him and wants him to be successful. I never had a relationship with a coach like that before and I know that without Doug I never would have become the quarterback I am today.

The Eagles lost their opener 34-24 to the Redskins but, the following week, came from behind to top New Orleans 27-17 to even their record at 1-1. This is the "regular" Eagles last game for more than a month. After the game, the players go out on strike and are replaced by "scab" teams. The "Eagles" lose all three of their strike games, including a 41-22 drubbing from the Dallas Cowboys, who have nine regulars playing, including quarterback Danny White and defensive lineman Randy White. Ryan is furious after the game, claiming that Cowboys' coach Tom Landry ran up the score.

Kenny Jackson and I were against going on strike. We didn't think a strike was necessary. We figured we could go out and play and collect our weekly paychecks under the old collective agreement and let the courts decide between the union and the NFL. We didn't think a strike would accomplish anything and that it would eventually have to be decided by the courts anyway and why should we, in the meantime, lose all that money? We weren't the only players on the team who felt this way, but we all agreed that whatever we did we would do as a team and so everyone went out on strike, except for three players who were on the injured reserve and needed to go in for treatment. We were the strongest team in the league, but later, as it turned out, we were the dumbest. Buddy figured that once the regulars came back, the strike games wouldn't count against our record. He was wrong and we wound up 0-3 during the strike games. We were 7-9 overall and without those three losses, we might have had a chance to make the playoffs.

The players finally gave in and came back, even though there was no new collective bargaining agreement. As fate would have it, the Eagles' first game back was against Dallas on October 25. Buddy and the Eagles were out for revenge and that's exactly what they got. With less than two minutes to play, the Eagles, who were ahead 30-20, had the ball on the Dallas 33. On first and second downs, Randall took the snap from center, stepped backwards and knelt down—standard operating procedure when a team plans to run out the clock. On the next play, on orders from Buddy, Randall dropped back and lofted a long pass downfield toward Quick. Dallas is called for interference, the Eagles got the ball on the Cowboys' one and Byars rumbled in for the score and a 37-20 win as time expires.

"That last touchdown was very satisfying," Buddy said after the game.

That was Buddy's way of getting the Cowboys back and rubbing it in their faces. I didn't care one way or the other; I did what Buddy told me to do. After that game, Dallas never beat us again with Tom Landry as coach.

In the Eagles next two games, Randall brought the Eagles from behind for last-minute wins. Against the St. Louis [now Phoenix] Cardinals, Randall hit Greg Garrity late in the fourth quarter with a nine-yard scoring pass for a 28-23 win. A week later, against Washington, Gary Clark scored on a long pass to give the Redskins a 27-24 lead with just over two minutes to play. The Eagles took over on their own 23 and began moving. "Right before we went out on the field," Randall said after the game, "I said, 'Hey guys, it's nothing different. We've been here before.'" Two completions moved the ball to the Washington 40 and Randall dropped back, looking for Quick.

"Mike went out and there was a guy there waiting for him," Randall said after the game. "I stepped up in the pocket. I didn't want to dump it off to the short guy, so I stepped back up in the pocket and converged the line and let our line get better blocking. I stepped back, rolled out, and there was Garrity in the end zone."

Randall rifled a perfect pass and Garrity—whose nickname is "Trash" because he scoops up anything close to him—grabbed it for the touchdown and a 31-27 Eagles win. Randall completed 18-of-31 passes for 268 yards and three scores and ran for another 80 yards, including a 45-yard dash.

The Redskins were impressed. "The guy's probably the most dangerous quarterback in the league," said cornerback Barry Wilburn. "We came out trying to contain him. Even trying to do that, we couldn't."

"It's like a running back playing quarterback," coach Joe Gibbs said. "That's bad news for the rest of us. We had a tough time getting our hands on him. We couldn't get him down."

At the end of the game, Doug Scovil came down from the booth and we hugged on the sideline. We didn't say a word, but I know that we were both thinking that all the hard work had paid off and that I was finally starting to understand everything Doug had been trying to teach me and that I was on my way to accomplishing some of the goals he had set for me. Someone took a picture of us hugging and later I got a copy of it and wrote "All the hard work we put in paid off" and signed it, framed it and gave it to Doug.

For the season, Randall completed 223-of-406 passes (54.9 percent) for 2,786 yards, 23 touchdowns and 12 interceptions. He also led the Eagles in rushing with 505 yards on 76 carries (6.6 per carry) and rushed for three scores. Randall was voted the Eagles' offensive MVP and was an alternate to the Pro Bowl. His quarterback rating of 83.0 was the sixth best in the NFC. Still, there were times when the offense struggled, especially when Buddy tried to establish the running game, even when it wasn't there.

In 1987, Buddy was the head coach, Ted Plumb was the offensive coordinator and Doug was the quarterback coach. Buddy's thing was he wanted the defense to be aggressive and set the tone for the game and come up with two or three turnovers. Buddy believed that defense won Super Bowls and was his first priority when he got here. The offense, and especially the offensive line, was something he built later. On offense, Buddy wanted to run the ball and have me come up with four or five big plays a game—either throwing or running the football. Doug drew up all these great plays that he gave to Ted and asked him to run. Every once in a while Ted would put one in and it usually worked—like sending a back into the flat for a quick toss, or running a receiver across the field to get open, using the other two receivers as decoys. Doug taught me how to make my reads when I dropped back—"Y" was the tight end, "Z" was the strong side flanker, which is the flanker lined up on the tight end side, and "B" was the back. Normally your read is B, Y and then Z, but Doug told me to go Y to Z to B. When we got inside the 20,

Doug told me to run audibles and throw the fade to either Mike Quick or Chris Carter, depending on who was being covered man-to-man. That play always seemed to work for us.

But we did get predictable in what we were doing on offense. The game plan was to establish the run and then make the pass work and other teams caught on to us. We would run on first down almost every time. Then, when we got behind, Buddy would let Ted and Doug open things up. That was Buddy's way of saying to me, "Run the offense and do your thing." We would run the two-minute drill and I would call the plays using the system that Ted and Doug had designed and we were very effective. They gave me my freedom and that's when I played my best.

1988

In July, Randall ended a one-day holdout and signed a three-year contract worth close to $4 million, making him the highest-paid player in the NFL.

The 1988 season was a breakthrough year for Randall and the Eagles, who finished 10-6 and won the NFC East championship. During the regular season, Randall completed 301-of-560 passes (53.8) percent for 3,808 yards, 24 touchdowns and 16 interceptions. Randall also ran for 624 yards on 93 carries (6.7 per carry) to lead the Eagles in rushing for the second straight year.

Randall was named the starter in the Pro Bowl, was named the MVP in the game, received the Bert Bell Award as the NFL Player of the Year from the Maxwell Football Club in Philadelphia, was named NFC Player of the Year by the Washington (D.C.) Touchdown Club, and was the Associated Press's runner-up to Boomer Esiason in the voting for NFL Player of the Year.

I took a big step forward in 1988. It was my fourth year in the league and my third year running Buddy's offense, so I felt very comfortable and confident about it. We had a lot of great young players and we began gaining confidence in ourselves and realized we could beat anyone in the league.

After beating Tampa Bay 41-14 in their opener, the Eagles struggled and lost their next three games. When they played Houston on October 2 at home, the Birds were desperate for a win to revive their fading playoff hopes. The Eagles quickly fell behind 16-0 as the Oilers blocked two punts—one for a touchdown and the other for a safety.

The Eagles clawed their way back into the game. With just over two minutes remaining in the first half, Randall hit Garrity with a 16-yard score to give the Eagles a 17-16 lead. In the third period Randall scrambled for a 33-yard touchdown and the Eagles never looked back on their way to victory. In the game, Randall completed 24-of-38 passes for 289 yards and two scores and ran for another 59 yards and a touchdown.

The Eagles did pay a price for their victory, as five-time Pro Bowl selection Mike Quick suffered a broken leg in the second quarter. This is the start of a string of injuries that would eventually force Quick to retire before the start of the 1991 season. Quick, who was voted to the Pro Bowl for five straight seasons (1983-87) finished his abbreviated career with 363 catches for 6,464 yards and 61 touchdowns.

Mike Quick and I clicked from the start. Right after I was drafted by the Eagles, they had me come to town for a workout. On one of the first plays, Mike ran a route and I dropped back. As soon as he made his break, I threw the ball and it hit him right in the ribs. He came back to the huddle and said, "Nice pass," and I could sense that I had gained his respect. We became good friends and Mike taught me a lot. He told me that I didn't need financial planners, that I should take care of my own income and put it in the bank where I knew where it was. Mike showed me around town my rookie year. Everywhere we went, people knew Mike and some of them even recognized me, even though I hadn't even played a game for the Eagles yet.

Mike was one of the greatest receivers in the history of the game. If he had played on grass, Mike might have lasted 15 years and set numerous records. If you put a ball in Mike's area, even if it was a very difficult catch, he would always come up with it, even if he had to make a one-handed catch. And Mike was so smooth, sometimes the defensive back didn't even know he had caught the ball. Mike was like a gazelle.

The following Monday night, the Eagles hosted the New York Giants. The game introduced a national television audience to the game's most exciting player as Randall completed 31-of-41 passes for 369 yards, three touchdowns and no interceptions to lead the Eagles to a 24-13 win.

Randall also showed his brilliant improvisational skills, as he turned a certain sack into a touchdown on a memorable play that was shown over and over during the 1988 season. Early in the game, with the Giants ahead 3-0, the Eagles began to drive and were faced with a third-and-goal from the New York four. Randall rolled to the right, but Pro Bowl linebacker Carl Banks was waiting for Randall and hit him squarely and solidly. Randall bounced backwards, but instead of going down, somehow kept his balance, regained his feet and fired a pass to tight end Jimmie Giles in the end zone for a 7-3 Eagles lead.

After the game, when he was asked if plays like that amaze him, Randall responded: "It amazes me; I amaze myself." He also amazed millions of people watching around the country. "God has given me a talent to throw and run with the ball, but things like that aren't supposed to happen."

Before Buddy came along, we always seemed to lose to the Giants. Buddy was supposed to change all that, but the first time we played them in 1986, they whipped us 35-3. Afterwards, Buddy told us we went into the game thinking we were going to lose and that's why we lost. He called us cowards. He challenged our manhood and I think that's when we started turning things around. Buddy brings out your best.

The next time we played the Giants in 1986, they were lucky to beat us 17-14. It was a very physical game, but this time, we were giving it as good as we were getting it.

In 1987 the Giants beat us 20-17 and 23-20 in overtime. Then everything came together for us on Monday night in 1988. I was sick the entire week before the game and dropped something like 15 pounds and was down to 180. Nobody thought I could play, but before the game I went out and warmed up and felt a little better and decided to give it a go. Once the game started I was OK and everyone else picked it up a notch or two.

Then came the Carl Banks play. On the play, a naked bootleg to the right, I made my fake and rolled to the right, but sure enough, Carl Banks was right there waiting for me. He hit me on my waist and I thought I was going down, but somehow I stayed up and threw it to Jimmie Giles. The whole stadium went crazy and at that point I knew that we were going to win. That game was a turning point for us in terms of us becoming an aggressive, physical football team.

The Giants are a team that is tough and physical and they try to intimidate you. For example, when they sack you, the guys who did it stand right over and high five each other. You're left under them trying to get up and they push you back down to rub it in your face. I'm not going to take that and I start pushing them off me and they push back and my linemen run in to protect me and everyone starts pushing and shoving.

Over the years, I've gotten to know a few of the Giants, including L.T., who I consider the greatest linebacker in the history of the NFL. When you get to know L.T., you realize he's a very humble, easy-going guy who you can sit back with and talk to. But he does have this one very annoying habit. He always seems to be wearing one of his Super Bowl rings and he likes to hold his hand up close to your face so that ring is flashing around next to your face, like he's trying to rub it in that he has one and I don't. Then he'll laugh about it and I'll laugh about it.

I've been to a couple of functions with Carl Banks and whenever people see us together they always ask us about the Monday Night Football play. Carl jokes about it, but I know he's sick of hearing about and seeing that play. I'm even tired of seeing replays of it.

The win ended the Eagles six-game losing streak to the Giants and evened their record at 3-3, which means they were tied with New York and Washington for second in the conference, a game behind the 4-2 Cardinals. Just when it looked like the Eagles had turned the corner, they lost 19-3 to the Browns to drop to 3-4. The following week the Eagles hosted Dallas. Although the Cowboys were out for revenge, it is the Eagles who rally from a 20-0 deficit to win 24-23. With the offense sputtering, Randall began calling his own plays in the fourth period and led the Eagles on a 99-yard drive that cut the Dallas lead to 23-17 with 6:23 to play. The next time the Eagles got the ball, Randall marched them 85 yards, capped by a 2-yard scoring pass to Anthony Toney for the winning points.

On the first scoring drive in the fourth quarter, Randall waved Keith Jackson out of the game after he dropped a pass and signaled in Jimmie Giles, who quickly made a key catch to keep the drive alive.

Earlier in the game, Keith had dropped a pass on a third-down play. Then he dropped another pass. I yelled over to the bench, "Give me Jimmie Giles." He was a 10-year veteran and I knew he'd hang onto the ball. I called for him, but Buddy had the final say on whether or not he came in. Jimmie just stood there until Buddy waved him in. Then I threw a pass to Jimmie, he caught it, and I waved for Keith and Buddy sent him back in so he'd know that I still respected his talents. Of course Keith got mad at the time, but later he realized it was best for the team at the time. After he came back in, he caught a pass. The main thing was I was in control of the offense—calling the plays and asking for and getting who I wanted on the field. That's what a quarterback must do—take control of the game and Buddy allowed me to do it.

Another instrumental part of us winning that game was Ted Plumb putting in a play that I asked for—a sprint-out pass to the fullback. It was the last play of the game and I hit Toney for the touchdown. If Ted and I weren't on the same page, he wouldn't have called that play.

The Eagles finished the season strong, winning five of their last six games to win the conference title, earn a week off and then they traveled to Chicago to take on the Bears—Buddy's former team—in the second round of the playoffs. Buddy wasn't bashful about returning to Soldier Field and when the Eagles' bus arrived, he had the driver circle the field and blow his horn to let everyone know the Eagles had landed.

In what has since become known as the "Fog Bowl" the Bears topped the Eagles 20-12. Late in the second quarter, the fog started rolling in and by the start of the third quarter, the field was covered by a dense, heavy fog that reduced visibility to little more than a few feet.

Despite the elements, the Eagles moved inside the Bears' 20 nine times and came away without a touchdown despite outgaining Chicago 430-341 in total yards. Two touchdown passes by Randall were called back by penalties and Keith Jackson dropped another sure touchdown with nobody near him. Another pass that would have given the Eagles a first down at the Chicago one was nullified by an offensive pass interference call on Kenny Jackson and another pass bounced out of Toney's hands and was picked off at the Bears' eight. In all, Randall completed 27-of-54 passes for 407 yards and three interceptions.

It was ridiculous, they should have stopped the game. I would drop back to pass and I couldn't even see Mike Singletary, their middle linebacker and he was only 10 yards away. You couldn't see anything downfield. We were on the sidelines when their offense had the ball and you couldn't see anything. They started driving and we didn't know they scored until we heard the announcement. The reason Chicago was able to do anything was that they were able to run the ball on us. We were behind and had to keep throwing.

1989

In their season opener, the Eagles crushed the Seattle Seahawks 31-7. A week later, a few hours before the Eagles took on the Redskins in Washington, Randall signed a five-year contract extension through the 1995 season worth $18-22 million with incentives that made him the highest paid player in NFL history.

We had been negotiating a contract extension with the Eagles, but I didn't think it was going to happen so fast. It was all very hush-hush, but word leaked out to the press that we were negotiating. Finally, right before the Redskins game, we agreed and I signed and went out and played the best game of my career. Afterwards, the big joke was, "We need to sign Randall to a new contract every week."

Once the game began, it looked as though the Eagles got themselves a bargain. Down 27-7 in the first half and 37-28 with 3:06 to play, the Eagles miraculously rallied for a 42-37 win. "We were down and we were out," Randall said at the time. "But we didn't hang our heads because we knew what we could do. And I kept walking along the sidelines saying, 'Buddy conditioned us too much. Those guys over there, they're tired.'"

The Eagles' conditioning, Randall's magic and a little bit of luck began to come together for the Eagles in the second half. The defense held the Redskins scoreless in the third period and the Eagles began edging their way back into the game. First Randall took the Birds 92 yards on 12 plays, hitting Keith Jackson with a five-yard scoring pass and it was 30-21. To start the fourth period, Randall moved the Eagles again, hitting Carter with a 5-yard scoring pass and suddenly it was 30-28.

Then Mark Rypien hit Art Monk with a 43-yard touchdown pass for a 37-28 lead with 3:06 to play and it looked like the Eagles' valiant comeback would be in vain. But Randall kept throwing and his receivers kept catching and the Eagles went 69 yards and scored when a ball intended for Carter bounced off his hands to Quick for a two-yard touchdown with 1:48 to play to cut the Washington lead to two.

Washington seemed to put the game away when Gerald Riggs burst through the defense and rumbled 58 yards to the Eagles' 22. Three plays later, with the game all but wrapped up, Riggs fumbled and the fun began. The bouncing ball headed toward the right sideline, where Eagle linebacker Al Harris scooped it up. An instant later he was tackled, but before Harris hit the turf, Wes Hopkins wrestled the ball out of his hands and began racing up the field and was finally hauled down at the Washington four by Ricky Sanders. The Redskins argued that Hopkins received the ball on an illegal forward handoff, but after the officials reviewed the play, it was allowed to stand and the Eagles were in business. Randall hit Keith Jackson in the end zone on the next play and the Eagles won 42-37.

Randall was magical, completing 34-of-46 passes for 447 yards and five touchdowns. More impressive was his presence of mind and leadership when the Eagles were down. "I guess he has a magic air about him that he gets the job done," said Byars, who caught eight passes for 130 yards. "I guess if anyone is wondering, 'Who's the best quarterback in the NFL?' they saw him out there working today."

The Eagles lost to San Francisco and Chicago in their next two games to drop to 2-2 and faced a crucial contest with the 4-0 Giants in New York in week five. New York took a 19-14 lead with six minutes to play on a field goal and it looked like the Eagles had one more chance for the win. As the Eagles huddled to start the drive, tackle Ron Heller looked into Randall's eyes: "You tend to look around the huddle and see what kind of mood other people are in, the people who are going to make the big plays. When you come back and see Randall sitting there nice and calm and thinking about what's happening, you just know that if we give him a chance, we're going to win."

Randall's passes begin finding their targets. First 23 yards to Chris Carter, then 21 to Quick and 15 more to Garrity. On third-and-4 from the Giants' 9, Randall took the snap out of the shotgun. Carl Banks charged around the right tackle, but Randall faked him off his feet with a deceptive swivel of his hips, pump faked to get another defender to jump up into the air and then Randall scrambled to the two before he was finally tackled. On the next play, Toney dove in for the winning score.

Earlier in the game, with the Eagles trailing 10-0 late in the first half, Randall scored on a five-yard run that showed his unique abilities. Chased out of the pocket, Randall's way to the goal line was obstructed by Giants' safety Terry Kinard, who was eagerly awaiting the fast-approaching Randall. "You can't go through guys when you're only 200 pounds," Randall said. "The best way is to go over guys." Randall tried to hurdle Kinard like he was a high jump bar. Kinard kept his feet and flipped Randall high into the air and he came down hard—on his head and in the end zone for a score.

"I don't want to make him a stereotype quarterback, he's too good a football player," Buddy responded after the game when he's asked about the risks of Randall's running. "He made some big first downs. If it hadn't been for Randall, we would have got beat 100 to nothing . . . There's nothing the matter with running the football if you're a great athlete. Roger Staubach kept Dallas in the win column a long time doing it. Tarkenton did too. So that's the kind of quarterback we always wanted; it's the toughest kind to defend."

When told of Buddy's comments, Randall smiled and said, "I know Buddy wants me to run. If I run it slows down the rush, makes us more effective. I'll run if they want me to. But I'd rather hand off."

"Why?" a reporter asks.

"Because," Randall said and paused for effect, "it hurts." Especially when you land on your head.

The Giants game is the first of four straight wins, followed by two losses and four more wins. The third win in the streak is at New York, 24-17, which ties the Eagles and Giants atop the NFC East with 9-4 records. The game's biggest play is turned in by Randall, but it's neither a pass nor a run. Early in the fourth quarter, on third-and-long, Randall is sacked back at the Giants' two. Buddy let Randall punt instead of regular punter Max Runager, and with the wind at his back, Randall booms a beautiful spiral that travels at least 60 yards downfield in the air—over Dave Meggett's head—and begins bouncing toward the end zone. Meggett finally tracks down the ball on the seven and returns it to the 16. The punt traveled 91 yards, making it the longest in Eagles' history, the third longest in NFL history, and pinned the Giants deep in their own territory. A few plays later, Mike Golic hit Phil Simms and caused a fumble. Mike Pitts recovered at the seven and two plays later, Byars ran in for the winning points.

On Saturday, December 9—the day before the Eagles host Dallas —Doug Scovil died from a heart attack. Stunned and shaken, Randall nevertheless had a game to play the next afternoon and he and *his teammates went out and beat the Cowboys 20-10. Randall completed 17-of-31 passes for 170 yards and a touchdown and ran for another 47 yards.*

All week, before the Dallas game, Doug seemed different, more serious. It was as if he knew our time together was running out. During the week, Bill Walsh, our offensive line coach, was running a meeting where he went over the blocking assignments. I was supposed to be in the meeting, but I knew all the assignments already, so I left to watch film with my receivers. Doug came over and started yelling at me. He said you can't show disrespect for Bill by leaving his meeting. I tried to explain that I already knew the blocking assignments, but Doug didn't want to hear about it. He told me that I was the quarterback of the team, the leader and that it was my responsibility to set the tone for the entire team and be in that meeting to show Bill and the offensive linemen that I cared about what they were doing. Doug was right. He stayed on me all week, telling me I had to drop back faster, key into my receivers and follow through. "If you want to be the best," he told me, "you have to work even harder."

The day before the game I got a phone call, from Otho Davis I think. He told me Doug had a heart attack. I asked if he was OK and Otho told me he was dead. I started crying. It was such a big blow to me and hurt so bad. Doug and I were like father and son and now it was like I was abandoned and all alone. I don't really remember much about the game; I was sort of in a daze the whole time. But I do know that I went into the game thinking that I wasn't going to let anything defeat me or the team. I had to win it for Doug.

I felt lost on the field without Doug. Before every game, he used to come up and give me a test. He'd grab my throwing arm and shake my wrist and say, "See, you're loose, now go out and complete sixty percent of your passes." It was a ritual, something to relax me. In the past, after every series, I would get on the phone to Doug, who was always up in the press box, and talk to him about what had just happened and what to expect. Now, every time I walked off the field, I still expected to pick up the phone and talk to Doug. I think that's when I realized he was really gone.

I love Doug and still think about him a lot and remember what he taught me, especially when things aren't going so well. Doug taught me to prepare totally for every game, work as hard as I can in practice and try to be a leader by example. I have to be a general so that other people will follow and I have to take control of the offense and the game. That's what Doug taught me.

After Doug died, his wife, Enid, gave me the picture of us hugging after we beat the Redskins in 1987 and now it's hanging in my office. Enid also gave me Doug's Cotton Bowl watch from 1964—the year after I was born. She said the watch was very special to Doug, but she was sure he would want me to have it. I keep it locked up—it's too precious to wear—and every once in a while I take it out and think about Doug and everything I learned from him.

The win over Dallas raised the Eagles record to 10-4 and two more wins will lock up their second straight conference title. But, in New Orleans, the Saints' defense forced four turnovers—two interceptions and two fumbles—and sacked Randall four times, once for a safety, and New Orleans won 30-20 to drop the Eagles a game behind the 11-4 Giants.

The following week, the Eagles needed a win to ensure a berth in the playoffs as a wildcard team and also had to hope the Los Angeles Raiders somehow upset the Giants, which would give the Eagles the NFC East championship. The Eagles did their part as they smashed the Cardinals 31-14, but the Giants won 34-17 and the Birds had to settle for a wildcard berth and a home game the following week against the Los Angeles Rams.

In the Cardinals' game, Randall completed 19-of-36 passes for 162 yards and a touchdown and ran for 41 yards. For the regular season, Randall completed 290-of-532 passes (54.5 percent) for 3,400 yards, 21 touchdowns and 15 interceptions and rushed for another

621 yards to become the first quarterback in modern history to lead his team in rushing for three straight years. Randall is named a Pro Bowl alternate and winds up starting after injuries force Joe Montana and Jim Everett to miss the game.

The pressure is on the Eagles to beat the Rams, but they come away with a crushing 21-7 loss. "I wanted us to take that one step forward, but today wasn't the day to do it," Buddy said after the game.

The Eagles' game plan was to run the ball early and often and it didn't work. The Rams stopped the Eagles' running attack and scored twice in the first quarter to take a 14-0 lead. The Eagles had to play catch-up the rest of the afternoon and this worked right into the Rams' defensive game plan, which was geared toward stopping Randall. Ram defensive coordinator Fritz Schermer came up with a unique zone defense that, at times, employed five linebackers and six defensive backs and no defensive linemen. Randall completed 24-of-40 passes for 238 yards and one interception and ran for another 39.

"It was a matter of saying, 'Hey this is what [Randall] does extremely well,'" Schermer said. "'We need to find a way to cope with it.'"

The Rams coped with Randall by staying in zone coverage all day, with as many as eight men dropping into the zone coverage and two or three others spying on Randall to prevent him from running the football. Behind and without a running attack or Mike Quick as a deep threat, the Eagles were limited in what they could do and could not find their rhythm on offense.

1990

Before the season, there was a lot of talk that we needed to get to the Super Bowl in order to save Buddy's job. This was the last year of Buddy's five-year contract with the Eagles. During training camp,

I was very open and verbal in support of Buddy and several times I told the media we needed to get his contract extended and taken care of so we could relax and have a very productive year. There was a lot of pressure on us to win for Buddy. By the time the season started, I figured there was nothing I could say that would get Buddy a new contract. Like I said before, I'm just a player and I don't have any pull with management. If I did, I would have gotten Buddy a contract extension. I figured I'd let my playing do my talking for me and if we could come together as a team and have a great year, then they'd have to bring Buddy back.

A big change came when Richie Kotite was hired as our new offensive coordinator. The first time I met Richie I didn't know what to think. When we met, it seemed like, right from the start, Richie took complete control of the situation and conversation, like he had something to prove to me and I really didn't know what it was. I guess he was trying to let me know he was in charge and his way was going to be the way it was. I wasn't used to anyone like that. In the past, with coaches, it had always been a mutual communication thing. But Richie came in, took over and said, "We're gonna throw the ball and we're not gonna have you running all over the place. Hey, as long as you're right seven out of 10 times, that's all I ask." Richie expects his quarterbacks to complete 70 percent of their passes, which is a lot, but certainly something to strive for.

After the meeting I walked out and said to myself, "I don't see how this guy and I are going to get along." It was like he was making a power play instead of saying, "Hey Randall, nice to meet you, we're going to have a lot of fun together, work hard and get the offense going." The tone of his voice and his volume kind of surprised me. It seemed like Richie was talking at me instead of holding a conversation with me. I learned that's just the way Richie is and the way he comes across to people. Richie is loud and later I nicknamed him "bullhorn" because you can hear his voice booming all over the field.

Right from the jump start, I didn't think we'd get along. But as the season went along, Richie's system was good and we began to eat up the league. I threw 30 touchdown passes and rushed for 942 yards and we scored more points in a season than any other Eagles' team. The key was that Richie designed the offensive system and tried to control everything, but Buddy was still the head coach and there were times when Buddy would tell me, "Hey, do your own thing, run the offense and make something happen." We had a lot of weapons—Keith Jackson, Keith Byars, Anthony Toney, Freddie Barnett and Calvin Williams—and we used them all. It was like we had the best of both worlds: Richie's system and Buddy letting me be me.

The Eagles lost their first two games of the season—27-20 to the Giants and 23-21 to the Cardinals and faced a must-win situation in game three against the Rams.

"The coaches told me before the game, 'Hey, don't sit back there and hold the ball,'" Randall said afterward. "I had been trying to be the consistent quarterback that they wanted me to be. I said, 'Fine, thanks for letting me be myself.'"

Down 14-10 late in the second quarter, Randall was himself. He dropped back to pass, saw his receivers were covered, side-stepped a defender, and began weaving his way downfield for a 27-yard gain. Two plays later he hit Calvin Williams for a touchdown and a 17-14 Eagles lead and the Eagles never looked back and won 27-21. Randall completed 18-of-29 passes for 248 yards, two touchdowns and an interception and ran for 44 yards.

Another key was the return of Keith Jackson, who had been holding out, demanding his contract be renegotiated. He signed the week before the game and caught four passes for 77 yards. "Randall definitely looks for me up the middle on the scramble, and he did a great job this time," Jackson said. "He also did a super job running the ball and picking out one-on-one coverages, not only to me but to Mike Quick and to the backs out of the backfield."

The Eagles continued to struggle, losing two of their next three games, before going on a five-game winning streak that included wins over Dallas (21-20), New England (48-20), Washington (28-14), Atlanta (24-23) and New York (31-13).

The New England game featured one of those plays that only Randall can come up with. On the play, Randall called an audible, a running play, but his receivers misunderstood him and tight end Mickey Shuler wound up in the backfield as the ball was snapped and this, in turn, led to Randall missing the handoff to Heath Sherman. Randall did the obvious—for him that is—and took off around the left end and went 52 yards for the touchdown. In all, Randall completed 15-of-24 passes for 240 yards and four touchdowns and ran for 124 yards and just missed the NFL quarterback single-game rushing record of 129 yards. Seven of Randall's eight runs were for first downs and four came on third down.

"Once he got rolling," Patriots coach Rod Rust said, "it was like trying to stop a snowball going downhill."

After the five straight wins, a poor start dooms the Eagles to a 30-23 loss at Buffalo, despite some heroics from Randall, including his most amazing play to date—and that's saying a lot. Backed up on his own five late in the first half, Randall dropped back, into the end zone and looked in vain for an open receiver while the blitzing Bills charged through the offensive line. It looked like a sack and a safety. Randall side-stepped one defender, who crashed to the turf, and then he began sprinting toward the far corner of the end zone, all the time looking downfield for an open receiver. Somehow, Randall either saw, smelled or sensed Bruce Smith coming from behind and ducked just before the Pro Bowl defensive end was about to crush him. Then, off balance, off his wrong foot and falling backwards, Randall launched the ball high and far into the windy Buffalo sky. It came down just past midfield, where Barnett outleaped a defender, who fell to the ground. Barnett gathered himself and went all the way for a 95-yard touchdown.

"I amaze myself," Randall responded after the game when a reporter asked him if he ever amazed himself.

In game 13, the Dolphins topped the Eagles 23-20 in overtime, after the Birds squandered a 10-point fourth quarter lead; their record dropped to 7-6. The following week, the Eagles improved to 8-6 and clinched a wildcard playoff berth with a thorough 31-0 destruction of the Green Bay Packers. Randall completed 13-of-27 passes for 241 yards and a touchdown and rushed for 56 more and a score. For the season, Randall has now rushed for 828 yards, and with two games remaining, he had a shot at becoming the first quarterback to rush for 1,000 yards.

"I think it's highly possible," Randall said after the game. "I haven't made it a goal yet, but if next game I can rush for a good amount of yards, I think it's possible to get 1,000 and then I might shoot for it."

In the final game of the season, with a wildcard playoff berth already clinched, Randall sits out the fourth quarter of the Eagles' 23-21 win over the Cardinals, despite the fact that he is only 27 yards shy of the all-time quarterback rushing record (Chicago's Bobby Douglass ran for 968 in 1972) and 58 yards shy of the 1,000-yard barrier.

"To come out after throwing a couple of touchdowns and winning home-field advantage [in the wildcard playoff game] is good enough for me," Randall said after the game.

In the game, Randall completes 13-of-19 passes for 172 yards, three touchdowns and one interception and ran for 60 yards. For the season, Randall completed 271-of-465 passes (58.3 percent) for 3,466 yards, 30 touchdowns and only 13 interceptions and rushed for 942 yards and five touchdowns on 118 carries (8.0 per carry). Randall won numerous awards in recognition of his amazing accomplishments (including several MVP awards) and is named to the Pro Bowl for the third straight season.

All the honors and awards are nice, but more than anything, Randall wants to take the Eagles to the Super Bowl. The Birds open the playoffs at home against the Redskins on January 5, 1991.

The game started off with a bang, as Randall hit Keith Jackson with a 66-yard completion to the Redskins' 11 on the third play from scrimmage. But the Eagles had to settle for a field goal and 3-0 lead. While the Eagles' offense struggled all afternoon, the Redskins calmly and methodically moved the ball up and down the field behind their great offensive line. On the other side of the ball, Randall was chased all over the field by the Redskins' fierce rush and wound up completing 15-of-29 passes for 172 yards and ran for 80 more on seven carries.

The game's key play came late in the first half with Washington up 7-6. Cornerback Ben Smith hit Earnest Byner, who fumbled, and Smith scooped up the loose ball and raced 89 yards for an apparent touchdown and 13-7 lead with just seconds left in the half. But hold everything. One of the referees ruled that the fumble was caused by Byner hitting the ground, and not Smith's tackle, and it was ruled a catch and tackle, with no fumble. The Redskins kept the ball and connected on a field goal for a 10-6 halftime lead.

After the Eagles failed to move the ball on their third possession of the third quarter, the Redskins took over and moved the ball into field goal territory again, connected and led 13-6. At this point, with 5:43 left in the third quarter, Buddy took Randall out and put Jim McMahon into the game. McMahon threw three straight incompletions and the Eagles punted.

"I thought that putting in a different pitcher would get things going, shake things up a bit," Buddy said after the game. "But it didn't make any difference."

After the Redskins got the ball back, they drove down the field for a touchdown and a 20-6 lead. Randall came back in, but the Eagles were unable to mount much of an offensive attack the rest of the way.

Richie came up to me, right before we were going back onto the field, and told me Jim was going in for a series. I was shocked, but I figured Buddy was doing what he thought was best for the team and I was all for that. Still, I wasn't happy with his decision. I'm a competitor and I wanted to be out there and do anything I could to help the team. I can't do anything from the bench.

After the game, a disappointed Randall said of the benching, "It was insulting." Buddy was on the hot seat, for losing his third straight playoff game and for pulling Randall, which many in the media labeled a desperation move.

Two days later, in the Inquirer, *Randall was quoted as saying that Richie Kotite would be a great head coach. Many interpreted this as a slap at Buddy and was Randall's way of lobbying for Kotite to be named the new head coach. This wasn't the case.*

People don't know the real story. Before the Washington game, we went to Tampa Bay to work out and get away from the cold weather in Philly. While we were there, we heard a lot of rumors that Buddy was going to get the Tampa Bay job after the season. And since Buddy was one of the lowest paid coaches in the league and I figured Norman Braman wasn't going to match the money Tampa Bay was going to pay him, I figured we'd lose Buddy for sure. And then I started hearing that Richie had a chance to get the Cleveland job. So I figured I'd say something nice about Richie to help him get that job, or to get the Eagles' job if Norman Braman let Buddy go. People were thinking I was mad at Buddy because I got yanked, but that had nothing to do with it. I'm not the kind of guy to stab someone in the back. Buddy did too much for me to ever stab him in the back. I mean, be realistic. Why would I want to hurt the man who made me who I am today. Buddy put his total trust in me as his quarterback by releasing Ron Jaworski and giving me the starting job. I'm still for Buddy 100 percent, wherever he's coaching [he was named defensive coordinator for the Houston Oilers after the 1992 season]. I would love to play for Buddy again because he gives a player respect after they've earned it.

The next morning, the Eagles did indeed announce that Buddy would not get a new contract. Later that afternoon, Kotite was named the Eagles' new head coach. The controversy didn't end, as many of the Eagles, especially the defensive players, expressed outrage that Buddy wasn't coming back and several said they didn't want to play for the Eagles any longer. The media played up every angle they could, trying to keep the controversy alive. Randall was a convenient scapegoat and was blamed for the team's playoff failures, for not being a leader and even for Buddy's firing. A three-part feature in the Daily News *claimed that the Eagles were a divided team and, "Privately, these players have complained that Cunningham is preoccupied with his statistics, that he doesn't mingle well with his teammates, that he is quick to take a bow when times are good but that he won't take the heat when he messes up." Everything came to a head during the Eagles' mini-camp in early April at a players-only meeting.*

Basically, even though nobody put their names to the comments, I knew who they were coming from. I went into that meeting knowing what was coming and I just sat there and listened and didn't say a word. Only two guys stood up and said anything negative about me. Keith Jackson stood up and said I was always running down the field when he was wide open. I didn't say anything. Afterwards Keith came up to me and we hugged and he said he just had to get it off his chest and now he felt better. The thing is, if I see an opening and can gain 20 yards, I'm going to run. I don't do it for statistics; I don't get paid to run the football; I want to help the team win. But I listened to what Keith said and decided to look for him even more than I already did.

Then Seth Joyner stood up and said that when I scramble around and make a big play, I act like I'm the only one out there helping the team. He was talking about the touchdown play against Buffalo and how afterwards, when the reporters asked me if I amazed myself, I said yes, sometimes I do. He said I was an "I" player instead of a "We" player.

What was I supposed to say, no, I don't amaze myself. That would have made me sound cocky and arrogant and I'm not like that. I also complimented Freddie and said that without his great catch the play wouldn't have been anything. But I can't control what the reporters write in the paper and nobody wrote what I said about Freddie. Or was I supposed to say, "we" dropped back, "we" scrambled around, "we" saw Bruce Smith coming, "we" ducked under him and "we" threw the ball downfield.

What Seth was saying, and I agreed, was that other players work hard and play hard and deserve some credit too. Along with L.T., Seth is probably the most talented linebacker in the league, but he wasn't getting the recognition he deserved—especially back in 1990. I can't control the media. I can't get Seth more publicity. The quarterback—every quarterback—gets the most attention. That's just the way it is.

Even Keith Byars got on me a little. He stood up and said I should have more of the guys over to my house. I agreed and have tried to do that since that meeting.

All during the meeting, I was biting my tongue and keeping my mouth shut. Some guys were waiting for me to talk back and then really jump on me. There were some guys defending me. Other guys got criticized, but nobody criticized Buddy and I think that shows how much respect we had for him. Overall, I think guys formed a more positive opinion of me because I stayed quiet and listened to what people had to say. Some guys might have thought they needed to bring Randall back down to earth, but I never left earth. People might say I'm not team-oriented, but that's a lie. Anyone who knows me knows I'll do whatever it takes to help the team win. People should look at themselves first before they start pointing fingers at others. Like the Bible says, why should you remove a speck from someone else's eye when you have plank in your own eye. First remove the plank.

Guys said I should be more verbal and yell at guys more. But that's not me. I don't ever want to embarrass a player out on the field or on the sideline. I encourage them. But the guys said I had to be more vocal and I decided I'd try.

A lot of people might not believe this, but Buddy and I are still friends. There was never any problem between us; the whole thing was made up by the media. After Buddy was let go, I called him up at his house and tried to explain that I didn't try to get him fired and that I thought he was a great coach. Buddy said, "Thank you, my friend," and then he hung up. Since then, we've seen each other a few times at various events and we talk and joke around. Buddy is a great guy and if he ever gets another chance as a head coach, he'll do a great job. Buddy is the type of coach that is loyal to his players and doesn't care what people think about him. He just wants to win.

CHAPTER 7

The Eagles' offense starts slowly during a dismal first two quarters in Dallas, but the Birds are only behind 3-0 at the half. Randall completes 3-of-8 passes for 13 yards and an interception in the first two quarters. The interception looks particularly ugly, as Randall throws the ball right into the hands of a wide-open Cowboys' cornerback. Three other passes bounce in front of receivers.

At the half, Kotite benches Randall and puts McMahon in the game. McMahon completes 10-of-19 passes for 122 yards and a score, but the Eagles lose 20-10 to drop to 5-3. In case you're counting, that's three losses in the last four games, games in which the offense has scored only 46 points, after scoring 107 in the first four games—all wins.

"I felt we had to make a change to get something clicking," Kotite says after the game at his press conference. Then he quickly adds that Randall will be back in the starting lineup the following week in the Eagles' home game against the Los Angeles Raiders.

Although he's upset with being benched, Randall is diplomatic after the game: "First of all, I want to state that I don't want to start any controversy. Richie runs this football team and whatever his decisions are, we live with it and that's the way it is. It's no big deal, man. We obviously weren't doing well, and whatever wasn't being done on offense, I take the blame for it. It's my fault."

While Randall is ready to accept the blame, there is plenty to spread around. Heller and Davis—the two starting tackles—miss the game with injuries, as does Keith Byars, who has a broken hand. Without the departed Keith Jackson at tight end, or Byars to catch balls out of the backfield or as a tight end, Randall is now without two of his prime weapons. Opposing teams are able to double their coverage on the wide-outs, blitz a linebacker or two and not worry about covering the middle of the field. Plus, the running game isn't effective, yet Kotite continues to go to it, setting up numerous third-and-long situations and making the Eagles a predictable, unimaginative team.

"I don't think Randall was the problem," lineman Mike Schad says after the game. "The whole offense was."

The week before the Dallas game we beat Phoenix 7-3 and the offense wasn't very productive. Richie called me into his office that Tuesday. "What's the matter with you?" he kept asking. "We have to get things going. Your timing is off, your focus is off. What's the matter with you? You have to concentrate, you're going against the system." Then he tells me that he heard that I wanted to run the two-minute [or hurry-up] offense more often, not just in the last couple of minutes of a half. We did this a lot in 1990 and were very successful with it. "We know you can run the two-minute drill, so stop fighting the system," Richie said. All I did was nod and say that I would do it his way and would work within the system. "Whatever you want coach," I said.

Richie's offensive system is designed for a drop-back quarterback who stays in the pocket and doesn't run. Like a Ken O'Brien-type who he coached when he was with the Jets. Or a Jim McMahon. That's not me. I can be that, and I will be that, if that's what Richie wants. But that's not what I do best. I've proven in the past what I can do when I'm let loose. People want to see Randall Cunningham rolling out, running, making things happen and being exciting.

In 1990, when Buddy was the head coach and Richie came in as the offensive coordinator, Richie adapted the offense to my style and we were very productive. I threw for 3,466 yards and 30 touchdowns and ran for 942 yards. Then I got hurt in 1991 and Richie put in a different system for Jim, and basically, we're using that same system again this year. "Stay within the system," he always tells me.

The whole time he was talking to me in his office, Richie didn't look me in the eyes. I left feeling very uncomfortable about my starting job. It was as though everything he had just said was a warning that I could be replaced. I walked out of his office and saw Keith Byars and said, "Tank, you don't know what's going on. Richie just called me into his office and it sounds like he's going to bench me."

"No way," Tank told me. "This is your team, your offense, you run the show and make things happen."

Tank hit the nail right on the head: let Randall be Randall. Because of Buddy, that's what Richie did in 1990 and we were very successful. For example, at the start of the 1990 season, Richie put in something called the 67 pass protection blocking scheme for the offensive line, in which only three guys go out and everyone else stays in to block. It's designed to pick up the blitz and provide maximum protection when the line breaks down. But my thing is, let them blitz: I'll read it and get the ball to the "hot" back coming out of the backfield, or make the guy blitzing miss me and throw the ball downfield or run it. When someone blitzes or beats a blocker, they vacate a spot and create a lane I can escape through. Don't tie my hands by keeping the tight end and running backs in to block and have so many people in front of me blocking that there aren't any lanes for me to run through.

I went to Richie and told him I didn't like the 67 and we didn't use it very much after that. When someone blitzed, I just flipped the ball to Keith Byars. I must have done that 50 times in 1990 and Keith wound up catching 81 passes for 819 yards. Richie and I were on the same page and our offense was ranked third in the entire NFL.

This year, Dick Wood, our running backs coach, is calling the blocking schemes. Dick came here in 1991. He doesn't know my style and he wants maximum protection, which is what you'd want for a drop-back, pocket passer. When I got hurt, they used the 67 blocking scheme to protect Jim. This year, even though I'm back, Dick keeps calling the 67. I went to him and tried to explain what we did in 1990, but he says, no, he's going to keep using the 67. Richie has to back him up because Dick is one of his coaches, which is what a good head coach does. The point is, we're still using the 67, which I hate.

I've been frustrated with this for a long time, but I haven't said anything. This is Richie's team, not mine, and I'll do whatever he tells me to do.

Against Dallas, I did what Richie wanted; I ran the system. We used the 67 a lot, even though Dallas wasn't blitzing. This meant we only had three guys running patterns, with everyone else in blocking and clogging up the running lanes so I couldn't escape upfield. Plus, Dallas had plenty of defensive backs in coverage and our receivers couldn't get open. On one third-and-long play, we sent two guys out to one side—Calvin Williams and Roy Green. Calvin ran an eight-yard stop route and there were two guys right on him. Roy releases upfield, runs a 12-14 yard hook route and there are two linebackers sitting right on him. I didn't have anyone open and didn't have anywhere to run. I got sacked. It felt like both my arms were broken. Another play was designed for Calvin to run a long in-and-go route. In practice I told the coaches I thought the play took too long—at least three full seconds. I had to take a full drop, pump fake when Calvin made his break and then throw it. I went into the huddle saying this was going to be a big play and I thought it was. Calvin ran his pattern, was about to make his break when—BOOM!—I got hit.

Calvin kept running and was wide open a split second after I got hit. It could have been a touchdown.

I'm not trying to make excuses or pass the blame. I didn't play well and that's exactly what I told everyone after the game. I made some bad throws and held the ball too long a few times. I can accept it if the coaches don't think I'm playing well and want to bench me, but then they started to question my intelligence, saying I wasn't calling the plays properly. After the interception I got second-guessed. On the play, Calvin went in motion to the left and the cornerback was supposed to be playing off him, which would get Calvin open for a quick six or seven out-pattern. But they changed up their defense—they were in a two-deep zone, which I read right away—and the cornerback was right up on my receiver. Calvin made the right adjustment and turned upfield and ran the fade. Normally, one of the running backs is supposed to release, but they both stayed in to block. Freddie was covered on the right side and for an instant it looked like Calvin was open behind the cornerback and in front of the safety. I tried to loop the ball over the cornerback to Calvin. My pass was too short and it got picked off. It was underthrown; it was my fault. But later I hear that everyone was saying I didn't make the right call, that I was trying to throw an out route when Calvin was running a different pattern. I'm not stupid. I've been in the NFL a long time and I know what I'm doing. I knew the play and the adjustment, it was just a bad pass.

We go into the locker at halftime of the Dallas game and Richie calls Jim and me into an office. "Randall, look at me," he said and I looked at him. "We're going to go with Jim in the third quarter, be ready to go back in the fourth quarter."

I said, "OK."

"Look at me," Richie said again.

"Richie, I don't have a problem with that," I said.

Jim looked like he couldn't believe what had just happened, but I hugged him and wished him good luck and I meant it.

I thought I was coming back in the fourth quarter, but I didn't.

Then, after the game, Richie comes out and says there will be no quarterback controversy, Randall will start against the Raiders. I figured that was that and I'd be back in and get things turned around against the Raiders. I was wrong.

MONDAY, NOVEMBER 2, 1992

When I got to the locker room this morning, Zeke came over and said Richie wanted to see me. I thought, "Oh boy, what did I do now?" When Richie calls you into his office, it's not to chat or joke around, it's because you did something wrong. And when you're in his office, you're not going to be in there but for a hot two or three minutes and then it's out the door. Richie is all business.

Richie sits me down and tells me he still doesn't know what's wrong with me and that he is going to sit me down this week and Jim will start, but that it would be for one week only and then I'd be back against Green Bay the following week. I just stared at Richie. I was emotionless. He kept talking and so many things started running through my head that I really didn't hear what he was saying. No one ever wants to get benched. And you don't expect it when, at the start of the season, your coach tells you that if anyone is going to take this team to the Super Bowl, it's you and nobody else.

I think that Richie lost confidence in me as a player. He kept asking me what's wrong and I didn't really say anything, but I was thinking, "You are the coach, you know me, you know I'm a strong individual and that nothing gets me down." At this point in my life, I'm the happiest I've ever been and if he knew me, he would know that there is nothing wrong with me.

Richie kept asking me what was wrong and finally I just got up and left his office. What did he want me to say, that I was happy about getting benched? I went to my locker and saw Jim and told him he was the starting quarterback against the Raiders. His jaw dropped like he was shocked or didn't believe me. Then Jim looked down at his throwing elbow. He had just had a couple of stitches put in, plus his neck was sore. Two injuries is nothing for Jim. I still don't think he believed me, but then Richie called him into his office and he found out I was telling the truth.

Then I told Dave Archer, our third-string quarterback, and I got the impression Dave was a little upset. Dave's a competitor and he did a great job during preseason when Jim was holding out and I'm sure he wanted a chance to play.

In the afternoon, Kotite told the press about his decision. "I thought about it all night and all this morning," Kotite tells the media. "I told [Randall] I'm gonna have Jim start this week and have him back off. I think the kid needs to back off and maybe take some pressure off himself . . . I just have a feel that a week off is going to help him. That's how I feel. I think he's trying too hard . . . I think he's pressing a little bit, which is natural when you're not having success . . . I stress a week . . . a week, OK. I don't want you to think this is going to be a week-to-week deal or anything like that. [Cunningham] is the guy. That has not changed."

Randall tried to contain his frustration when the press surrounded him after Kotite's announcement, but a little of it spilled out.

"If he thinks a week off will help me, he doesn't know me as well as I thought he knew me," Randall told the press.

"Do you want to start?" a reporter asks.

"You got that right. I don't want to sit on the bench and it's not because of the splinters."

Kotite's announcement sets off a firestorm of controversy that rages out of control the entire week—in Philadelphia and around the country.

"It's started," Randall says. "The quarterback controversy has started." Instead of getting upset, Randall instead decided to have some fun with the situation.

The headline in the Inquirer *on Tuesday, November 3—Election*

Day!—reads: "Kotite to bench slumping Cunningham for Sunday's game." Below this story is the number two story of the day: the presidential election. The Daily News *has a field day with the situation. On Monday the headline on the back page blares: "Pine Time." The next day, after Kotite announces Randall will be benched, the headline reads: "It Doesn't Sit Well: Cunningham irked as Kotite says he'll start McMahon on Sunday." The next day the headline is: "Earth to Randall" and suggests that Randall's problems are in his head. The resident psychologist at the* Inquirer *likes this theme and adds his analysis: "Randall Cunningham keeps saying nothing is wrong . . . What's wrong is the apparent inability of Randall Cunningham to understand that something is wrong."*

WEDNESDAY, NOVEMBER 4, 1992

Every Wednesday night Randall tapes his television show, which airs Sundays at 11:30 A.M. on the local CBS affiliate. It's standing room only in the large studio and the audience is pumped. Almost everyone is wearing some sort of Randall shirt or hat. There are hand-painted signs and one woman baked a cake for Randall. When Randall finally walks out from the back of the studio and through the audience to the stage in front, the audience erupts in cheers, rises to its feet and begins chanting: "Randall, Randall."

Randall is upbeat and smiling and eager to talk with his fans. "If you come to my show, you can't be going to Richie's show," Randall jokes. Kotite's show is taped Thursday nights in the same studio. Everyone laughs.

"I heard Keith Jackson on television say that the reason I'm having problems is that he isn't here," Randall continues. "Is that true?" The audience cheers. "That's right, he's the best tight end in football."

"Randall, how's your knee?" someone shouts from the back.

"My knee is fine. If you listen to the media, it's not my knee, it's my head. I have a mental problem."

Randall is positively beaming. He's thoroughly enjoying the give-and-take with the audience, who are all Randall Backers. There's not a Randall Basher in the bunch. Several times he has said, "If fans want to know the real me, they should come watch my television show being taped. They don't see the real me on television when I'm being interviewed by the television reporters or read about the real me in the newspapers. That's the professional Randall, being careful not to say anything controversial. They have to come here and see the real Randall, the fun-loving Randall who likes to joke around and have fun."

This is the real Randall and his fans are loving it as much as Randall.

"Do you still get paid when you get benched?" someone shouts and everyone roars with delight as Randall shouts, "You bet I do."

"It's true I haven't played as well as I can, but when I have a mediocre day, all you hear about is what's wrong with Randall."

"It's the conservative play calling," someone shouts.

Randall smiles, nods knowingly and the cheers reach a new level.

"Don't worry, I'm a very strong person in my heart. I won't let anyone change the way I feel. I'll be strong. I got a book coming out next year where I'll break it all down for you. Are you going to buy it?"

Everyone shouts yes.

"How about if there were a couple of naked pictures in my book like Madonna has in hers. Would you buy it then?"

The women in the audience scream.

"I heard there's a picture of Madonna kissing [super model] Naomi Campbell and there's even a picture of her with a dog in there and . . ."

Someone interrupts to ask a football question and another member of the audience tells him to shut up. "I want to hear more about

Madonna. Why don't you put a picture in there of you and Naomi naked?"

"I would but I'm a Christian and can't have any of that in my book."

A little kid in the front row asks a question, but Randall can't hear him. "Come on up here," Randall says with a wave and the shy boy, with a little nudge from his father, walks onto the stage. Randall sits him on the edge of his chair and puts his arm around his tiny shoulders.

"Why don't you run more fake punts and onsides kicks," the kid asks.

"We only do onsides kicks when we're losing and we try not to get behind. What's your name?"

"Chris."

"How old are you?"

"Seven."

Chris, in awe of Randall, doesn't want to get up and stays seated by Randall as he fields a few more questions from the audience. Finally it's time for the show to start and Chris reluctantly goes back to his seat.

Randall's guest tonight is Kenny Jackson, one of Randall's closest friends. Jackson played for the Eagles from 1984-88 and was with Houston in 1989. Buddy Ryan brought him back in 1990 as a special teams player, reserve wide receiver, and, as many suggested, Randall's personal psychiatrist. Jackson remained through the 1991 season and was released during training camp before the current season.

Before the show, while Randall and Kenny munched on dinner, someone suggested that it would be a great idea to have Jackson come out dressed like a doctor. "That's right," says Jackson, who is far from shy. "Everyone always says I'm Randall's psychiatrist so why don't I dress like a doctor."

When Jackson is introduced he comes out in a white doctor's

gown, with a stethoscope around his neck, which he holds up to Randall's head as if he's examining him to find out what's wrong. "There's nothing in here," Jackson says with a smile and he and Randall crack up.

Kenny Jackson: When Randall first got here, I knew he would be in for some tough times because he was black and there weren't many black quarterbacks in the NFL. We had to be a family for him; we had to be there for him because he was eventually going to be in a position where he had a lot of pressure on him. I realized this right away because I went to a school—Penn State—where we were a family. Certain people in the family need more attention. Randall, as quarterback, a black quarterback, was going to have more pressure on him and his job was a lot tougher than ours. A lot of guys won't look at it this way because they are jealous Randall got so much attention so quick. But the thing is, Randall worked hard for what he has and never took his talents for granted. If Randall hadn't been dedicated and determined to do anything to help the team win, I wouldn't have been there for him.

When coaches let Randall do his thing and be himself, there's nobody else in the NFL that can touch him. It got to a point where the other guys on the team figured there wasn't anything he couldn't do. So, we almost took it for granted that he would come up with the big play. Our job is to put him in position to make the big play. The only coach who totally understood this was Buddy. Buddy knows that if you have a great thoroughbred, you can't corral him. Buddy knew that he had to put the pressure on Randall, that pressure brings out the best in Randall. A lot of people say he shouldn't run because he'll get hurt. I told them they were full of it. He better run or he's going to get hurt. If he had a line like Miami's line, he might not have to run. But when Randall got here, he had one of the worst lines in the history of the NFL. But he never complained—not one word. He got beat up every single game and never complained or blamed anyone. He never said or did anything to make someone else on the team look bad. He never took away from another player to make himself look better.

SUNDAY, NOVEMBER 8, 1992

The controversy continues right up until game day at Veterans Stadium, when NBC—which is televising the game—devotes most of its pregame coverage to the situation. O.J. Simpson (the same O.J. Simpson an awed nine-year-old Randall Cunningham once asked for an autograph at the Rose Bowl) has spent the week covering the story. "It has been an interesting week in Philadelphia," O.J. begins, stating the obvious. "In fact, it's been an interesting year. The Eagles started off 4-0 and looked invincible, but a lot of bad things have happened lately, including the benching of an all-pro quarterback."

The screen is filled with Randall's face and he begins answering a question from O.J.: "We started out of the blocks 4-0 and we were doing great. And then I started playing average football and the [critics] said, 'Hold on a second, Randall's playing terrible, he's not doing what he should do, he can't read defenses'—all these crazy things."

"You were quoted as saying," O.J. says, " 'If Rich Kotite thinks sitting me on the bench is gonna make me a better quarterback, that isn't so.' "

"That isn't so," Randall insists. "If you look at the quarterbacks who have proven themselves—the Marinos, the Montanas, the Kellys, the Kosars, the Everetts, the Moons, none of these guys get benched and I look at it and say why am I getting benched?"

Cut to Kotite: "He didn't say very much [when I told him]. He didn't say anything at all as a matter of fact, but that's Randall."

Cut back to Randall: "Previous to that week [in Dallas] he had come in and said, 'You're not playing the way [we want],' and he wouldn't look at me and he basically said, 'What's wrong?' And he really believed it was me and he said, 'You have to play better, you're fighting the system. Don't fight the system.' I'm like, 'No problem.' So, when I was told Jim's going to come in for the third quarter [against Dallas]—be ready for the fourth quarter—I figured, hey, they'll try Jim, I'll be back in the fourth quarter and be ready to play. Then I didn't go in and I was like OK."

"Were you surprised Monday when you found out you weren't going to start this week?" O.J. asks.

"Monday I came in and Richie calls me into his office and says Jim's gonna start this week; what's wrong, you got to tell me what's wrong, and he goes through all the reasons, 'You're throwing balls in the dirt, this and that and you got to tell me what's wrong,' and I'm completely emotionless; I have no emotions left. First I get benched, then I'm coming back in the fourth quarter, then I don't come back, then I'm starting, then I'm on the bench. My mind is spinning. What's occurring here? But, [then Kotite says] 'We're gonna start you in Green Bay.' So now I'm like, am I really going to start in Green Bay or am I actually going to be on the bench?"

"What if [McMahon] goes out there and throws for 400 yards and four touchdowns?" Simpson asks Kotite.

"I got that one a number of times," Kotite says. "Still, I feel the same way. We need to get back on track, both for ourselves and Randall and when we [play the Packers], Randall is going to be the quarterback. People don't want to believe me when I give them the answer, but that's the answer."

"If you go out and have a great game this week and you guys win, it's gonna be kind of tough for you to go back to that backup position," O.J. says to McMahon.

"There's no doubt about it," McMahon says. "I know I'd be upset and I know [Randall would] be upset if they continued to play me."

Cut to Randall: "The can of worms had been opened. The quarterback controversy is starting now."

"Can Randall Cunningham be a backup quarterback?" O.J. asks Randall.

"I won't be a backup quarterback. I'll back Jim up this week, but I don't think Norman Braman pays me the money he pays me to sit the bench. If he wants to pay me $2.5 million or $3 million to sit the bench, I don't see that happening."

To fan the flames on the fire even further, Buddy Ryan joins NBC's panel discussion.

"I believe in benching anybody who is having a bad game," Buddy begins. *"I don't believe in punishing 44 other guys who are trying to win a game by leaving a guy in there who is having a bad day. But you don't carry it on into the next week. I've benched some great players . . . but I let them play the next week, that's important and I think Randall should be playing."*

"In general, the past few weeks Cunningham has looked out of rhythm," Bob Costas asks Buddy. *"In his previous four quarters he was just 5-for-17 for 24 yards. Is there something wrong with their approach?"*

"I think they are kind of tying his hands a little by trying to get a 1,000-yard rusher, when really, if they want to put those people out there and split them out and let Randall do his thing with Keith Byars, and of course they did have Keith Jackson playing tight end—a great talent—that's the way we used to play offense and Randall got the rushing yards for us along with the back that remained in the backfield who would also pick up a blitzer if they came."

"How much has Keith Jackson's absence hurt him?" Costas asks Ryan.

"I think it hurts them a great deal. You don't lose the best tight end in football and not hurt yourself. He takes the pressure of those two wide-outs. They're doubling them and it makes it a lot different game."

"You know Randall," Costas continues. *"Is he going to be shaken by this?"*

"No, Randall is a lot tougher guy than people give him credit for," Buddy says. "He comes from a tough background, he really prepares to win and he'll do a good job this week if he gets in and Jim will do a good job."

The game finally, mercifully, begins and the Eagles' defense seems to take out all the frustrations of the week on the hapless Raiders' offense. The Eagles' offense gets the ball in Raiders' territory on its first four possessions, McMahon does an average job—completing 12-of-24 passes for 157 yards, one touchdown and one interception—and the Eagles win 31-10.

After McMahon's touchdown pass to Barnett, Randall is the first to congratulate McMahon as he trots off the field. The two embrace and smile as Randall says something to McMahon. "I said what the heck was that play," Randall says. "Jim just laughed and said he told Freddie to run a dig and go, which is not even in the game plan, but it worked, so what can the coaches say: Jim you can't do that. No. It worked and was a touchdown. Jim made something happen."

Late in the game, with the Eagles running out the clock. McMahon calls an unnecessary audible on 3-and-3 with the Eagles way ahead. Herschel doesn't hear McMahon, runs to take the handoff and slams into the back of McMahon's knee. The quarterback goes down, calls a timeout and jogs slowly off the field. "It was scary there for a little while," McMahon says. "I checked [the defense] at the line and changed the play and Herschel didn't hear it—so it was my own damn fault." McMahon is OK and goes back into the game after the timeout. Walker is stopped short on fourth down and the Raiders take over the ball.

After the game, the huge horde of reporters crowds into the interview room across the hallway from the Eagles' locker room waiting for Kotite and his customary post-game press conference. There's only one question on everyone's mind: Who will be the starting quarterback the following week in Green Bay? Cunningham or McMahon.

My first game back after my knee surgery was on September 6, 1992, and we managed to beat the New Orleans Saints 15-13. (LAURENCE KESTERSON / SPORTSTOCK)

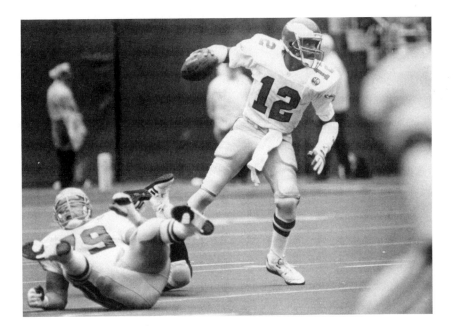

Through a lot of hard work, I was able to rebuild my knee and come back scrambling. (LAURENCE KESTERSON / SPORTSTOCK)

My faith in God is an important part of my life. After every game, players from both teams get together to pray. (STEVE WARTENBERG)

It's important to be on the same page as your receivers. Here I am talking things over with Heath Sherman, Roy Green and Calvin Williams. (STEVE WARTENBERG)

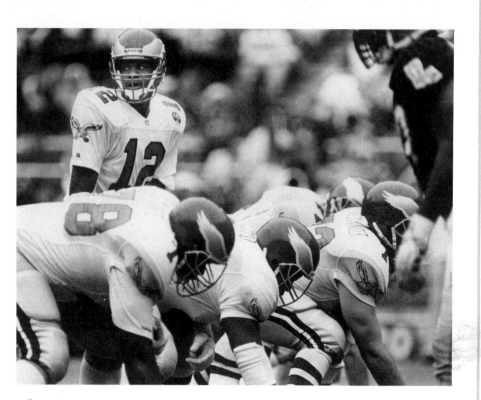

A key to our success in 1992 was our offensive line, which developed a nasty attitude.
(LAURENCE KESTERSON / SPORTSTOCK)

Don't listen to rumors. Whitney Houston and I are just good friends. (LARRY BUSACCA / RETNA)

I've always enjoyed getting to know the fans in Philadelphia. (PHOTO BY MICHAEL MERCANTI / PHILADELPHIA DAILY NEWS)

𝔽elicity is my gift from God, my dream come true and now she's my wife. (FELICITY DE JAGER)

Whenever we play the Giants, we expect a hard-hitting game. (PHOTO BY MICHAEL MERCANTI / PHILADELPHIA DAILY NEWS)

"Can you imagine," one reporter says, "the Eagles win 31-10
the only thing everyone wants to ask Kotite is who will be his q
terback. Unbelievable." But true. "I think Rich Kotite will start F
dall next week, but in my opinion that's the wrong thing to do,
television reporter announces during his live post-game coverage
the game, trying to further fan the flames of the controversy.

Kotite strides into the room, makes a brief opening statement,
which he praises his team's intensity, and fields the first questio
"Who is your quarterback next week?"

"I'll answer that one time," Kotite responds testily. "I answered
45 times last week. Cunningham's playing next week. Next question.

"Are you convinced everything is straightened out with Ran
dall?"

"I'm convinced the week off did him some good and that now
we'll get back to practice as a team and be ready for Green Bay."

"What do you think [Randall] learned from this?"

"I don't know, you'll have to ask him."

"Any concern among the players that the team is rolling under
Jim [and now you're switching back to Randall]?"

"No concern at all."

"Does the offensive line respond better to Jim?"

"You'll have to ask them."

After answering a few more questions—some of which even concern the defense or other aspects of the game besides Cunningham
and McMahon—Kotite departs and McMahon enters for his press
conference.

"Fire away boys," says McMahon, who is clad in his undershirt,
funky sunglasses and a baseball hat with a large "O" on it.

"Jim, what's your reaction to going back to the bench next
week?"

"Well, it's just something I can't worry about. It's a coach's decision. I just wanted to go out and get a win for the club, and I think I
did some good things today and unfortunately I guess I'll be sitting
next week, but I can't really worry about it. I'll do whatever I can to

help the team, whether I'm playing or helping Randall when I'm not in there."

"Did you see this as an opportunity to win the job?"

"I wasn't worried about next week. I just wanted to come out of this game [with a record of] 6-3 and that's what we did.

"How do you avoid a situation where half the team wants one guy and the other half wants another?"

"We're not gonna worry about who's supporting who. I think the whole team is going to support whoever is playing . . . If we start complaining about who's playing and who isn't, it's gonna divide the team and that's what we don't want."

"Do you believe you won the starting job?"

"I'm not worried if I won the starting job. I can't worry about things I don't control. When I get my opportunities I try to make the most of them."

"How much was said between you and Randall [during the game]?"

"We were talking a lot about what was going on. He was telling me what defenses they were in and joking around. When I came off after I hurt my knee a little bit I told him he had to go in and he wasn't too happy about that. We had fun today. We have good rapport."

"Is there more pressure on Randall now to keep you on the bench?"

"Like Randall said last week, he puts a lot of pressure on himself to play well and so do I. When you're in a position like Randall where you're making a lot of money, the pressure will be on him every day no matter what the situation is. He'll be all right."

The instant McMahon is finished, the pack of reporters races to the locker room to talk to Randall. Normally, after a game, Randall will hold his own press conference, but today, since he didn't play, he doesn't. Randall is standing in front of his locker, dressing, when the swarm arrives, buzzing with questions, microphones, film crews and

Mr. Braman (left) and I got off to a rocky start, but over the years we've come to respect one another. (PHOTO BY MICHAEL MERCANTI / PHILADELPHIA DAILY NEWS)

We always enjoy the challenge of playing the best team, and that certainly included Joe Montana and the San Francisco 49ers. (PHOTO BY MICHAEL MERCANTI / PHILADEL-PHIA DAILY NEWS)

blinding lights. The crowd is so big that only about a third of the press (about 30) can get close enough to Randall to hear him. After the first group of 30 finishes, the next group of 30 surrounds him and when they are done, the final group of 30 crowd around Randall, whose head towers above the group of men and women assembled around him.

Archer heads to the shower with a warning to the reporters, four or five of whom are standing in his locker, stepping on his clothes as they reach their microphones over the top of the divider between the two locker stalls in order to hear Randall. "That's too much boys," says Archer, already grumpy because he's the third-string quarterback. "By the time I get back from the shower you better be out of here."

While this is going on, McMahon returns to his locker, which is next to Archer's and two away from Randall's. All the reporters ignore him as they crowd around Randall. McMahon begins removing his padding, which includes braces on both knees, a flak jacket to protect his ribs and a thick black rubber tube around his tender right elbow. Under the tube is a bandage and under that is a nasty gash he suffered the week before against Dallas.

"Did my stitches get pulled out?" McMahon asks no one in particular as he tries to get a look at his elbow.

"I don't think so," someone answers.

"Thanks," says McMahon, who finishes undressing and heads to the showers.

"Randall," a reporter begins, "Richie said you're starting next week."

"Well, I'll be ready," Randall replies calmly.

"Would you have been upset if he said Jim was starting?"

"Jim should start. He did well. Just let us know up front who is starting."

"Did Kotite handle this well?"

"What am I supposed to say?"

"Can this thing split the Eagles?"

"It just depends on how the head coach handles it."

"Did the week off help?"

"I don't think I'll be a better quarterback [because of it]. Hopefully, he'll allow me to get in sync."

"Did you know that Buddy Ryan said on TV that the Eagles should just turn you loose?"

"I'll tell you what—Buddy knows me very well. That's what he did in the past. He allowed me to create the numbers I did in the past. I don't want to create anything, but he said it, so I'll go along."

On and on it goes, the same questions over and over. In the midst of the onslaught, Archer returns from the shower to find four reporters standing in front of his locker. He glares, not saying a word, and they move out of the way. He dresses quickly while Randall continues answering questions.

"It's not a Jim-versus-Randall thing," Randall says. "It's that Randall sat the pine. I'll pull the splinters out and I'll be OK. We won and that's the main thing . . . I'm glad Jim went out and did a great job . . . I don't want to get pulled again, a quarterback can't play looking over his shoulder . . . I have to go out and have fun like I used to. I saw what Jim did. He changes plays and makes them work. He does things he's comfortable with. Sometimes the coaches can't see what's happening on the field. So, when I see something, I'll go with my instincts."

After Randall finishes he heads to the showers. While he's gone, McMahon returns from the showers, walks into Randall's locker stall, grabs his deodorant stick, rubs some under his arms and puts the stick back on the shelf in Randall's locker.

"He did what?" Randall says the next day when someone tells him about it. "Jim and Archer did that all during training camp. Finally I went out and bought them both their own deodorant. I guess he's out and I'll have to get him more. I don't mind if Jim uses mine; he doesn't have any hair under his arms anyway."

WEDNESDAY, NOVEMBER 11, 1992

I don't even know how to begin to describe the last 10 days. So, let's just say they put me on what we call THE BENCH. I rode pine for one game and didn't get any splinters. We have heated benches, but when I went to sit down right before the game, they were covered with a layer of ice. They couldn't turn on the heat because that would just melt the ice and we'd all be sitting in water. Some maintenance guys came over, chipped off all the ice, turned on the heater and I sat down. Right then I knew it was going to be a long day.

I have to admit I didn't like the experience of being benched. All week there was the hype about how Jim would play and how the offense would play. Everyone wanted to see if our offensive slump was Randall's fault or if it was the entire offense's fault. For the game, we changed the game plan, simplified the offense. We cut out a couple of formations and took out some of the motions and kept an extra running back in the backfield to block on passing plays. The coaches changed it for Jim, not because he didn't understand it, but to take advantage of his style of play. Jim makes quick drops and throws to the guy who should be open. He doesn't run. They built the offense for Jim.

In Bible study the night before the game I said a prayer for Jim to be successful and for God to protect him and keep him safe. Before the game I hugged Jim and wished him good luck. I meant it. I don't like phoney people. I'm a person who speaks from the heart and when I pray for something, I'm very sincere. I wanted Jim to play well and I wanted us to win. Jim and I are friends and we both want the other to do well.

The defense played great and the offense got the ball 10 times in Raiders' territory. The line played well, Heath and Herschel ran for a lot of yards and Jim did what he had to do. He orchestrated the offense very efficiently and that's what everyone expected him to do.

There is one thing I have to apologize to Jim about. First you have to understand Jim. For the past few years, during practice, Jim's always coming up to me and saying, "My arm's a little sore today. Why don't you grab all the reps?" It's become a joke between us. This week in practice, I went up to Jim and said, "I'm a little tired. You have to help me out and take all the reps. You're on your own."

Late in the game, Herschel ran into Jim's knee and he went down, but he came off the field and I didn't think he was hurt. In fact, I thought he was joking around. Earlier in the week I had told him, "Why don't you put thirty points on the board and then give me a little playing time." But, after Jim came off the field with about two minutes left, Richie told me to start warming up and I might have to go in for Jim. I never had to warm up before, so I didn't even know what to do and panicked a little. First I had to find a ball and then I didn't know if I should throw it to someone or take snaps from center. The timeout went by and I hadn't done anything. I wasn't used to being benched. But Jim was OK and went back into the game. When Jim came back to the sideline, I said, joking around, "Are you OK? Don't pull that joke, I'm not going into the game to mop up for you." Jim didn't really say anything, he was worried about his knee. Then a few seconds later I find out his knee really might be injured. Then he starts dropping back on the sideline, testing out his knee, and I'm really confused—is he OK or is he injured?

Then Richie came up to me and says I have to put you in the game if Jim can't go. He said he couldn't put Archer in since he was inactive for the game and if Archer went in, that meant neither Jim or I could go back in. I'm thinking, so what, there's only a minute left to play and all we're going to do is hand off the ball anyway—what does it matter who goes in? I said, "Richie, I'll do anything you need me to do. If you need me to go in, I'll go in. I'm no kid." I couldn't believe he was so worried about me getting upset at having to go in. But Jim said he was OK and went back in to finish out the game.

After the game, when the reporters asked me about it, I joked around about Jim getting hurt. Then, on Monday, the day after the game, Archer comes over and tells me I shouldn't have been joking around, that Jim really was hurt. As soon as Jim got in, I went over and said, "From my heart, I'm sorry. I thought you were just kidding." He said no big deal and that was the end of it.

I think this whole week has helped Jim and me become even closer. I really like Jim; there's no one else in the world like Jim McMahon. He's courageous and will play hurt and do whatever it takes to get on the field.

Right after the game I didn't know if I would be starting against Green Bay. I told some of the reporters that I thought Jim should start. I knew Richie had already said all week before the game that I was going to start against Green Bay, but who really knew? So I said Jim should start as a courtesy to Jim and to let people know I appreciate his talents. But then I got the word that Richie said I was starting and I thought, OK, he said I'm the starting quarterback again and if we're going to go to the Super Bowl, I'm the one who's going to take this team there. If you pull me out again, I'm not going to be Mr. Nice Guy: I'm going to react differently. Because, if you do it again, what you're doing is questioning my character and showing a lack of confidence in me. Every starting quarterback in the NFL needs to know he's the man, that we're going with you, so he can just go out, relax and play football. If you go out there and second-guess your talent and have to be looking over your shoulder toward the bench all the time, you can't be your best.

The only thing I learned from sitting on the bench is that I don't like sitting on the bench. But I am going to start doing what Jim did. If he doesn't like the play or doesn't think it will work, he changes it. He told me that if you don't like the play and don't change it and it doesn't work, it falls on your head when it's unsuccessful. He made up a play and it went for a touchdown to Freddie. I used to do that all the time, especially in 1990. This year, I've been doing what the coaches want and staying within the system, but now I'm going to have to go out and create some things on my own like I used to do.

Yesterday, I went to Richie and gave him about 12 plays—plays that were already in his playbook—and told him these were plays I liked and felt comfortable with and thought would work. I also told him I didn't like the 67 pass protection scheme. It seems like Richie and I are on the same page; at least I hope we are. He listened to what I said and told me he would sprinkle some of the plays into the game.

Richie and I don't talk that much. He's all business and when he calls you into his office, it's boom, boom, boom, two or three hot minutes and you're out. Buddy was totally different. His door was always open and guys were always going in there to hang out and joke around. I'm not saying one way is better than the other. Everyone's different and has their own style; I just wish Richie and I talked more.

I'm glad this week is over and I'm starting again. From the beginning, I tried to have some fun with it instead of getting all upset. I tried to give the reporters a few things to think about, but of course they tried to turn everything I said into a controversy.

In one paper, the headline on the cover was, "If I'm Sittin' I'm Splittin' " and they made it seem like this was a quote from me, even though I never said those words. What I said was: I don't look forward to getting put on the bench again. I don't think I'd react the same way if they put me on the bench again. If they want to put in Jim, that's their decision. But then I'll have another decision to make after that. A reporter from that paper came up to me the next day and said that was one of the stupidest headlines he'd ever read. But I sort of liked it. They were saying something I didn't say and trying to make it look like I said it. I figured I'd let people believe what they wanted to believe and have fun with it.

Then someone tells me that on the all-sports radio station in town, someone called in and said he saw me with a beautiful woman the night before a game buying booze and that I was an alcoholic and hung over the next day at the game. I had to call in and say, "Nice try, but no." The truth is that Felicity was in town and one of her best friends was coming to visit and stay in the house. I don't drink, but we wanted to make her feel welcome, so Felicity and I went out and bought her something. This was before our curfew and afterwards I went back to the team hotel and made it in time for bedcheck, played some video games with the guys and went to sleep early. But because someone saw me in a liquor store with a beautiful woman, they had to make it into something more than it was.

Here's another example. A bunch of reporters were gathered around my locker the week before the Raiders' game, asking me the same old questions about Jim and Richie and the whole quarterback controversy. I decided to give them something to think about, so I said the world's a confusing place. There's a new President, there are earthquakes, hurricanes, wars, the economy's bad, there's recession and all kinds of problems: the world's coming to an end. All they wrote was that Randall's crazy and is predicting the end of the world because he got benched. They missed my point, which was that we shouldn't spend so much time focusing on minor things like me getting benched. Instead, we should be focusing on the important things in life and be reading the Bible to find out what God wants us to do and how he wants us to lead our lives.

I know how I want to lead my life and I'm working toward that goal so that one day I'll go to heaven, where the streets are paved with gold and God says there is a home for me. My point was my faith in God makes me strong and will lead me through any problems I face. But they didn't understand. I guess that's what happens when someone is looking for controversy.

I'm trying to understand why I've been picked to go through this adversity—my parents dying, friends dying, coaches dying, my knee surgery, getting benched, plus all the controversy I always seem to be involved in. I think the reason is that God is trying to tell me that I'm a strong person, but that sometimes even strong people can be broken down, and that I have to be even stronger when these times come. I look to the Bible for guiding answers. The situation that gives me strength now is the story of Job.

Job was blameless and upright. He feared God and shunned evil. One day the angels came to present themselves before the Lord and Satan also came with them. The Lord said to Satan, "Where have you come from?" Satan answered, "From roaming through the earth and going back and forth in it." Then the Lord said to Satan, "Have you considered my servant Job?"

"You have blessed the work of his hands," the Devil said to God. "So that his flocks and herds are spread throughout the land. But stretch out your hand and strike everything he has, and he will surely curse you to your face."

God said to Satan, "Very well then, everything Job has is in your hands, but on the man himself do not lay a finger."

The Devil then goes about destroying everything Job has—his farm, his crops, his cattle and his family. Job doesn't understand why all these terrible things are happening to him, but he never loses his faith in God. He remains a righteous man. The Devil loses his challenge with God, who returns to Job everything he had lost—and more.

I know that I'm nowhere close to being as righteous and strong as Job, but that's my goal. If this is what God wants me to go through, if this is what God thinks will make me a better and stronger person, then I'll go through it praising God.

I grew up with religion and went to church every Sunday with my family—whether I wanted to or not. But I don't think I really understood it or had a personal relationship with God. I had a feeling inside me that God was with me, but I didn't read the Bible very often and when I did I didn't understand what it said or what God wanted from me or how I was supposed to live my life. I was too young to understand.

When I first got to the Eagles, Reggie White, who is an ordained Baptist minister, was running weekly Bible study classes. You have to understand Reggie and how strong he is and how much he wants to bring people closer to God. At the time, I didn't understand this and Reggie didn't understand me and how much of an infant I was in Christ. Reggie put pressure on me and said you have to come to Bible study class and you have to get to know God and develop a personal relationship with him. Reggie is a very strong man, and I'm not just talking about his physical strength. I was young and immature and resisted Reggie and what he was trying to teach me. A couple of years later, Reggie came to me and apologized. He told me he wanted to help people so much that sometimes he came on too strong and pushed too hard. I told him I understood and that I had also begun to understand what he was trying to teach me about God.

I was saved in 1987 and, believe it or not, it happened at Spanish Trails, a golf course in Las Vegas—which ironically is nicknamed "Sin City." I was with Tommy Cameron, a friend from my college days, and after we were finished playing 18 holes and were walking toward the car, Tommy asked, "Have you been saved?"

I said I didn't know, "What does being saved mean?" Tommy explained and asked if I wanted to be saved and I asked how long would it take. He said the time wasn't what was important; the important thing was whether or not I wanted to be saved and wanted to commit myself to a life of God and let him come into my life and make me the best possible person I could be. I said I wanted to be saved and Tommy said to repeat the Prayer of Salvation with him— which I did—and if I truly believed in the words and let God enter my heart, then I would be saved. I did believe what I was saying, but I asked Tommy, "How do I know if I'm saved?" He said I would know.

Some people get a sign from God, but, for me, there was no immediate sign. For me, it was a feeling deep down in my heart that I knew I wasn't perfect, but, with God's help, I would strive to live the way he wanted me to live and by doing that, I would be fulfilled and be permitted to go to heaven, where it says the streets are paved with gold and there is a place reserved for me. Little by little, this feeling grew and grew in my heart and now I have complete faith and it's an important part of my life.

After my parents' deaths, I was hesitant to get close to people because I was scared we wouldn't be friends forever. But once I opened my heart to God and got close to Him, I was able to get closer to other people. I know now that when my days on earth are over and my flesh is in the ground and rotting away, my spirit will be in heaven where everything is good and I'll get to see my mom and pop again. Now I'm not afraid to get close to people and I'm able to open my heart to my friends and family.

In 1988 I was doing a weekly radio show that was broadcast from a local restaurant. After one show, a lady came up to me and gave me a student Bible, which I put on the table along with all the other gifts people gave me. At the end of the show, everyone swarmed around me to ask for autographs, shake hands or wish me luck in our next game. After a while, I started heading out the door to my car, signing autographs and talking as I walked. Right before I got to the car, the same lady who had given me the Bible approached and, carrying the Bible I had left on the table, said, "You celebrities are all alike. You don't care about anything. All you care about is yourself." I tried to apologize and explain that I had forgotten the Bible in all the confusion and was sorry, but she didn't want to hear it and said she was going to take the Bible back. I convinced her I really wanted it and she finally gave it to me. I began reading it every day —a few pages at a time. I wore that Bible out because I took it everywhere with me and read it every day. I had to buy another one for me and I've given several others to friends. I have no idea who the lady was who gave me my first student Bible or if she'll ever read my book, but I hope she forgives me and believes me when I say I'm sorry and that I learned a valuable lesson from her.

Now, my faith is what keeps me going. People ask why I play so recklessly and don't seem to be afraid of getting hurt. The answer is I'm not afraid of getting hurt because of my faith in God. How about this for a sign—the name Randall means "protected." So now, when there is adversity in my life—like my injury—I remain strong and work hard and know things will be all right. I still have a long way to go—I know the road to heaven is a long one and there are many temptations—but I think I'm on the right path.

When I came to Philadelphia, I needed to find a church and a teammate took me to St. John Baptist in Camden. Right from the start I got a very warm feeling about the church and its minister, Pastor Townsend. I began to realize there was something missing in my life and it was attending church on a regular basis. It's a joyous feeling when you're connected with the Christian people of a church. At first, when I attended St. John Baptist, I could feel everyone staring at me and afterwards a lot of people would come up and say hello and introduce themselves and that gave me a very warm feeling. I guess that's why St. John Baptist is called the "honeycomb" church and everyone sticks together and everyone is welcome. Now, after attending for a few years, everyone knows me and I'm just another member, which I enjoy.

There was this one guy at St. John Baptist who used to stand up and say, "I know there are some people out there who haven't been saved. God's calling you to be saved, so come on up if you wish to be saved." Then he would look around the room at everyone and I could feel him staring at me. I was confused. Even though I had already been saved, he was so forceful and seemed to be talking directly to me. I thought I might have to go up and be saved again. I went to Reverend Townsend and asked, "Since I had already been saved, did I need to get saved again?" He said, "No," and I let out a big sigh of relief. Then Reverend Townsend told me once you've been saved, your relationship with God is set if you think about him every day and make him part of your life. After that, I knew this was the church for me and that Reverend Townsend was a very wise and strong person who could give me guidance. His sermons are incredible. He combines wisdom and humor and teaches you a lesson all at once. Plus, St. John Baptist is known for its music and singing and the services are very joyous and uplifting.

Once I began attending St. John Baptist on a regular basis, I began giving my tithe, which is 10 percent of all the money I make. It makes me feel good that I'm able to give the money to the church and to God. Over the past few years, my tithe has gotten to be such a phenomenal amount that Reverend Townsend and a few other members of the church came to me and asked what I wanted them to do with the money. I said the money is what God told me to give and the money is the church's money. It belongs to God and the church and I can't tell you what to do with it. They said I had to give them a suggestion and I tried to search my heart and figure out what God would want me to do with the money. There are a lot of problems in the world and I thought we should start with solving some of the problems in Camden. This is a tough, poor area, but there are a lot of great, intelligent, strong people here and they're trying to climb out of a hole. What we needed to do was give something back to them, especially the kids, and try to give them some guidance. Kids today face so many problems—single-parent families, drugs, crime, teen pregnancy—and they need some help. I thought back to when I was growing up and how important the West Side and Santa Barbara Boys Clubs were to me and all the people there who gave me guidance and kept me out of trouble. So I asked if they would use my tithe to build a youth center and everyone agreed and thought it was a great idea. It's going to be an 18,000 square-foot facility with a day care center, a gymnasium, library, game room, a kitchen so kids can learn to cook, and lots and lots of classrooms. Kids will be able to come here after school. First they have to do their homework and then they can play in a good Christian setting. There won't be any fighting or cursing and the kids will learn to get along with each other, better themselves mentally and physically and be good Christians.

This year, before training camp, Felicity went with me to St. John Baptist. She got saved and I officially joined the church. Before that day, I just attended regularly, put my money in the collection plate and gave my tithe, but had never officially become a member.

Mr. Braman (left) and I got off to a rocky start, but over the years we've come to respect one another. (PHOTO BY MICHAEL MERCANTI / PHILADELPHIA DAILY NEWS)

We always enjoy the challenge of playing the best team, and that certainly included Joe Montana and the San Francisco 49ers. (PHOTO BY MICHAEL MERCANTI / PHILADEL-PHIA DAILY NEWS)

Whenever we play the Giants, we expect a hard-hitting game. (PHOTO BY MICHAEL MERCANTI / PHILADELPHIA DAILY NEWS)

At the end of the service, Reverend Townsend, like he does every week, said anyone who wanted to could join the church through Christian experience, baptism or just being there and joining. Felicity nudged me and there were tears in her eyes and she said she wanted to go up and be baptized. She wanted me to go up with her, but I was scared to do it. I know I play in front of 75,000 people every week and millions more on television, but I was scared to walk up in front of everyone in church. But Felicity just walked straight up there and I was very happy for her. Afterwards, they took about 10 people to the back of the church to arrange for their baptisms and, as Felicity walked by me, I grabbed her hand and went with her. As we walked out, everyone started clapping and to me this was a sign from God that Felicity was someone special. I knew then I would ask her to marry me.

Since I had already been baptized when I was a baby, I joined the church through Christian experience and everyone congratulated us and the whole day was a very joyous experience and brought us closer together and closer to God.

I believe that God gave me a special talent and put me here on this earth to be a football player and a good person and help educate people about God. It's especially important for kids to understand this, because I know that a lot of them look up to professional athletes as role models. When they look at Randall Cunningham, I want them to look at me as more than just a football player. Kids must realize they can grow up to be anything they want to be. A few years ago, I made a poster that has a drawing of me with four kids looking up to me. The important part of the poster is this message:

God gives each and every one of us a special talent. It should be the main focus for each of us to realize that talent in order to fulfill our God-given potential. To do this, we must all make the most of our opportunities, meet all challenges, and be prepared to overcome adversity. Don't be afraid to reach for the stars. It doesn't matter whether you're a boy or a girl, or whether you're black, white or yellow. Once you have the opportunity to achieve success, you should always try to come out a winner. However, the road to success is not always easy. There are many stumbling blocks out there to trip you up, such as drugs, alcohol, teen pregnancy, peer pressure, and many others. These obstacles are like the hurdles in a track event and it is up to you to hurdle them in order to continue on the proper path. On your road to success you are apt to discover that you need guidance and assistance. For this you should look to your parents, your family and your friends. You may not always think they are right, but your parents want what is best for you. I know. I lost both of my parents while I was in college. They had guided me while I was growing up. Without them I might have been lost and strayed off course. It was the strength of my brothers and family, and the caring of my friends that enabled me to keep going and to keep growing. So remember, to hurdle life's obstacles, look to your family and friends. In doing so, you can help them as well. Together you can jump these hurdles and become winners.

CHAPTER

8

Controversy continues to surround the Eagles, but this week it's a "coaching controversy," not a "quarterback controversy" and it begins immediately after the Eagles' 27-24 loss to the Packers in Milwaukee.

I felt so much pressure all week in practice, like I had to do everything perfect on every play. I worked hard and everyone tried to build my confidence and by game time I was ready to go. I wanted to go out and have fun and make some plays and help us win a game.

The Eagles receive the opening kickoff and begin moving down the field. On first down from the Green Bay 37, Randall drops back and goes deep to Barnett, who is streaking down the right sideline and has two steps on rookie cornerback Terrell Buckley. An instant before Barnett reaches up to catch the ball at the goal line, Buckley pushes him from behind, knocking Barnett off stride and the ball deflects off his fingertips. No penalty is called.

An offside penalty moves the ball back to the 42 and, on second-and-15, Randall throws a quick out to Byars, who is coming out of the backfield. Buckley steps in front of Byars and almost picks the ball off, but the high pass deflects off his fingertips. Another incompletion and the Eagles have to punt.

I don't want to make any excuses, but on the deep ball to Freddie, Buckley interfered and the refs should have thrown the flag. I noticed right away that Buckley was jumping on the short routes, so I told Freddie when I audibled, he should just run a go. I called the audible and Freddie ran the go and had Buckley beat. The pass was on target and Freddie would have caught it, but Buckley pushed him from behind. That would have given us a big lift to score right off the bat on a long pass.

On the throw to Keith coming out of the backfield, Buckley jumped right in front of him. Luckily I saw him and threw the ball high, hoping Keith could somehow come up with the grab. If I had thrown it low, like I'm supposed to, Buckley would have picked it off and would have been off to the end zone. It was like he knew what play was coming. So I said to myself, "If this guy knows what play we're running, if the offense is this predictable, then maybe the problem isn't with me like everyone is saying. Maybe the problem is with the offense."

On Green Bay's first possession, the Eagles recover a fumble and Randall and the offense start out on their own 47. On third-and-11 from the Green Bay 42, Randall takes off up the middle, fakes out a linebacker and runs for 18 yards and a first down at the 24. On first down, Herschel is stopped for no gain, and on second down, Randall hits Pat Beach for a seven-yard gain. This is the first pass caught by a tight end since October 18. On third-and-three from the 17, Herschel is stopped for no gain on an off-tackle run. The Eagles settle for a field goal and a 3-0 lead.

The Packers, behind a very hot Brett Favre, march right down the field and score to take a 7-3 lead a minute into the second quarter. The Eagles take over on their own 34 and on third down, Randall hits Calvin Williams over the middle for a first down at the Eagles' 45. On first down, Walker runs for a yard, followed by a two-yard gain by Byars, setting up a third-and-7. Randall drops back, but his receivers are covered and, under pressure, flips the ball to Byars in the flat, who is tackled for a two-yard loss. The Eagles punt and the Packers march down the field again and take a 14-3 lead with 2:21 left in the half.

The Eagles come out in their two-minute offense and begin moving the ball. Randall hits Vai Sikahema for seven, Herschel runs for 10 and Randall hits Sikahema for another six yards to the 45. About to be sacked, Randall throws the ball out of bounds, but then connects with Barnett for eight yards and a first down at the Packers' 47 with 1:14 to play. Randall immediately goes deep to Barnett, who has a chance for the ball in the end zone, but drops it as he's hit just as the ball arrives. On second down, Randall hits Walker for six yards, but on third-and-4 from the 41, Randall is sacked and the Eagles are forced to punt. In the half, Randall completes 9-of-17 passes for 59 yards and is under a lot of pressure, even though Green Bay is only rushing three men on obvious passing situations. Despite Randall's plea to Kotite the week before the game, the offense is still conservative and predictable. Until the last possession, when the Eagles were in their hurry-up offense, they ran the ball seven times on first down and threw it only twice. The Eagles trail 14-3 and the big question is: Will Randall start the second half?

Once you get pulled you start to worry that it will happen again. I didn't know what to think at halftime. It was kind of quiet in the locker room and I was wondering if I was going to get pulled. The coaches were in their room talking while we waited, and I'm thinking to myself, "Are they talking about putting Jim in for me?" I decided if that happens, forget it; I'm not going through that garbage any more. There is a sense of respect that a coach should have for his quarterback, especially one who has done it for him in the past.

Richie comes out of his meeting and doesn't say anything to me. The coaches make a few minor adjustments, nothing major, and we head back out onto the field. On the sideline, Richie comes over to me and says, "Come on big fella, let's get it going." That was a big relief and gave me a boost of confidence.

Green Bay gets the ball to start the second half, but the defense holds and forces a punt and the Eagles take over on their own 24. On first down, Heath Sherman is stopped for no gain. Randall hits tight end Maurice Johnson for three yards and then Roy Green for 10 and a first down at the 37. Two plays later, Randall hits Green again, for 21 yards over the middle, and a first down at the Green Bay 47.

On first down, Sherman is dropped for a one-yard loss as the seemingly endless string of runs on first down continues. On the next play, Randall is chased out of the pocket, runs right and tightropes down the sideline for 12 yards before going out of bounds, where he is hit late. The personal foul gives the Eagles a first down at the Green Bay 21. On first down Walker runs for three yards and then Sherman bursts through a hole and gallops 18 yards for the score to cut the lead to 14-10.

But the Packers answer right back with a long drive to take a 21-10 lead four minutes into the fourth period.

When we scored on our first possession of the second half, that really boosted up the offense and we started having fun. I think that's what had been missing from the offense. In the past, we used to be loose and confident and made things happen. We got the ball back after Green Bay scored to make it 21-10 and we went with a screen pass where I fake a throw to the left and throw it to the right to Heath. He caught it and had three blockers in front of him and went 75 yards for the score and we were down 21-17 with plenty of time left.

Andy Harmon came up with a huge sack for us and the Packers had to punt and we got the ball back on our 11. Heath ran for four on first down and then I had Freddie run a deep route down the right side. He had Buckley beat, but right before Freddie was set to catch the ball, Buckley ran right up his back and knocked him down and then their safety really laid a hit on him. This time the ref called the pass interference and we had a first down at the Green Bay 46. Freddie came back to the huddle with his face mask all messed up. The bars were bent out of shape so that the opening to his face was twice as big as it was supposed to be. And he didn't even know it.

On the next play we ran a flea-flicker. I gave Byars the ball and he faked like he was going to run and then he turned around and tossed it back to me. I went deep to Freddie again and he had his man—Roland Mitchell—beat. Just as Freddie went for the ball, Mitchell grabbed him by the shoulder pads and pulled him down. It was so obvious the ref had to call it and we had a first down at the two. Herschel broke two tackles and plowed his way in for the score and we were up 24-21 with 5:45 to play.

After two incomplete passes, Favre was picked off by Byron Evans who returned the ball to the Green Bay 20 and it looked like the Eagles had the game wrapped up. On first down, Sherman broke off left tackle for eight yards, but fumbled as he hit the ground and Green Bay recovers at its own 12 with 5:08 to play. Replays clearly show that Sherman's knees were already on the ground before the ball popped loose. A 34-yard completion to Sterling Sharpe took the ball into Eagles' territory, but the defense finally stopped the Packers at the 13 and Chris Jacke hit a 31-yard field goal to tie the score with 1:31 to play.

The Eagles take over on their own 11 after the ensuing kickoff and Randall was ready to take the Birds down the field for the winning field goal or touchdown. On first down, Herschel ran for nine yards to the 20. With the clock ticking under a minute, Herschel gets the ball again, fumbles and Green Bay's Johnny Holland recovers at the 23 with 45 seconds to play. A play later, with no time left on the clock, Jacke kicks the game-winning field goal.

In the second half, Randall completes 5-of-6 passes for 110 yards. In the game he is 14-of-23 for 169.

After the game, Seth Joyner is furious: "Any time you play conservative in this league, you're setting yourself up to lose. You don't win when you're just playing not to lose . . . I just think you've got to be all-out. You've got to have some guts, sometimes, to step up and call a play, you know? Call the unexpected play. When you run what they expect you to run, they're sitting there waiting on you with an eight-man front. How far do you think we're going to get with eight guys up there on the line?"

According to Byron Evans: "We played not to lose. We always played to win under Buddy Ryan. Once you do that, you take the whole intensity away from what you're trying to do."

Fred Barnett adds: "Were we here to win a game or not? If I could call the plays, maybe it would be a little different. But I can't."

According to Kotite, he was playing to win: "I was going for it. We had everyone set on the sidelines and everything [ready for the hurry-up offense]."

When asked by reporters about the conservative play calling and two consecutive handoffs to Herschel at the end, Randall refuses to answer. "No comment. Next question."

While we were waiting on the sideline to get the ball back for our last possession, Richie calls a couple of plays out of our quarter package, which is where we go with four wide receivers and no tight ends. First we were going to throw short to Vai on one side and then come back and hit Vai short on the other side and get some yardage. Then, right before we go out on the field, Richie tells me to call a running play to Herschel out of a formation with two tight ends. Herschel gains nine yards, and I'm thinking, now we're going to send in the extra wide receivers, take out the two tight ends and start running the two-minute drill.

We rush and get set at the line of scrimmage and I start shouting, "Quarter right, quarter right," which means we're in the two-minute drill and in the quarter formation with four receivers. I looked over to the sideline for the play and they're signaling in Slant 30, which is another running play to Herschel out of the two-tight-end formation. I say to myself, "We don't have this play out of the quarter formation," and then I look over and, sure enough, the two tight ends are back in and Vai and Roy are heading off the field. So now I start yelling, "thirty, thirty." Meanwhile time was running and everyone's confused about what formation we're in and what play we're going to run. I called the play and made sure everyone heard it. Herschel gets the handoff and gets hits, fumbles and they recover the ball.

We all walked off to the sideline disgusted. Guys were angry and throwing up their hands and cursing. That's when the finger-pointing started, with guys saying we should have done this or run that or thrown and so on. I just sat on the bench and didn't say a word. I was so upset tears came to my eyes. Then they kick the winning field goal and we walk off to the locker room. Richie comes in and starts yelling, saying we stunk and didn't play well on offense, defense or special teams. Then the reporters come in saying some of the players had questioned the play calling. They want my opinion and I'm not about to say a word. I just got through 10 days of controversy and I'm not about to get in the middle of another.

What Seth and some of the other guys were saying was that we were playing too conservatively and you can't do that in the NFL and win. His point was we had to be aggressive and attack all the time. We have weapons like Freddie and Calvin and Keith and myself and we have to use them to win football games. That's what we've done in the past and it's worked. That's the attitude that Buddy taught us and it's still here.

In 1990, when Buddy was the coach and Richie was the offensive coordinator, we were a totally different offense. There were times when Buddy would say, "Just give the ball to number twelve," and he'd turn the offense over to me and say, "Do what you have to do to win the game." We'd run the two-minute offense for long stretches of the game and I called my own plays, within the system that Richie designed. It seemed like Richie and I were on the same page and the offense clicked.

The way I see it, what happened at the end of the game shows me that either Richie didn't have the confidence in me he used to or he's still afraid I'll get hurt and it will be 1991 all over again with a series of revolving quarterbacks. So, he's structured an offense that he controls and is geared toward protecting me. Guys were saying, "Let Randall be Randall" and I agree. Richie put in a couple of the plays I suggested, but not in the formations I wanted. Some of the guys on the team tell me to take control of the offense and just change the plays, but realistically, you can't do it. It's not that simple. If I call an audible, I better have a good reason—like the defense is set up to stop that specific play. I can't call an audible just because I want to run a certain play—like a bootleg. At the end, on the play Herschel fumbled, we had two tight ends in the game and I couldn't just turn around and call a passing play. This is Richie's team and Richie's offense and I'll run it the way he wants me to run it.

As if all this weren't enough, the Monday, November 16 edition of USA Today, *reports that NBC's Will McDonough said on the air before the Eagles-Green Bay game: "The Eagles' coaches wanted to run a drug test on Randall Cunningham because of his disappointing play."*

What McDonough actually said was: "The Philadelphia coaching staff is going to be looking at this in the game today—is he doing what we want him to do? This has been a big beef behind the scene in that whole situation. I was told, on the plane down from Dallas a couple of weeks ago, when he had the bad game, the next day they

*wanted to test him because they weren't sure he knew what he was
supposed to do in the game."*

*"It's ludicrous," an angry Kotite responds. "Ludicrous, ridicu-
lous, a lie, whatever [word] you want to use. Absolutely incorrect.
That's the farthest thing from the truth you could ever say."*

Nothing that's written in the newspapers or said about me on
radio or television surprises me anymore. When I first got to Philadelphia, everyone told me, "Be careful what you say to the media.
Don't trust the media. The media will screw you every time." I
listened and I'm careful. Just like football players, reporters are competitive and unfortunately, it seems the only way for them to get
ahead or prove themselves is to create controversy.

My first few years everyone in the media treated me great. They
wrote and said all kinds of nice things and said I was the quarterback
of the future and brought a new dimension to the game and stuff
like that. Then, after I was established in the NFL and starting to get
recognition as a good quarterback, they changed their tune. One bad
game and they were all over me, looking for reasons for my slump,
saying I couldn't read defenses or held onto the ball too long or ran
too quick or was too sensitive to criticism and on and on. In this city,
and probably a lot of other cities, the media loves you when you're
on the way up. But once you get there, they love to tear you down
and create controversy. This is especially true when you play a high-
profile position like quarterback. The saying goes, quarterbacks get
all the fame and glory when their team wins and take all the blame
and shame when their team loses.

Every well-known athlete in this city has gone through it. Ron
Jaworski got booed all the time and he was a great quarterback who
always gave it everything he had. Mike Schmidt, the greatest third
baseman in the history of baseball, got booed all the time. Look what
happened to Charles Barkley. They couldn't wait for the 76ers to get
rid of him. Now that he's gone, guess what? We wish he was back.

My thing is to give the media the time they need and be polite and professional. During training camp, I have a press conference four days a week during our lunch break between practices. During the season, I'm available before practice and give a conference call once a week for the press from the city we'll be playing that week. After games, I have a press conference, where I can answer all the questions at once instead of having to answer the same question nine different times.

For the most part I get along with the media. I look at it as part of the business of being a professional football player, and I approach interviews like a businessman. In fact, people always tell me that I seem so serious when I'm being interviewed and that I should loosen up and be myself and joke around and have fun. But I decided to take a business approach to the media and answer questions in a certain way and always be positive and noncontroversial and never criticize anyone. The media doesn't know the real Randall, even though they may think they do and write and talk about me like they know every intimate detail of my life and have spent hours and hours with me. They're always trying to analyze me and say I lack confidence or that I'm too sensitive and that I have to be more vocal and more of a leader. When the truth is, they don't know who I am. They only see the part of me I want them to see when I'm being interviewed. After I was injured and was doing my rehab, I spent about fifteen minutes talking with a reporter from one of the local papers. He was new covering the Eagles and after we were done, he thanked me and said he was glad he had a chance to get to know me. I didn't say anything, but I was thinking, "You can't get to know me —the real me—in fifteen minutes." But that's how reporters think. If they interview you for long enough, they think they know you and feel free to write or say anything they want about you.

I'll meet people when I'm out at an event or shopping and they'll come up and say hello and I'll say hello back and we'll talk for a few minutes. A lot of times they say, "You're nothing like I thought you would be. I thought you were so serious and aloof." See, that's the image of me the media gives people and it's not the real me. Those of you reading this book will get a chance to get to know the real me and see that I'm a nice, easy-going guy, a Christian brother who can be serious when I have to be serious, but who also likes to have fun when it's time to be fun. If you see me somewhere, you don't have to be afraid of coming up to me and saying hello. I'll be glad to talk to you.

CHAPTER

9

NOVEMBER 22, 1992

The Eagles are at the Meadowlands on a rainy afternoon and quickly fall behind 10-0 to the Giants. The offense isn't able to get much going the first two times it touches the ball and Randall starts off 1-of-3 for 13 yards and an interception. After the Giants score on a 14-yard pass from Jeff Hostetler to Dave Meggett, Sikahema makes a nice return of the ensuing kickoff and the Eagles take possession at the New York 46. On first down Randall's pass is batted down at the line of scrimmage and on second down he's sacked for a nine-yard loss, setting up a third-and-19 play.

Randall rolls right and Byars makes a nice block on a charging linebacker to give him more time. Randall continues to roll out and just before he crosses the line of scrimmage, he throws a perfect pass all the way across the field to Barnett for a 29-yard gain and a crucial first down just when it looked like the offense was about to sputter out again.

On the next play, Randall is on the move again. This time it's a naked bootleg to the left, but Giants' lineman Erik Howard isn't fooled and he's waiting for Randall, who somehow manages to avoid him and, in the same motion, sidearm a pass to Herschel for four yards. On the next play, Randall drops back and quickly hits Herschel in the left flat. Herschel is uncovered and scampers 21 yards for the touchdown to cut the Giants' lead to 10-6 after the extra point is blocked. The Eagles finally let Randall out of his cage and the result was a touchdown.

We finally got back to doing some of the things I like to do on offense. We were behind and had to open things up and Richie called a sprint out to the right side. I rolled out, but the receivers were covered and Keith Byars made a beautiful block to buy me some more time. Then I looked over at Freddie, who was my fourth read on the play and saw him cutting back the other way, away from me. When Freddie sees I'm in trouble he tries to make something happen to get open and then he tries to make eye contact with me so he knows I see him. I saw Freddie was open and fired the ball across my body and all the way across the field—which is exactly what they teach you not to do. If you throw the ball across the field, it gives the defense more time to react to the throw and come up with the interception. But that's my style and I'll do whatever it takes to win. I could have run for 10 yards on the play, but it was third-and-19 and we needed the first down.

Then Richie called a naked bootleg left, another play I like. A lineman came right on me unblocked, which is the worst-case scenario for that play. He was right on top of me, but still, I was able to get the ball off to Herschel for a few yards. My point is, let me do my thing and I'll make something happen. On that play, I could have avoided the defender and run for four or five yards, hit Herschel and let him try to make the big play, or, at worst, I could throw the ball out of bounds. But give me the option to run or throw and give me the opportunity to make things happen. Make the defense defend the entire field and have to be worried about what I'm going to do.

Then I hit Herschel in the flat with a quick pass and he made a nice run for the score. That's another play I'm very comfortable with and I told Richie before the game, "Please call that play 20 times." I saw Green Bay run it against the Giants when I was watching film this week. It's a very simple, but effective play. You release a tight end inside, and when the linebacker moves over to pick him up, that leaves the running back open in the flat. If the linebacker goes over to cover the running back, I'll hit the tight end. Once teams see us run this play successfully, they'll be watching for it. So what we have to do is run it, but run it out of a different formation or run it to the opposite side of the field.

I'm to the point now, where I'll say to Herschel, "I know what the coaches say you're supposed to do on this play, but go out and run a hook pattern in an open hole so I can see you if I run and I'll get the ball to you." That's what we did in 1990, but we've gotten away from it. When Herschel first got here, he had to learn the offense and ran the plays exactly the way they were drawn up. Now he knows the offense and he knows me and we're starting to get in sync and create big plays. A lot of people misunderstand Herschel because he's quiet. But Herschel is very intelligent and has a great sense of humor. Herschel's also very business-like when it comes to football. He's very fast and powerful and we're just starting to learn how to take advantage of his talents. As good as he is running the ball, I think he's even better catching the ball. Herschel knows how to get open and, with his speed and strength, once he's in the open field, he's very hard to bring down.

On the ensuing kickoff, Meggett goes 92 yards for a 17-6 New York lead, and, on the first play of the Eagles' next possession, Herschel fumbles and the Giants recover at the Birds' 23. The defense stiffens, but the Giants kick a field goal and lead 20-6 three minutes into the second quarter.

After the Eagles are stopped on three plays, the Giants take over and look to put the game out of reach. But Wes Hopkins blitzes and forces Hostetler to rush his throw to Meggett. Joyner makes a perfect

read, steps in front of the intended receiver for the interception and races 43 yards for the score to cut the lead to 20-13.

The Giants are stuffed on their next possession and the Eagles take over on their own 48. On third-and-10 at the Giants' 40, Randall drops back to pass and is chased to his right. He sees Byars with a step on his defender and tries to loop the ball over the defender's head to Byars. The pass is high, but Byars reaches up with one hand, tips the ball down, catches it, takes a few steps and then dives for the first down at the 27. Sherman dances for 16 yards to the 11 and then Herschel runs into a wall at the line of scrimmage, bounces left and races into the end zone. The extra point is good and the score is 20-20.

The Eagles get one more scoring opportunity late in the half, as they drive down to the New York 18, but under pressure, Randall forces a pass into the end zone that is picked off.

All of a sudden it was 20-6 and everyone is saying, "Those Eagles are going to lose again," and "Randall's garbage, get him out of there." But we knew we were going to come back and we did. Seth came up with the big play to get us back in the game and I told the offense, "Relax, let's have some fun out there." We did and started coming up with some big plays.

The Eagles get the ball to start the second half and Sikahema comes up with another beautiful return, all the way to the Eagles' 45. On first down, Sherman gains 11 yards, but on the next play, the Giants have eight men on the line of scrimmage and stuff Sherman for a two-yard loss. Randall hits Calvin Williams for eight, setting up a third-and-four from the New York 38. Randall drops back, but there is pressure coming up the middle. Randall avoids one would-be tackler, but linebacker Corey Miller has him dead in his sights for a loss. Just as Miller hits Randall, he flips the ball to Byars, who grabs it and races in for a touchdown and a 27-20 Eagles' lead.

"I was supposed to be in blocking on the play," Byars explains after the game. "I picked up my man. But I saw Randall scrambling. [Randall and I] are on the same wavelength when he scrambles. I don't know how he got the pass off to me. He's such a great athlete, great player. I was able to get my hands under it before it hit the ground. Then Calvin Williams had a big block to spring me."

It has been a tough year for Byars, who started off the season filling in for Keith Jackson at tight end. After two games, Byars was moved back to fullback, but then he broke his hand and missed a few games. In his absence, Heath Sherman came into his own as a fullback. After the Green Bay game, in which he alternated at tight end and fullback, Byars, the ultimate team player, went to Kotite. "I said, 'Leave Heath in there. Heath's got the hot hand. He's playing well. Let him stay in and play. I'll go to tight end and I'll make some plays there.'"

That touchdown to Keith shows you how important it is to have someone who is on the same page as I am. Keith and I are in sync. Keith Jackson and I were in sync like that for four years. When you take a Keith Jackson away from me, it hampers my performance. When you take Keith Byars away from me, that further hampers my performance. A crucial part of our offense is third-down situations. When Keith is in, he knows what I want; I tell him what to do and he does it, even if the play isn't in our playbook. Keith knows that when I scramble, he's supposed to help the center block. But once he sees me start to run, Keith gets open. On the touchdown play, I was moving around in the pocket and was all set to run when I saw Keith out of the corner of my eye. He started hollering to let me know he was open and I flipped him the ball and then I got tackled. I thought the ball was too low, but Keith caught it anyway and when I got up, I saw him running in for the touchdown.

Already, I think Keith is one of the best tight ends in football. By next year he could be the best in the league. The thing about Keith is that he is so versatile. He can run, catch and block and he's an

intelligent player who easily picks up any new position he's forced to play. On our offense, because he does so many things and does them so well, Keith is our most valuable player. I think he should make the Pro Bowl this year, but because of his number—41—most of the defensive players in the league still think of Keith as a running back. I keep telling him he's got to get a number in the 80s.

The Eagles defense continues its strong play and forces the Giants to punt. Kenny Rose breaks through the line cleanly and blocks Sean Landeta's punt, picks it up at the three and stumbles into the end zone for the touchdown and a 34-20 Eagles' lead. The defense stops the Giants again and forces another punt. This time Landeta gets it off, but Sikahema, who is in the midst of a great game, fields it at the 13, jukes out one defender and heads up the right sideline behind a wall of blockers. At midfield he puts a move on Landeta, who falls to the turf with a knee injury, and races in for the score and a 40-20 lead. Sikahema, a former Golden Gloves boxer, runs over to the goal post, which is covered with padding decorated with the Giants' logo and begins working on the padding like it's a heavy bag before his teammates track him down and mob him. The following Wednesday, Sikahema is the guest on Randall's television show and enters the studio wearing a robe and boxing gloves to the theme song from "Rocky." Sikahema, a ham at heart, dances and shadow boxes while the audience howls. "I want you," he signals to Randall, who just laughs.

The Eagles score one more time, on a 30-yard Sherman run, and win going away 47-34. The key play in the drive is a 41-yard completion from Randall to Herschel on the same quick pass in the flat that was good for a score earlier in the game. Although Kotite doesn't call the play 20 times as Randall requested, Herschel does catch four passes for 79 yards and runs for another 61. Sherman runs for 109 and Randall completes 10-of-21 passes for 209 yards and two touchdowns.

After the game, Randall faces the media. "I felt great today,"

Randall begins. "I felt better than when we were 4-0. I'm doing everything within the system, but I'm being myself. I'm having fun. The quarterback controversy and all that garbage is over with."

The Eagles are now 7-4, two games behind Dallas and a game ahead of the Redskins, who will drop to 6-5 tomorrow night after they lose to New Orleans 20-3 on Monday Night Football.

It was nice to be able to just play a football game and not have to get involved in any controversies. After Seth's comments after the Green Bay game, Richie told us loudly and clearly that we had better look in the mirror before we go pointing fingers at anyone else. He didn't tell us to stop talking to the press, but Seth and I decided to take a week off from the media and they started reporting that Richie had the "gag rule" in effect. That wasn't true. I just felt like concentrating on football and figured it was someone else's turn to get all the criticism and be involved in all the controversy. I had fun with the whole "quarterback controversy" thing for a week or two, but now it's over and it's time to play football.

10

NOVEMBER 29, 1992

It would have been the perfect ending to a perfect week if we could have come from behind and beaten the San Francisco 49ers today in Candlestick Park. But we lost by an inch.

Although I'd rather not have to relive the game—especially our last offensive play—I'll get to it in a couple of minutes. First, guess what I did on Thanksgiving Day?—besides eat turkey that is. I got engaged! Felicity agreed to be my wife and she made me the happiest man in the world.

During the week before the Raiders game, when I was benched and going through all that controversy garbage, I woke up one morning and decided I'd fly my entire family in so we could all spend Thanksgiving together. One of the things I learned during all the adversity is how important my family and friends are to me. I wanted us to all be together on Thanksgiving and I wanted my family to be there when I proposed to Felicity.

Because of football, this was going to be the first Thanksgiving we were all going to be together since I was 10 years old. The only thing that could have made it better was if Mom and Pop were there. All three of my brothers—and their families—came in and so did my Aunt Nettie, who is my mom's sister. Aunt Nettie is like a second mom to me. Also, Felicity's two sisters, Karen and Johreen, flew in from Johannesburg, South Africa, a few days before Thanksgiving to celebrate with us. Lynn Swann (Sam's college roommate and still one of his best friends) and his wife, Charlie, were in town and we invited them to join us. A few other close friends stopped by.

We had a beautiful and delicious dinner at my home and it was wonderful to have everyone sitting at the same table enjoying themselves. I felt very thankful for all my blessings and had such a warm feeling in my heart the whole day. After dinner, all the ladies were in the kitchen cleaning the dishes. I had already told my brothers that I was going to propose to Felicity after dinner, but nobody else knew. I showed them the ring and told them to play dumb, which they're very good at. I pulled Felicity out of the kitchen and told her I needed to speak to her in private. We went upstairs to the bedroom and I hugged her and told her I loved her, but right as I was about to pop the question, one of my nieces came in the room and started playing around. I told Felicity we had to go down to the media room to get a little privacy. I was so nervous, but I kept saying to myself, "Be strong, be strong Randall."

Felicity: I could tell Randall was very nervous about something, but I thought it was just because there were all these children running around his house. Randall is very meticulous about his house and I thought he was worried they were going to break something. I had no idea what he was up to.

We were in the television room and again I was just about to ask Felicity the big question, when I heard people laughing and playing pool in the next room. So I said to Felicity, "Let's go for a walk around the block." We stepped outside on the porch and it was drizzling. It was beautiful, with the mist coming down from above caught in the lights outside my house. We stood under an overhang so we wouldn't get wet and I hugged Felicity again and told her I loved her. I was getting more and more nervous by the second, even more nervous than I get before a big game. Finally I said, "You're the best thing that's ever happened to me (pause, pause, pause while I tried to get the words out). You know I really love you a lot. And I would like to spend the rest of my life with you (pause, pause). Will you marry me?"

For a second Felicity didn't say anything.

Felicity: I was shocked; I didn't know what to say. There are a million things that run through your mind in a second.

She just stood there and didn't say anything and I said, "Baby, don't do this to me. You're making me very nervous. Just say yes or no." Finally she shook her head yes and I said, "That's not good enough, you have to verbally say it." Then she shook her head yes again and kind of mumbled "uh-huh" and I said, "That's not good enough" and then she said, "Yes, yes, yes" and we hugged.

Felicity: I kept asking myself, "Is this the right thing for me?" and I knew the answer was yes. But still, I was so nervous I couldn't say anything and finally the words just came out and I started crying.

Then I pulled the box with the ring in it out of my pocket and handed it to her and Felicity opened it. When she did, the ring almost fell out, so I grabbed it back and went to put it on her finger, but before I did, just to be sure, I asked her to marry me again and she said yes. I put the ring on her finger and we hugged and kissed. There were tears streaming down her cheeks and we went upstairs so she could wash up before we went and told everyone. I was trying to be strong and not cry, but I do have to admit, my eyes were a little misty.

Felicity: He was crying too and had to wipe his face off when we went up to the bathroom.

I wasn't crying, that was sweat.

Felicity: Randall doesn't sweat from his eyes; he was crying.

Don't be saying that. You know I was sweating and was telling you to stop crying before I started crying.

Felicity: He did say that, but I still say you were crying.

Don't believe her. After Felicity washed up, we went downstairs to tell everyone the news and we were both really nervous. I told everyone to come out in the dining room, we had something to tell them. Aunt Nettie runs out of the kitchen and starts following me around the house, tugging on the back of my jacket saying, "You're getting engaged, you're getting engaged!" I said, "No Aunt Nettie." I didn't lie, because she asked if we were getting engaged and since we already were, I was telling the truth. Then she said, "You're having a baby, you're having a baby," and I said, "No, Aunt Nettie, we're not having a baby. Just relax and we'll tell everyone our news." Finally everyone came into the dining room and I said, "I've asked Felicity to marry me and she said yes." Everyone started clapping and hugging us. I asked Sam to be my best man and he said yes and then Anthony and Bruce said that all three of them should be the best men. I said, "How are three of you going to give me the ring?" Bruce pulled off his wedding band, each of them took a turn holding it and passed it on to me and Bruce said, "like this," as he handed me the ring. Felicity asked her sisters to be her bridesmaids and they said yes.

Wow, that was a big step in my life, but I knew it was the right one. I had met the woman of my dreams and now she was going to be my wife.

Two days after his engagement, Randall and the rest of the Eagles were on their way to San Francisco to play the 49ers. As is becoming their habit, the Eagles get off to a slow start and fell behind 10-0 at the half. In the first half, Randall is 9-of-16 for 83 yards, the running game was nonexistent and the Eagles seemed to face third-and-long on every first-half possession.

When Mike Quick was with us, I used to try to get him the ball early to get Mike into the flow of the game. I try to do that now with Freddie and Calvin. I think it's important for me to get into the flow early too, but we always seem to start the game trying to establish the run. Every possession seems to be run-run-pass and the defense knows what to expect. So, in the second half, we came out firing and we started moving the ball. I could have done the same thing the second half at Dallas, but I never got the chance.

The Eagles got the ball to start the second half and Jeff Sydnor returns the kickoff to the 49ers' 48. On first down, Randall hits Williams for 14 yards; then he hits Sherman for 11 more yards and a first down at the 23. After Sherman runs for three yards, Barnett goes deep down the left side and gets a step on the cornerback. Randall lofts a perfect spiral over the fingertips of the leaping cornerback and Barnett cradles it into his arms in the back of the end zone and the 49ers' lead is cut to 10-7.

Later, San Francisco marches down the field, but has to settle for a 28-yard field goal and a 13-7 lead with 3:57 to play in the third quarter. The Eagles get the ball and begin moving. Randall hits Barnett for 10 and Sherman rips off a 10-yard gain. Then Randall is sacked for a seven-yard loss and a pass to Herschel in the flat gains only two yards. On third-and-15 from the Eagles' 33, Randall drops back and looks for a receiver. The rush comes right up the middle and Randall has to side-step one lineman to buy himself some time. Finally he spots Byars in the flat and hits him in the midsection. Byars breaks a tackle and sprints down the right sideline toward the first-down marker. A 49er has the angle on him, but Byars dives and appears to have the first down; but the official on the sideline rules he stepped out of bounds two yards short of the first down. The Eagles have to punt and the 49ers march down the field and score on a 43-yard bomb from Steve Young to Dexter Carter and lead 20-7 with 13:04 to play.

Randall continues his hot second-half play when the Eagles get the ball back. First he hits Byars for nine yards, then Byars for another seven and a 13-yard pass to tight end Maurice Johnson gives the Eagles a first down at the 49ers' 29. After an incompletion, Randall hits Byars for seven and Barnett for 11 for a first down at the 11. On the next play, Byars lines up wide to the left and sprints down the field. Randall throws a bullet and Byars stops a yard short of the end zone, comes back and catches the ball and dances into the end zone and the Eagles are back in the game 20-14 with plenty of time to play.

After the 49ers are stopped twice and the Eagles once, the Birds get the ball back on their own 47 with 4:13 to play. On first down, Randall drops back to pass, sees a huge lane open up in the middle and takes off for 12 yards and a first down at the San Francisco 42. From here, Randall hits Herschel for two yards, Williams for seven and Sherman gets a yard on third-and-one to give the Eagles a first down on the 32. Randall drops back to pass, is chased to the right and finally runs upfield. After gaining four yards he is sandwiched between two players and crashes to the ground. But Randall leaps up, calls the next play and hits Herschel over the middle for seven yards and a first down at the 20. On first down, Randall is chased out of the pocket again and is forced to throw the ball away. On second down, Herschel catches a short pass for three yards and on third-and-seven, the 49ers catch Randall for an eight-yard loss and the Eagles call timeout.

The game is down to one play—fourth-and-15 from the 26 with :53 to play.

Richie called a quarter right 17X corner with left protection, which means the line slides to the left to pick up anyone who might be coming on my blindside. I checked for the blitz coming on the right side, but nobody was coming. Freddie had a corner route and he was covered on the outside by the cornerback and on the inside by the safety. He was double-teamed and I couldn't go to him. Vai released into the flat on a fan route and was open, but I could see he wouldn't have been able to run for the first down—there were too many guys between him and the first-down marker. Then I looked to Calvin and saw him running a seven-yard crossing pattern. He wasn't deep enough for the first down either, so I looked toward Roy Green, who had a 16-yard in route, but he was covered. I looked back toward Calvin, who, after running the seven-yard crossing route, turned it upfield and was close to the first down. There was a guy on Calvin, but I thought I could sneak it in to him, so I fired it. Calvin made a great catch and it looked like he was tackled right at the 10, which should have been enough for a first down.

I was sure we had the first down, so I start sprinting up to the 10, thinking we'd line up fast and I'd spike the ball into the ground to stop the clock. There was no doubt in my mind that we were going to take the ball into the end zone. Then, as I'm running toward the line of scrimmage, I can see there's all sorts of confusion. First of all, there wasn't a referee anywhere near Calvin when he caught the ball. One referee runs over and takes the ball and marks the spot with his foot. Where he marked it would have been a first down. Then another referee comes running up and takes the ball and puts his foot down to mark the spot. I could see this spot was six inches behind the first spot and I got worried. The first referee looked at the first-down marker and saw how close it was and kind of walked away, like he was saying, "I'm not getting involved in this." Freddie and Calvin and I are all arguing with the referees and then they brought the chains out and stretched it out for the measurement. It was so close the referee had to kneel down and put his eye right up to the pole. I think they leaned the top of the pole forward so it would make it harder for us to get the first down. We were all signalling first down, but then the referee signals it's San Francisco ball. I was so mad I just threw my helmet down and ran off the field. Then Steve Young did a very smart thing. He ran out on the field and picked up the ball and put it back down. This meant the referees couldn't remeasure the ball even if they wanted to. The 49ers ran out the clock and we lost.

We were all very frustrated and angry. The thing was, we knew we would have won, but the referees took the game away from us.

John Madden, who was broadcasting the game on CBS: "To me the officials didn't hustle . . . When he got down there, how does he know where to put his foot?"

Randall wasn't the only angry Bird. "They moved it back once, and then another official moved it back again," Schad said.

"I started back to the huddle," Heller said. "Even their defense started back to the huddle. Everybody out there thought we had it."

"If the refs put the ball where they should have put it, we would have won," Barnett said.

"[The referee] leaned the stick," Davis added. "I know it's a game of inches, but if they hold the stick up straight, it's a first down."

Kotite took a more philosophical approach and said that, despite the loss, the game showed that the Eagles were back after struggling the past several games. "I think we're back," Kotite said after the game. "We were hitting on all cylinders against a very good team."

Randall was also back and was the old rambling, scrambling Randall that had led the Eagles to so many come-from-behind victories in the past. "I haven't felt this good since, probably, 1990," Randall said immediately after the game. "I really felt great, in sync."

In all, Randall completed 28-of-42 passes for 257 yards, two touchdowns and no interceptions and rushed for 13 yards on three carries.

Even though we lost, we knew we played a good game and should have won. After the game, on the airplane ride back, Heller came up to me and said, "Hey Bubba, I don't know what you did, but if you play like this after getting engaged, maybe you should get engaged every week. You played great and had fun and you're back." Schad and Alexander told me the same thing and I think they were right. Now we have to carry this over to the next game.

CHAPTER
11

DECEMBER 6, 1992

The 7-5 Eagles host the 9-3 Minnesota Vikings this afternoon at the Vet and desperately need a win to stay alive in the hunt for a wild-card playoff berth. Before the game even starts, Randall is involved in another controversy. Why should this week be any different from the previous ones? Fortunately for Randall, this controversy never makes the newspapers.

The night before home games, the entire team stays together in a hotel in South Jersey, which is just a 10-minute drive from my house. This season, they finally gave Byars and me our own rooms, but still, even though I don't have to listen to Keith snore all night long, I don't feel comfortable staying in a hotel when my own house is right down the road. I paid a lot of money for my house and I'd like to sleep in my house and in my own bed. What I do is check in with everyone else at the hotel, attend the team meeting and Bible study, and then, after the 11 P.M. bed check, I leave and go home. It's no big deal—a lot of guys do it, but I won't name any names. There's a team breakfast the next morning—game day—but only about half the guys ever show up for that anyway, so it's no big deal if you're not there.

Last night I checked into the hotel and attended all the meetings and Bible study, was in my room for bed check and was all set to leave and go home a little after eleven. There's a security guard who sits in the hall, but we don't pay much attention to him. On my way out I stopped in McMahon's room to hang out for a few minutes. Jim doesn't go to sleep until about 2 or 3 A.M. and then sleeps a couple of hours. Jim was in his room playing video golf with Archer and Alexander. You have to understand, when Jim plays any game— and especially video golf—he is very competitive. And loud. Jim screams and curses up a storm when he makes a bad shot and whoops it up when he makes a good shot. You can hear him all the way up and down the hall. We don't think much of it; we're all used to Jim.

I hung around for a few minutes and Jim wasn't doing too well. That meant a lot of screaming and cursing and the rest of us were having a good time laughing with Jim. Eventually, I said good night and left. The guys knew I was going home, but like I said, a lot of guys do it and it's no big deal. I've done it before and never been caught, but if I ever am, I figure I'll just pay the fine and that will be that. So I drove home and made sure to obey all the speed limits. The last thing I needed was to get pulled over or get in an accident and have it make the newspapers the next day that Randall was out the night before a game. Then Richie would definitely know I had skipped out of the hotel. I made it home safely and thanked God. The next morning Felicity made me breakfast and I got to the stadium around ten, watched film and then went into the training room. Richie walked by and didn't say anything, so I figured I didn't get busted. I went over to my locker and Richie walks by and says he wants to see me. I figured he wanted to talk about the game. We went into the equipment manager's office and Richie closes the door and says, "I can't believe what you did," and goes on to say he got a note the first thing this morning from the security guard saying I left the hotel at 11:16 P.M. the night before, got in my car and never came back. Then Richie says, "I can't believe you, the disciplined person you are, the guy we always count on, could do this." I think Richie was waiting for me to explain why I left, but I just sat there and didn't say a word. Then he says he's going to have to fine me and I said OK, I understand. Then he stood up, like he wanted me to leave, and said, "Hey, have a good game." Richie walked out of the office first and I thought he was going to hold the door open for me, but he didn't and it kind of slammed shut in my face. Now, all of a sudden, I have this on my mind a couple of hours before we're about to play one of our biggest games of the year.

I walked back to my locker and Casey Weldon, our rookie quarterback from Florida State, was standing at his locker, which is next to mine. I guess he could see that something was bothering me and Casey said, "What's the matter?" and I told him what just happened. Casey had a stunned look on his face.

"He told you this right before a big game?" Casey asked.

"Yeah, but I won't let it bother me," I said.

You have to understand Richie, which I do. He's a perfectionist and covers everything from making sure everyone has their shoelaces tied to preparing for the last few seconds of a game. Nothing slips by Richie. That's just the way he is and I've learned to understand him in that way. It's a good quality for a head coach to have. I figured I brought the situation on myself by skipping out of the hotel, but I did wonder why he had to tell me about it two hours before the game. It could have waited until the next day during practice.

Archer came in a few minutes later and tells me that he and Jim had been up until three playing golf and that at six-thirty, Richie called, asked for Jim and started hollering at him, "What did you say to upset Randall and make him leave the hotel and not come back?" Jim said he didn't say anything, that I had stopped over to visit and then went back to my room. See, Jim was covering for me and didn't tell Richie I went home. Richie was still mad and hung up.

Here's what must have happened: the security guard saw me go into Jim's room and then he heard Jim hollering and cursing at the video golf game and he figured Jim and I were fighting. He bought into the media hype that Jim and I don't get along and are enemies, when really we get along great. Then the guard saw me leave Jim's room and leave the hotel and somehow came to the conclusion that I was upset. Richie bought into all the media bull that I'm too sensitive, when he should know me by now and know that I'm a strong person and get along just fine with Jim.

Jim came into the locker room a minute after Archer and I told him I got fined for leaving the hotel. We both started laughing and that helped loosen me up. Then Jim complained about how Richie had called and woken him up so early and interrupted his sleep. The next thing I know, Jim's laying down in his locker and is asleep. About an hour later, Richie came out of his office. Normally, at this point, he'll come over and tell all the quarterbacks the first couple of plays he wants to run the first time we get the ball. But Richie walked right by us and over to the offensive linemen and gave them the plays. Then he walked right by us and didn't stop. As he went by, Jim starts shouting at Richie, "Hey, hey," trying to get his attention, but Richie kept on walking. Jim and I just looked at each other and laughed. Later, right before the game started, he did give me the plays.

I was really looking forward to playing the Vikings. They are a very talented team, especially on defense, but we saw a few things on film we thought we could take advantage of. Richie told me that the Vikings' defensive line came hard—real hard—and what I had to do was either deliver the ball fast or take off through the lanes they vacated when they rushed. That's always been my philosophy and it was great to hear Richie say the same thing.

Randall does indeed come out running. The Vikings, who went into the game with a league-leading 30 quarterback sacks, put a lot of pressure on Randall. But their all-out rush often leaves lanes open for Randall to run through, and, without a spy watching Randall or a couple of linebackers sitting behind the line of scrimmage to block his running lanes, Randall is free to roam around the Minnesota secondary. Randall takes advantage of this new-found freedom and rushes for 121 yards and two touchdowns on 12 carries and completes 16-of-23 passes for 167 yards and the Eagles win 28-17.

Things don't start off well for Randall as defensive end Chris Doleman blindsides him on the Eagles' first possession, forcing a fumble that the Vikings recover deep in Eagles' territory. But the defense stops the Vikings and a field goal gives Minnesota a 3-0 lead. On the Eagles' second possession of the game, on third-and-15 from the Eagles' 25, Randall runs out of the pocket and scampers for 30 yards to the Vikings' 45. Four plays later, Randall is on the loose again, this time for 18 yards. The Eagles go for it on fourth-and-one from inside the Minnesota five and Randall dives for the first down on a quarterback sneak. The drive ends when Randall scores from the one and the Eagles take a 7-3 lead.

The Vikings come back to take a 10-7 lead, but the Eagles roar back, marching 79 yards in 14 plays in the second quarter. This time Randall does it through the air, hitting Sherman for 17 yards and Walker for 14 more. Sherman dives in from the one and the Eagles led 14-10.

Later in the half, Randall has the Birds moving again as he races 16 yards on third-and-10 from the Vikings' 45. The drive ends when Ruzek misses a 40-yard field goal attempt.

In the third quarter, the Eagles drive 84 yards on 10 plays, including completions to Sherman (18 yards), Byars (13 yards) and Williams (13). The play to Sherman is a masterpiece. Randall rolls left on a bootleg, with Sherman running ahead of him to either block or receive a pass. As Randall nears the line of scrimmage, he flips the ball to a wide-open Sherman, who rumbles for 18 yards and a first down.

The Eagles put the game out of reach when Joyner goes 24 yards with an interception for a 28-17 lead early in the fourth quarter.

Right before the defense went out on the field, Seth turned to a couple of guys and said, "I'm going to make a big play." When Seth says something like that, you pay attention. Seth studies more films than any other player on the team and is totally prepared for every game.

The Eagles get the ball back with 2:54 to play on the Minnesota 42. On third-and-two from the 32, Randall runs a bootleg to the right and races down the right sideline for 24 yards to go over the 100-yard barrier for the first time since November 4, 1990, and the Eagles run out the clock and improve to 8-5 and remain tied with Washington for the second wildcard playoff berth behind New Orleans (10-3).

"I think this was Randall's best game," Kotite says afterward. "I liked his decisiveness, not just running the ball, but throwing the ball . . . We had him on a number of bootlegs, which is a run-pass option. Some of [his runs] were scrambles, the last play was a bootleg."

According to Heller: "[Randall] wanted to make things happen and he was having a good time, and when he has success it kind of steamrolls . . . He wants to go out there and show everyone he's a great quarterback and he did that today."

At his press conference after the game, Randall is upbeat. "Was this vintage 1990 Randall today?" a reporter asks.

"It felt great," Randall responds. "The thing that makes me feel comfortable is guys on our team being confident. When the offense is doing its job, it's a mix. We all have to collaborate and that enhances what the team does . . . The thing I told the guys when we were warming up was let's go out there and have some fun."

The only thing Randall wasn't happy with were the three quarterback sneaks he ran during the game—two for touchdowns and the other for a first down on fourth-and-one. "I don't like quarterback sneaks," Randall says with a smile. "You get hurt. Those guys come full speed and try to knock your helmet off. Heath Sherman and

Herschel Walker are great running backs and I'd rather see them run the ball."

It was nice to run again and get back to my old style of play. Now it seems that people are jumping back on the Randall Cunningham bandwagon and I appreciate that. But I wish that people would stay with me during the good and bad times. During the past month, I've learned that my true friends are the ones that stuck with me through thick and thin. Sometimes things get so negative, that even some of the people who you thought were your friends start believing the hype. True friends are the ones who stick with you no matter what. It's a great feeling to know I have a lot of true friends who are there for me when I need them.

After our fast start this season, teams were trying different things against me and I wasn't hitting my passes like I needed to be hitting them and the entire offense struggled. The coaches kept me locked in the pocket and we didn't do the things we needed to do to get me out of there and the offense moving again. Now we're doing those things. We went into the Minnesota game with a great game plan that was designed to take advantage of my skills. Richie was the one who designed the game plan and he deserves all the credit for our success. Richie called the bootleg about four times and every time it worked. He called another one of my favorites—the 19 special—at least eight times and it was there all game. I would tell you what the 19 special is, but it's probably our best play and I don't want to give away any secrets. We didn't use the 67 blocking scheme once the entire game and I had plenty of escape routes to run through, which were usually right inside the two tackles—Heller or Antone. The rollout where I threw the ball to Heath was a perfect call. That play gives me different options and really stretches out the defensive coverage. I could have run for 10 or 15 yards, but Heath was open, so I got the ball to him. Heath is a very talented player and can make things happen when he's in the open field. I only wish we would start off games running plays like that, instead of waiting until we get behind and have to open things up.

At one point in the game while we were waiting for the television timeout and were real anxious to get the game started again and run the next play, I could feel our confidence growing. I think the team's confidence starts with the quarterback. If a team doesn't have confidence in its quarterback, there will be confusion and that's what happened earlier in the season when things weren't going so well and I was in and out of the lineup. But today they were saying, "Randall is doing his thing and making things happen." And I thought to myself: this is how we used to play in 1990. We used to believe that other teams couldn't stop us, that only our mistakes would. At one point during the game I called a running play in the gap between Heller and Schad on the left side and then, while we were still in the huddle, Alexander started talking since we had plenty of time left before we had to run the play. Alexander called out the blocking assignments for the offensive linemen and said if so-and-so stunts I want this guy to do this and crash down on this guy and we'll clean out everyone in the hole. You could just sense the confidence of the line and see them working together to get the job done. You can't ask for anything better than that.

Sure enough, we ran the play and Heath got five or six yards. Then I rolled out and Keith Byars and Freddie geeked a couple of defenders and I got big yardage and we went in and scored. The Vikings' defense was worried about where I was going to be and what I was going to do, which is when things start to open up for us. It felt great. We were back in the groove that we were in in 1990, when we were the number three offense in the NFL.

CHAPTER

12

In Seattle today, an incredible string of penalties turns a potential blowout into a close game, with the Eagles finally prevailing 20-17 in overtime. The Eagles are flagged 17 times for 191 yards and are just a call or two away from topping the NFL record for the most penalty yards in a game, which is 209. While the Seahawks' offense is woeful, the defense, led by Cortez Kennedy, is all over Randall, stunting and blitzing and sacking him 10 times and knocking down six of his passes. Finally, late in overtime, Randall hits Roy Green for 20 yards and Byars for 21 and Ruzek connects on a 44-yard field goal to put the game out of its misery and give the Eagles a 20-17 win to raise their record to 9-5. Randall completes 27-of-44 passes for 365 yards and rushes for 38 yards and a touchdown.

Despite the constant heat, Randall refuses to blame the offensive line after the game. "If you look at the situation, it looks like I didn't have a lot of time," Randall tells the media after the game. "But Seattle had some great schemes. The offensive line did a great job. They were very productive. Sometimes I should have thrown it away. But I don't like to throw it up for grabs. That's when teams get touchdowns."

No matter how much pressure he's under, Randall will never blame the offensive line—in public or private. When he says he is pleased with the play of the five men in front of him, even though he was just sacked 10 times and had to run for his life on several other occasions, Randall means it. But a simple study of game films reveals that the offensive line does a good job of run blocking, but gets beat far too often on pass protection. Defensive ends or blitzing linemen are able to run around the tackles and opposing tackles are able to collapse the pocket and force Randall to improvise. On a team without such a mobile quarterback, this would spell disaster. With Randall Cunningham pulling the trigger, the Eagles survive. The only question is, how long can Randall survive if he has to take many more beatings like the one he took today.

"Seattle has a good defense," Kotite says after the game. "But they shouldn't have had that kind of penetration, shouldn't have been knocking balls down like that. That's the first time I've seen that all year."

"We can't ignore the sacks," Antone Davis adds. "We've got to go in and look at the film and see what we can do to correct it."

Any problems in the offensive line are overshadowed by a feature on Seth Joyner in the New York *Times* that is published the day of the Seattle game. In the article, Joyner is quoted as saying: "Buddy cared about winning and Braman cared about making money. Buddy did not get the chance to complete the job. Braman wanted a puppet and that's what he got [in Kotite]. Much of what Buddy said has come home to roost. We lost Keith Jackson because of money. Free agency is coming and this team could be ripped apart."

Joyner adds that Randall's knee injury in 1991 may have been God's way of punishing him for lobbying Braman to fire Buddy and hire Kotite.

"One reason [Buddy was fired]," Joyner is quoted as saying,

"was because Randall lobbied for Rich to Braman and deserted Buddy. Buddy gave Randall the chance, as a black quarterback, that no other coach in this league would. Buddy built the entire offense around Randall. I told Randall that he would pay for what he did, and I don't know if him missing all of last year with the knee injury was it, but God works in mysterious ways."

After the game, reporters tell Kotite about the remarks and ask for his comments about being called Braman's puppet. "I didn't know that," Kotite said. "But I don't worry about those statements. Let's talk about the football team and the game. I think it's ridiculous."

Next, the reporters swarm around Randall, hoping he'll say something to fan the fires of a brewing controversy. For the media, there's nothing better than two teammates going at it in public. But Randall isn't playing along. "I've got a lot of respect for Seth," Randall says. "Don't believe everything you read. I'll never lose respect for Seth."

As for Joyner, he's not denying the quotes, but is saying they were taken out of context and used to paint an unfair portrait. He says he was describing the past, not the present situation on the team. "I should learn my lesson and not say anything," Joyner says after the game as he's surrounded by the media. "Because it's amazing how you guys take little bits and pieces of what you want and you piece it together where you want it. It wasn't a matter of being off the record. The article started off being an article just on me. Not an article on Randall Cunningham or Richie Kotite or Norman Braman. Then again, like I always said, things always seem to get misconstrued when I open my mouth and say something. Something's always misprinted and misread, you know, and then it always seems like I'm the bad guy."

Two days later, Joyner holds a press conference to put an end to the controversy. Joyner doesn't come out and actually apologize for what he said in the article, but continues to say that it was a mistake to have spoken at all and that his words were turned around to make *him look bad. How about his quote about Randall? "My quote is, 'Hey, God works in mysterious ways,'" Joyner says at the press conference. "And, hey, if you do somebody wrong, sooner or later you have to pay for it. That goes for me and everybody in this room."*

Once again, this is an example of the media trying to make something out of nothing. There is no friction on this team. There was some in the past, right after Buddy got fired. But all of that is history. We respect Richie and we respect each other. Seth and I are cool. We straightened things out between us after the 1991 season and since then, little-by-little, we've become better and better friends. I got to know Seth better during training camp this year. In the shower room there's a hose that's used to clean the shower. One day I was in there with a couple of other guys after practice and Seth comes along and turns on the hose and gets us all pretty good with freezing cold water. Then Thomas Sanders grabbed the hose and started spraying guys too. I had to get them back, so later, while Sanders was dressing, I threw a cup of cold water on him. He wasn't happy, but he knew there was nothing he could say since he got me first.

Just because Seth always seems so serious and has such a scary expression on his face, everyone thinks he's angry all the time. But I thought, I don't care, I'm getting Seth too. So I got a cup of water and went into the locker room where all the defensive players dress. I took Keith Byars and Kenny Jackson with me—I didn't want to be in there alone. Seth was naked and about to put on his clothes when I threw the cup of water at him. He saw it coming and ducked and the water went all over his clothes. Seth got all mad and started cussing at me and I said, "What are you gonna do, fight me? You started it and now I ended it." Seth looked like he wanted to hit me, but I walked away and nothing happened.

The next morning, Seth walked up and said he was sorry about the other day and we laughed about it. So, you see, Seth is totally cool. People may think he's mean, but he's a down-to-earth guy with a sense of humor. He cracks jokes just like everyone else. Seth also takes his job as a football player more seriously than anyone else on the team. And he takes it upon himself to speak out if he thinks someone isn't working hard enough or if he sees something is wrong with the team. We've all come to understand that when Seth says something critical, it's because he wants to win so much and we respect him for it.

By the way, I did get fined for leaving the hotel before the Minnesota game, and not $1,000 like I thought. It was $2,000. Richie said it would be double if I did it again. I told him, "Don't fine me. If you catch me again, just tell me and I'll give you $2,000." I was joking when I said it, but Richie didn't laugh and said, "I don't want your money." Maybe next time I'll just hire someone who looks like me to stay in my room at the hotel. Stay tuned to find out what happens before our next home game.

DECEMBER 15, 1992

Randall is making an appearance at Wanamaker's, a large downtown Philadelphia department store. The appearance is on behalf of the Quarterback Club, of which Randall is a member. The Quarterback Club includes the NFL's top quarterbacks (Randall, John Elway, Dan Marino, Warren Moon, Phil Simms, Troy Aikman, Jim Everett, Bernie Kosar, Boomer Esiason, Jim Kelly and Bubby Brister), who signed a licensing deal with NFL properties and do endorsements and appearances. The Quarterback Club also has its own clothing line, which is what Randall is promoting today. A percentage of the profits from the sale of the clothing goes toward the Club's primary charity—the Children's Miracle Network. The Quarterback Club is one of Randall's many business ventures. For Randall, who is as competitive off the field as he is on, business is another sport and he is driven to succeed, not so much for the money but for the satisfac-

tion he gets from putting together a deal or negotiating a contract. Several years ago, following the advice of Jaworski and Quick, Randall formed his own company—Scrambler, Inc.

I started Scrambler so I could keep track of all the money I was making off the field. That way I can deduct my expenses, pay my taxes and keep everything organized. Scrambler handles all my endorsements, card shows, commercials, appearances, my television show and so on. All the income I make off the field goes through Scrambler and I take 10 percent of this, plus 10 percent of my Eagles' salary, and donate it to my church.

At the beginning of my career, Terry Bender, who owns Sneaks-N-Cleats, a sporting goods store in Allentown, and who used to put together a lot of card shows, hired me to do a card show. After the show, Terry told me he could get me a lot more things and I told him to keep bringing them to me. The income Terry was bringing me started adding up and I figured this man knows the card business; I can hire him to work for Scrambler, put him on salary, plus a bonus, and he'll more than pay for his own salary with all the income he brings. That's exactly what's happened. Over the years, Terry has become my closest friend off the football field. He has taught me about collectables, the merchandising business and the retail side of things, which we have used at Scrambler to start our own line of hats, tee-shirts and water bottles. I've helped educate Terry on negotiating contracts.

The other employee of Scrambler is Suzanne Cossaboon, who handles the day-to-day operations of the company and keeps my schedule. Suzanne is very intelligent and a perfectionist, which I like. She and I have become like brother and sister, but without all the fighting. Terry, Suzanne and I have been together for a long time and the key is that we all have a lot of respect for each other and are very loyal towards one another. As long as I have this company, they'll always have a job.

Randall and Terry Bender arrive at Wanamaker's two minutes past noon and pull up to a loading dock behind the store. A corps of security guards and Wanamaker executives whisk Randall up a back freight elevator, through stock rooms and into the store where a mob of more than 400 people are lined up. Another 75 people are gathered behind a rope barrier.

"Hey Randall, over here," a woman shouts and when Randall looks she snaps a photo.

"Hey Randall, keep scrambling," someone else yells and everyone cheers.

"Hey Randall, you gonna beat the Redskins?"

Randall moves through the mass of people, shaking hands and smiling and takes a seat at a desk. The first person in line—a thirty-ish white woman—shrieks with delight when the security guard waves her forward to meet Randall and have him sign a photo.

"I've been waiting here since eight o'clock," the woman says as she approaches Randall. "If you don't believe me, just ask the security guard."

The security guard nods.

"You played an awesome game," the woman continues. "Are you gonna win Sunday? We might win a few games if Rich Kotite doesn't keep you in a cage."

A little kid with a haircut vaguely similar to Randall's steps up for an autograph while his mother snaps photos. Randall pats the little kid's hair.

"Do you have to blow dry that to keep it neat too?" Randall asks. The kid is too nervous to speak, so he just nods. Randall laughs and signs his name. "Can you sign that 'to your best pal'," his mother asks and Randall obliges.

A few minutes later, a reporter and a television crew from Channel Six interview Randall, who continues to sign while he talks to the reporter. The interview starts off pretty innocuous, but then comes the zinger as the reporter asks about Seth's quotes in the Times article. Randall smiles politely, looks into the camera and says: "I *really have a lot of respect for Seth." The reporter keeps digging and asking about any friction between the two, but Randall just smiles and keeps signing.*

A mother brings her young son up and she's so nervous she's shaking as she hoists him up next to Randall and steps back to take a picture.

"You have to take the lens cap off," Randall says politely, and the woman, her hands shaking even more, removes the cap. "Don't be so nervous," Randall says. "Relax. We have plenty of time for you to take a picture."

Another woman asks about the cross Randall wears during games. "I have it on now," Randall says and fishes it out from under his shirt. "I always wear it."

"Praise God," the woman says and hands Randall an ornament for his Christmas tree—a black Santa Claus.

"God bless you," Randall says.

The next woman in line asks Randall to sign a photo to her boss. "This could get me a promotion."

"He could fire you if he knows you skipped work to come here," Randall jokes and they both laugh.

A middle-aged gentleman asks Randall to sign a dollar bill, which he does. "Now it's worth $100," the man says.

An elderly woman approaches and latches onto Randall's arm in a death grip. "I pray for you," she says and Randall thanks her. "I'm a true believer," she continues. "Do you know what a true believer is?"

Randall says yes he does and that he is a true believer.

"I'm 83 years old and I pray for you," the woman continues and then asks Randall to sign the shirt she is wearing. "I really do pray for you and when you donated that car to your church [which Randall won in a golf tournament] I cried."

The woman doesn't want to leave and finally the security guards have to gently escort her away in order to keep the line moving.

"Can I ask you a question?" asks a man in his mid-20s.

"Sure."

"Is the dissension in the locker room as bad as they say?"

"Don't believe what you read in the papers," Randall answers.

"I don't."

"You must, otherwise you wouldn't be asking that question."

"How about you and Seth?"

"We're cool. They just have to write all that bad stuff to sell papers."

The line continues to grow longer and is snaking back through three departments of the store. The chief of security approaches Randall and asks him to sign only one autograph per person in order to keep the line moving. Randall nods, but whenever someone asks for two or three signatures, he'll sign them.

An excited little boy bounces up to Randall. *"I caught a touchdown pass in my game,"* he gushes.

"You did? That's great."

"I had to dive for it."

"That's what I love—receivers who make diving catches."

"Hey Randall," someone shouts out and Randall looks up. *"There's a longer line here for you than there was for Santa Claus."* Everyone laughs.

Another woman brings up an empty Randall Bar wrapper for Randall to sign. Early in the season, the Morley Candy Makers introduced the Randall Bar, a chocolate, caramel, and nut confection with a wrapper that includes a photo of Randall and an anti-drug message.

"How did you like it?" Randall asks.

"I couldn't eat it. I'm on a diet," the woman says.

"You can eat one every once in a while. You need 30 grams of fat every day."

"Maybe I'll try one," the woman says.

Finally, after signing close to 500 autographs, it's time for Randall to leave. The security guards form a circle around him and lead him back to the door from which he entered. But there aren't enough

security guards and a throng of women rush forward and start grab-
bing Randall, tearing at his clothes, trying to get a piece of him.
Finally Randall makes it through the door unharmed.

I enjoy being out in public, meeting people and talking with
them. Sometimes, players have a tendency to get caught up in all the
negative publicity that comes out in the media and forget there are a
lot of great fans here in Philly. Today everyone was positive and
friendly and they were congratulating us for beating Seattle and
wishing us luck against the Redskins this week. The funniest part
came when I was leaving. This one lady grabbed me and wouldn't let
go. She was strong, as strong as Reggie White. I had to put my best
move on her to break free.

DECEMBER 16, 1992

Those of you who think you're tough, this is not where it's at.
You come in here, you'll be eaten alive. I've seen numerous
stabbings. I've seen people being killed. I even saw guys get
their heads cut completely off and hung up on the fence.
This is not a place where you can just come in here and do
time and get out. It's not like that. It's rough, it's nasty. You
may think you're hot shit out there—as long as you got them
guns—but in here you don't have those guns. So it's every
man for himself.

Gary "Gang War" Bates

Today, Randall travels to Graterford Prison, a maximum-security
prison located 30 miles outside of Philadelphia, to tape a one-hour
special episode of his weekly television show. Teammates Andre Wa-
ters and Mark McMillan are Randall's guests and the three walk
together into the prison, down a long corridor and through a sliding

steel door into the receiving area, where a guard takes all their valuables, puts an identification bracelet on their wrists and an infra-red stamp on each of their hands. "Don't lose this band or we won't let you out," the guard says and he's serious. Then, after the first steel door slides shut, the door on the other side of the receiving room slides open and the three Eagles walk through a metal detector and down another long corridor. On each side of the corridor are endless rows of cell blocks that house the 4,200 inmates of Graterford. The door slams shut behind Randall, Waters and McMillan, the locks click shut and they begin walking down the long hallway.

"That click, click sound's a terrible sound," Waters says.

At the end of the corridor is a door and the three walk through it and are suddenly in the prison's auditorium surrounded by a sea of inmates in brown uniforms. When they see Randall, the prisoners spring to their feet and begin stamping, clapping and shouting at him.

"You better beat the Redskins, Randall, I got eight packs of cigarettes bet on the game."

"Don't stay in the pocket Randall, run, always run when you get in trouble."

"Hey Randall, how's Whitney?"

The trio of Birds makes their way to the stage that is set up in the front of the auditorium. Along the way, they are mobbed by the inmates, who all want to shake Randall's hand and pat him on the back and touch an NFL quarterback. Although there are several guards in the auditorium, they keep their distance and there is nothing between the three Eagles and the swarm of inmates who all press forward into the aisle until there's only a foot of space for Randall, Waters and McMillan to walk through. Graterford is where hardened criminals serving life sentences for vicious crimes spend the rest of their lives.

Randall, Waters and McMillan make it to the front, but then word comes down from the director of Randall's television show that they didn't get the shot and he asks Randall to make another en-

trance, this time down the center aisle. The three Eagles comply, head back up the aisle through the sea of inmates and then back down again. Unbelievably, this take doesn't work either and they have to make the long walk back up the aisle and down again for a third time. This time it's a go and Randall takes a seat on the stage with co-host Ron Burke, who explains that the purpose of the show is to send the message that kids don't want to end up in prison.

"This is real, there is nothing phony here," Randall says. "There are a lot of brothers here who have something to tell the kids and we need to share that message."

The show also includes a behind-the-scenes look at prison life and interviews with several of the inmates, all of whom describe the horrors of incarceration.

In here, everything is so bleak and dark. You're not really a man, you're not really a human, and who wants to constantly look over their back worrying about someone trying to have sex with them. It's just frightening, you know, a big guy like me having to worry about someone attempting to take your manhood. People in here don't care how big or how small you are. The strong survive off the weak. If you think you can come to prison and survive, you're mistaken. People will eat you alive in here.

Gregory "Beetle" Lowe

Going into the prison, the thing that surprised me was that I didn't have any fear. It was just an experience that everyone should have, to come in a place like this that you can't get out of until they let you out. Going in, the main thing I was thinking was that I had to treat everyone with respect. There aren't animals in here, these men are people. Sure they've committed crimes and deserve to be punished, but we need to understand where these individuals came from and the terrible lives they led before they came to prison, and we need to turn this around so another generation of kids don't end up in prison. God put us here on earth to live together and to understand one another and we need to come together and love one another the way God intended.

There is more talent in that prison than you could ever believe. There are musicians and artists and athletes. A long time ago, I think it was during my rookie year, we played a charity basketball game at Graterford and there was this one guy who went up and down the court like Michael Jordan. And nobody will ever know his name.

The only bad moment came at the very end when we were walking back up the aisle to leave. There were guys all around us, crowding us, wanting to shake our hands and talk. A lot of guys wanted to know about Whitney Houston, but I told them there was never anything real between us. A lot of guys wanted to know about my fiancée. And a lot of guys told us we had to beat the Redskins. But there were also a lot of Cowboy fans in there, which surprised me. On the way out, I suddenly felt this burning sensation on the back of my leg. I thought someone had set my pants on fire, but it turned out someone spilled hot coffee on the back of my jacket and all over my pants. It wasn't a very pleasant feeling, but overall, I was glad I went to Graterford. I learned a lot. Guys, thanks for everything.

CHAPTER

13

A year ago, in the fifteenth game of the season, the Eagles hosted Dallas, with the winner clinching a wildcard playoff berth. The Cowboys won 17-3. This year, in game 15, the Eagles host Washington, and like last year, the winner will clinch a wildcard playoff berth, while the loser, if Green Bay wins its final two games, is out of the playoffs.

A lot of people were saying this was put up or shut up time for us. They were saying we couldn't win the big game and that I couldn't win the big game or take a team to the playoffs. Richie read us some quotes from the newspapers and that got some of the guys even more fired up. My thing is, I don't care about that stuff. We have a reason to play hard every week, regardless of who we play. We have to be ready every week to play our best. I thrive on pressure and I know Reggie and Seth and Clyde and Herschel and all the guys on our team are the same way. When people said we couldn't beat the Redskins, that just put more pressure on us and we play better under pressure.

Richie was expecting the Redskins to blitz a lot, but in my mind, I didn't think they would. Since Seattle blitzed us so much the week before and had a lot of success with it, you would expect the Redskins to do the same thing. But Joe Gibbs is such a smart coach, he knew we would make a lot of adjustments and be ready for the blitz, so I figured he'd think he didn't have to blitz us. The first time we played them this year they didn't blitz that much. Today, they rushed four guys and sent a linebacker every once in a while. The Redskins stayed in their lanes and tried to keep me locked up in the pocket. But the difference was that Richie designed some plays for me to escape with blockers in front of me—rollouts and bootlegs.

The game was televised nationally by CBS, with John Madden and Pat Summerall calling the action. Before the game, Madden said, "It all boils down to the quarterbacks . . . I think Randall Cunningham has to do it for the Philadelphia Eagles. He has to have a big day . . . [The Redskins] don't want to rush him, they don't want to give him lanes. They want to keep him in the pocket and don't let him run or don't let him run and throw."

After the Eagles' defense stops the Redskins on the first possession of the game, the Eagles begin marching down the field. On third-and-four from the 27, Randall hits Byars over the middle for seven yards and a first down. On third-and-three from the 41, Randall hits Calvin Williams on an in-route for 10 yards and another first down. On third-and-nine from the Washington 49, Randall hits Byars along the sideline. Byars lunges for the first down but is pushed out of bounds a yard short. On fourth-and-one, Kotite decides to go for it, but Herschel is stuffed at the line of scrimmage for no gain.

The Redskins kick a 29-yard field goal early in the second quarter and the Eagles take over on their own 20. Herschel runs for 14 on first down and then Randall escapes the rush and flips a pass to Byars for three yards. After Herschel is stopped for no gain, setting up a third-and-seven situation, Randall spots Barnett streaking down the right sideline and loops a perfect pass that hits him on the numbers for a 33-yard gain to the Washington 30. On the next play, Randall runs his first bootleg of the game. He fakes a handoff to Sherman and then rolls left. But the defensive end isn't fooled and is right on top of Randall, who flips the ball over his head to Sherman for a nine-yard gain to the 21. On the next play, Sherman bursts through the middle, breaks three tackles and scampers into the end zone for a 7-3 Eagles lead.

Washington answers right back as Rypien hits Ricky Sanders with a 62-yard scoring pass. Later, the Redskins kick another field goal to take a 13-7 halftime lead.

The Eagles get the ball to start the second half and begin moving the ball. On second-and-four from the Eagles' 37, Randall rolls left on the bootleg, picks up a block from guard Brian Baldinger and races 24 yards down the sideline to the Washington 39 before stepping out of bounds. After Sherman is dropped for a one-yard loss, Randall calls an audible at the line, drops back to pass and looks downfield for Williams, who is double-covered. Still, Randall throws the ball, Williams comes back for it and catches the ball for a 28-yard touchdown and a 14-13 Eagles' lead.

On the touchdown play, I called a 16 audible, which basically sends Calvin to the corner of the end zone and Freddie has an option to run any eight-yard route. Calvin was double-covered, but I could see that the defensive back had his back to me and the safety was still a few yards away from Calvin. So I threw the ball right at the back of the defensive back's head, so he wouldn't see it coming and the safety wouldn't have time to get over. Calvin saw the ball, adjusted his route and went up for it. It hit him in the chest just as the safety hit him and the ball dropped out of Calvin's hands, but he stayed with it and caught it in his lap.

My receivers know me and they know I have enough confidence in them to throw them the ball even when they're covered. My thing is, they might be covered, but if I can put the ball where my receivers have a chance to catch it, but the defensive backs don't, I'll still throw into coverage and rely on my receiver to make the adjustment and come up with the big catch. I used to do that a lot with Greg Garrity. Greg was a very talented receiver with great concentration. He'd run a fade and the defensive back would think he had him covered, but I'd just throw the ball at the back of the defensive back's head and Greg would stop, make the adjustment and catch the ball. Calvin and Freddie are talented enough to do that too. They are both very good athletes—loose, flexible guys who can stop and cut and leap and make those kinds of catches. Plus, Freddie is tall and can go up and grab the high ball.

On the Eagles' next possession, they are stopped by the Redskins and forced to punt. But Brian Mitchell fumbles the punt and Sherman recovers at the Washington 35. On first down Sherman runs for two. Then Randall is chased out of the pocket, cuts up the middle and is able to run for five yards to set up a third-and-three at the 28. From the shotgun formation, Randall hands off to Herschel, who is stopped for no gain. Ruzek comes in and attempts a 45-yard field goal, misses and Washington takes over. A CBS camera pans over to Braman, who was sitting in his box with a disgusted look on his face.

"[Braman's] still shaking his head," Madden says. "[It] looks like he's wondering, 'Why did we go third down and get into the shotgun and run a delay to Herschel Walker. Let Randall do something—he's the guy we're paying all the money to.'"

The defense stops the Redskins on their next possession and the Eagles take over on their own 16 and begin moving. First Sherman runs for four yards, then Randall hits Byars for nine and a first down. Then Sherman rips off runs of eight, 12 and eight yards to set up a second-and-two on the Washington 45. On the next play, Sherman fumbles a yard past the line of scrimmage, but the always-alert Heller falls on the bouncing ball and the Eagles have a first down on the Redskins' 43. After Randall is dropped for a one-yard loss on a bootleg, he throws a perfect spiral to Barnett for 20 yards and a first down on the 23. But the offense sputters and Ruzek misses a 47-yard field goal attempt.

After the defense stops the Redskins again, Sikahema breaks off a 47-yard punt return all the way to the Washington 25. On third-and-six, Randall drops back and looks for a receiver, can't find an open one and throws the ball out of the end zone. But the Redskins are called for holding Byars as he tried to get open and the Eagles are awarded a first down at the 16. After Sherman gains two yards, Randall rifles a pass to Barnett in the back of the end zone, but the ball goes through his hands. On third-and-eight, Randall runs the bootleg to the left and loops a touch pass over the linebacker to Byars who lunges for a first down at the six. After Walker gains three, Randall rolls right and hits Sherman for two more yards, setting up a third-and-goal from the one. But Heller jumps offside and the ball is marched back to the six. From here, Randall drops back, can't find an open receiver and throws the ball away. Ruzek connects on a 23-yard field goal with 3:35 to play to give the Eagles a 17-13 lead.

The Redskins have one more chance and need a touchdown to win. Behind Rypien, they begin methodically moving the ball down the field. On a fourth-and-10 from the Eagles 20 and with time running out, Rypien hits Ricky Ervins over the middle and he runs to the Eagles' five for the first down. But there are only about 10 seconds left in the game—probably not enough time for the Redskins to get to the line of scrimmage and run another play—and they don't have a timeout left. But safety John Booty picks up the ball, saying later he thought the game was over. It isn't and the officials stop the clock until they can retrieve the ball and spot it on the five with five seconds to play. By this time the Redskins are lined up and as soon as the referee blows his whistle to start the clock, Rypien takes the snap and throws the ball into the ground to stop the clock with two seconds to play.

On the game's final play, Reggie White breaks through the line and forces Rypien to get rid of the ball quicker than he would have liked. Rypien steps up to avoid Reggie and throws a low pass over *the middle toward Gary Clark, who is two yards deep in the end zone. It looks on target, but at the last instant, Eric Allen reaches across Clark and bats the ball to the turf. The Eagles win and lock up a playoff spot.*

"We did it as a team," Randall tells the media after the game. "No individual stood out today. A lot of people made great plays, but we did it as a team."

Indeed, there were plenty of heroes today. Randall completed 13-of-24 passes for 149 yards and ran for another 29, Sherman picked up 96 yards on 18 carries and caught two passes, Byars caught six balls for 41 yards, Williams came up with the big touchdown reception, Barnett had three receptions for 59 yards, Sikahema had a huge punt return, Joyner had nine tackles, a sack and an interception, and Simmons and White each had a sack.

If you're wondering whether I snuck out of the hotel last night before the game, I'll tell you what happened. I figured that there would be someone outside my door to catch me leaving, so I decided to lock the door from the inside so nobody could get in and then I'd go out the window and make them have to cut the door down the next day. McMahon and a couple of the guys said to come down to their room and they'd show me how to tie bed sheets together so I could climb out the window. I was all set, ready to tie the bed sheets together and make my break, but I was really tired and wound up falling asleep in my hotel bed. The next morning I woke up at eight o'clock, drove home and Felicity made me breakfast and then I drove to the stadium early and watched film.

CHAPTER

14

The Eagles close out the regular season with a workmanlike 20-10 win over the Giants to finish the season 11-5 and clinch the second wildcard playoff berth. The following Sunday they will travel to New Orleans to play the 12-4 Saints. In the Giants game, Randall completes 11-of-21 passes for 125 yards, including a 34-yard touchdown to Williams, and runs for another 35 yards, including a 20-yard touchdown scramble. Herschel runs for 104 yards to finish the season with 1,074 yards.

For the season, Randall completed 233-of-384 passes (60.7 percent) for 2,775 yards, 19 touchdowns and 11 interceptions and ran for 549 yards on 87 carries (6.3 yards-per-carry). However, after leading the Eagles in rushing from 1987-90, Randall is third on the team in 1992 behind Herschel and Sherman (570). Barnett is the team's leading receiver with 67 catches for 1,083 yards and Byars has 56 receptions for 502 yards.

Of course, the season ends with a minor controversy.

Normally, on Tuesdays, the entire team is off—except for me. I come in at some point during the day to pick up the game plan. But this Tuesday was the Tuesday before Christmas, my only day off and I had a lot to do, including all my Christmas shopping. So I decided I'd take care of everything on Tuesday, come in real early on Wednesday and get the game plan and start studying it before practice. Since we already had the playoffs clinched, I wasn't even sure at that point if or how much I was going to play.

Felicity and I went to New York to do our shopping. While we were walking down the street, I saw this homeless person with a sign saying he had AIDS and needed help. He looked very tired and sad. I stopped a couple of yards past him and reached in my pocket to give him $5, but all I had was a $100 bill. I asked Felicity if she had a $5 or a $10, but before she could even look, something inside me told me to give this man the $100. I folded it up so only he could see it, handed it to him and said, "Merry Christmas." He was very quiet, kind of stunned I think, and just said, "Thank you." As I walked down the street, I got a very joyous feeling. It felt great that I could help someone. I turned to Felicity and said, "We are truly blessed." And we are. We have our health, our faith and each other. We have problems, but compared to other people, our problems are nothing. Praise God.

Of course, the next morning when I got to practice, I was in trouble. I got in early and went to Zeke's office to get the game plan and then walked back to my locker. Richie walked by me, but I don't think he saw me. Five minutes later, Zeke's phone rang and it was Richie, telling Zeke he wanted to see me. Whenever I go into Richie's office, I keep my mouth shut and let him do all the talking. He says he had called all over looking for me and was pretty upset I didn't come in to get the game plan. It might have been a good idea to have called Richie to tell him I wasn't coming in, but I knew if I did, he would have made me come in and I wouldn't have gotten my Christmas shopping done. I let Richie holler and didn't say anything and I thought to myself, "My week has started off bad again, just like before the Minnesota game, so maybe I'll have another good game."

Later in the week, something nice happened. Before practice, someone brought down a little kid who was dying. I had met him before at Children's Hospital of Philadelphia and had given him a jersey and he had said that when he died, he wanted to be buried wearing my jersey. When they brought him down to see me and Herschel, he couldn't move at all and seemed pretty sad. He couldn't even shake my hand. Some people are scared of things like this and don't want to get too close. But God opened my heart and I hugged him and told him I loved him. He didn't say too much and didn't seem too happy. It was like he had already accepted the fact that he was dying and just wanted to get this over with. My only hope is that he knew God. I hugged him again and said, "God bless you." His mother was standing behind us and I could see the tears streaming down her cheeks and she kept thanking me over and over. I told her I was the one that should be thankful, thankful that she had brought her son to see me again. When they left I wanted to cry and could feel the tears coming to my eyes.

Christmas Day turned out to be a great day. We practiced, and afterwards, everyone wished each other Merry Christmas and headed home. I was so tired I didn't even take a shower. We call that "cowboying it." When someone doesn't take a shower after practice and we catch them trying to sneak out, we start yelling, "Yahoo" and jump on their backs and ride them like a horse. Reggie sometimes goes in the training room and gets Otho's big leather whip and starts cracking it on the ground. I always take a shower after practice and I'm one of the biggest critics when someone else doesn't. Or, if I see someone taking a real short shower, I shout, "Hey, you have to use soap."

I tried to sneak out without anyone seeing I was cowboying it, but Eric Allen spotted me and said, "Come on over here, I want to talk to you." I fell for it and headed over toward Eric and he started going "Yahoo" and tried to grab and pull me back into the locker room. I got real strong with him and picked him up and carried him out of the locker room with me. Eric starts saying, "I can't believe you're cowboying it." And Alexander joined in: "Yeah, you're the guy who always rips on everyone else; you're the last person to cowboy it." I finally got out of there and laughed all the way to my car. There were a lot of people waiting around for autographs and I signed them. I couldn't believe people were waiting outside the stadium on Christmas Day for autographs.

When I got home I was tired and sore and Felicity rubbed my neck and I wound up falling asleep for a few hours. After my nap, Felicity and I played a few games of chess. She wins all the time and she likes to rub it in to try to make me mad. She says, "Who's the champ? Who's the champ?" I tell her she is, but only for today.

That night we went to a dinner party at the house of Charlie and Marsha Foulke, who are like a second family to me. Charlie Jr. and his sister, Michelle, were also there. Charlie Jr. bought his fiance a Rolex watch and made the rest of us look bad. We had a very nice, relaxing Christmas dinner, but Felicity and I couldn't stay too late because I had practice the next morning. That afternoon, when I got home from practice, I gave Felicity a few of her presents to open and after we got back from the Foulke's, I gave her a few more. I gave her a mink coat, jewelry and all sorts of beautiful clothes, but the present she liked most was an electric toothbrush. A few times when we had been out shopping, she mentioned that she wanted an electric toothbrush and every once in a while I would crack a few bad breath jokes on her. The fact that I remembered and got her the toothbrush meant a lot to her. Felicity is the type who doesn't ask for much. All she wanted for Christmas was a toiletry bag and I made sure to get her one because she was always borrowing mine. In fact, she always borrows my clothes—especially my nice jackets and sweaters. She'd probably borrow my shoes if they weren't so big.

Felicity gave me all the things I needed for Christmas. I love ties and have about 200 of them. Felicity bought me an electric tie rack that spins around real slow so you can pick out the tie you want to wear. She also gave me a guest book to keep in the celebrity quarters guest room so our friends could sign their names and leave their addresses. I always ask for underwear and socks and she got me a black and a white pair of Calvin Klein jock straps. Felicity said they were for working out. I was going to wear one of the pairs in the Giants game, but I forgot to bring them to the stadium with me. I'll make sure to wear one in the New Orleans game.

Later, after Felicity thought I had given her all her presents, I went down to my office to get the last one and hid the box in her stocking. Then I told her to come downstairs and look in her stocking. She pulled out the box and thought it was a platinum watch to go with her engagement ring that has a platinum setting, but I told her a platinum watch was too expensive, but that one day, maybe, I'd get her one. She finally opened it and her jaw dropped. It was a platinum and diamond bracelet that I helped design. We sat down at the dining room table and I put it on her wrist and she started to cry. I told her I loved her and that I wanted to make her happy forever and not just in materialistic ways. I told her what we had was real love and this was how I always wanted it to be. "Sometimes," I said, "when we have little problems, we should remember this time and this day and how much we love each other and we'll be able to get through any problems that come up. People say that after five years of marriage, couples aren't as lovey-dovey as they were when they first got married, but I want us to be lovey-dovey forever. God has blessed me and he's blessed me with you and we're blessed to be together. Let's focus on God and what he's teaching us. Felicity, I love you more today than I did yesterday and my love for you can only grow."

CHAPTER

15

We felt very confident heading into the New Orleans game. The night before the game, I went out to dinner with Kenny Jackson and his fiancée, Ruth Ann, and Alan Pinkett and his wife. Alan plays for the Saints, but he's been out all season with a knee injury. I told him not to worry, that he'd be back next season. After dinner, I went back to the hotel and tried to go to sleep early. But, in the middle of the night, I kept hearing this tick, tick, tick sound. It wasn't the clock by my bed or the phone on the night stand. Then I remembered the big fire at the Moorestown Mall near my home. It started with an electrical problem. I was on the twenty-third floor of the hotel and got a little worried, so I called the front desk and told them about the strange sound in my room. They said they would send someone up to check it out. Before they came, I went into the bathroom and discovered the phone in there was making the ticking sound. I unplugged it and the ticking stopped. I thought, maybe they're messing with me, trying to keep me up all night so I have a bad game. Then the maintenance guys came in and before they looked at the phone, they wanted autographs at two o'clock in the morning. They finally fixed the phone and about an hour later, after I fell asleep, the phone rang. It was the front desk. They said of course they were Saints fans and didn't want to disturb me, but they just wanted to check and make sure the noise had stopped. I said it had and went back to sleep.

The next morning, I ate breakfast and read the Bible and watched the first half of the Houston-Buffalo playoff game. When I got to the locker room, I saw that the equipment guys had taken everything from Jerome's locker (which we've kept intact at the Vet as a shrine to Jerome) and set it up in our locker room in the Superdome. When I saw that, tears came to my eyes. I said, "Jerome's here with us." Jerome represents a lot to us and is still a big part of this team and will always be with us. I walked over to Reggie White and he was looking at Jerome's locker too. "Hey, Big Dog," I said, "You know we're going to win—J.B. is with us." Reggie nodded and said, "That's right." Then I walked over to Seth and asked if he had seen Jerome's locker. I told him I had almost started crying when I saw it and he nodded, which to me meant he felt the same way. The whole thing made me very emotional and a little confused and I wasn't sure what I should be doing to get ready for the game. I went into the training room and got some tape and then went over to my locker and taped my ankles. I always do that myself.

A couple minutes later, McMahon came in. Before we go out on the field to warm up, McMahon and Archer go out and have a field goal kicking contest. I could tell Jim was psyched for the game. He was carrying on and laughing and joking and was saying something like, "Baby, baby (something, something) till you taste some gravy." I had no idea what he was talking about. Then Jim pulls this article out of his locker and shows it to me. It says that Mike Ditka—who just got fired by the Chicago Bears—says he wants Jim back with him when he gets his next job. "See, I'm not going to be here next year," Jim said.

"You're not going anywhere," I said. "We'll both be back here next year having fun."

The Eagles flew in Jerome's father for the game and before we went out on the field, he spoke to the team. Mr. Brown is a minister and a very strong and deep man. He told us that we should focus on God, because God will bring you through anything and he's always there for you. And then he told us he loved each and every one of us. We were pumped up and ready to play.

The Saints receive the opening kickoff and come out throwing. Bobby Hebert is on target and marches his team 73 yards on eight plays for a 7-0 lead. After each team's offense is stopped, the Eagles take over on their own 20. On first down Sherman runs for four yards and then Randall rolls right on a bootleg. He hurdles one tackler, but is hit from behind and knocked to the turf. The ball squirts loose, but the referee rules Randall's knee was on the ground before the ball came loose, setting up a third-and-two from the 28. Randall takes the snap from the shotgun formation, steps back and then races through a seam in the middle of the line and runs for 15 yards and a first down at the 43. On the next play, Barnett runs straight down the right sideline, gets two steps on the cornerback and Randall hits him in stride for a 57-yard touchdown to tie the score 7-7.

On the touchdown, I faked a handoff to Herschel, who then had to stay in and block in case someone blitzed. But nobody blitzed. Ricky Jackson picked up Heath coming out of the backfield, the cornerback was playing way off of Calvin, who was running a corner route, so he was covered, and I saw Freddie with a step on his man and decided to throw the long one to him. I know from studying film and practice that if I drop straight back and throw the ball as far as I can, it will go over Freddie's head. But if we use a play-action fake and then I drop back, which takes an extra second, I can throw it as far as I can and Freddie will catch up to it. Freddie is like a magnet and goes right to the ball. He likes it a little bit to the inside and that's where I put it.

The Superdome is loud. I can stand at the line of scrimmage and scream as loud as I can and only the center and maybe the guards can hear me. The tackles can't hear me and the receivers don't have a clue what I'm saying. When we audible, I give the signal first to Dave Alexander and he passes the play to the other linemen. I'll use hand signals to give the receivers the play and then I'll turn around and shout it out to Herschel and Heath in the backfield.

The touchdown to Barnett is all the offense the Eagles can muster in the first half, as the Saints take a 17-7 lead behind Hebert, who passes for 187 yards in the half.

The Saints were controlling the clock on us in the first half. But we're not quitters. We were down, but we knew sooner or later the offense or defense would come up with a big play and we'd be back in the game.

The Eagles receive the second-half kickoff and the offense takes over on the 20. Kotite finally opens up the offense and Randall begins throwing and the offense begins moving the ball downfield. Randall completes four straight passes and then Sherman runs for 11 yards to give the Eagles a first down at the Saints' 25. On the next play, Randall drops back, but Ricky Jackson races around the right tackle and slams into Randall, knocking the ball loose. The Saints recover on their own 31 and promptly march down the field and kick a field goal for a 20-7 lead with 7:28 to play in the third quarter.

After the Eagles' offense is stopped on three plays, the defense finally comes up with the big play that Randall predicted as Eric Allen picks off a Hebert pass and the Eagles take over on their own 38. The offense begins moving again and Randall keeps throwing and connecting with his receivers, but the drive ends at the New Orleans' 23 and Ruzek hits a field goal to cut the lead to 20-10 with 1:01 left in the third quarter.

The Eagles' defense continues to gain momentum and stops the

Saints on three plays. The offense takes over on its own 36 after a 12-yard punt return by Sikahema. On first down, Randall goes deep to Barnett, but he is well covered and the pass is incomplete. Still, this stretches out the Saints' defense and opens things up for Randall and he remains hot. On second down Randall hits Sherman for five yards and then connects on a quick out to Williams for eight yards and a first down. Sherman runs for seven and two yards on the next two plays, setting up a third-and-one on the Saints' 42. From the shotgun, Randall hits Byars for seven yards and a first down at the 35.

After an incomplete pass, the Eagles are called for holding and face a second-and-20 from the 45. Randall connects with Byars for nine yards and then goes deep to Barnett one more time. Barnett is double covered as he races down the left sideline and into the end zone. But Randall throws the ball anyway and Barnett leaps up, grabs the ball at the apex of his leap and clutches it to his chest for a spectacular catch that cuts the New Orleans' lead to 20-17 four minutes into the fourth quarter.

As soon as I walked up to the line of scrimmage, I could see the blitz coming from the left side. I looked over at Freddie and gave him a nod. He could see the blitz and he knew what I wanted him to do: run a fade. I could see the safety leaning in Freddie's direction, so first I gave a pump fake toward Calvin to freeze the safety for a second and then I threw it to Freddie. As soon as I let go of the ball I got nailed from behind and went down. I threw the ball where only Freddie could get it and he went up in the air and made a great catch. That shows how much confidence I have in Freddie. I know if I put the ball in a position where he can go up and get it, nine out of 10 times he'll make the catch.

Fred Barnett: Randall puts the ball up because he has faith in me that I'll go up and get the ball.

The funny thing is, on the sideline right before that series, I was sitting next to Freddie. We looked at each other and I said, "You know we're going to win this game," and he smiled and said, "I was just about to say the same thing." We just knew we were going to win.

On the Saints' next possession, the big plays continue for the Eagles. Seth Joyner picks off an Hebert pass and returns it 20 yards to the New Orleans' 26. From here the Eagles' offensive line—Heller, Brian Baldinger (who is filling in for an injured Schad at left guard), Alexander, Floyd and Davis—begin to take over the game. On first down Sherman runs for two yards and after an offsides penalty on the Saints, Sherman bounces outside for four yards and a first down at the 15. Two more Sherman runs set up a third-and-one from the six. Sherman gets the ball again, and behind an excellent block from Baldinger, races into the left corner of the end zone for the score and a 24-20 Eagles' lead with 6:48 to play.

The Saints get the ball back on their own 20 and immediately begin moving backwards. On third down, Hebert drops back to pass, but Reggie White storms around the left side and drops him in the end zone for a safety and a 26-20 Eagles' lead.

The Saints are forced to kick off from their own 20 after the safety and the Eagles take over on their own 38 and begin running the ball right down the Saints' throat before Ruzek comes out and nails a 39-yard field goal to give the Eagles a 29-20 lead with 2:36 to play.

On New Orleans' next possession, Allen comes up with another big play as he steps in front of a Hebert pass and races 19 yards for a touchdown. The Eagles—who have just scored 29 straight points— lead 36-20 with 2:17 to play.

After completing just 5-of-15 passes for 77 yards in the first half, Randall completed 14-of-20 for 142 yards in the second half—19-of-35 for 219 in all. After the game, Randall tells the media: "It was great. It's just great to win. We've been through a lot of adversity this year, but now we just go out and have fun and enjoy the game. We love it. I think when you're enjoying whatever you do for a living, you're going to be successful at it. We don't panic when we get behind. When you panic, it seems like you take yourself out of your own element. But we just keep on plugging and having fun and that was the difference."

All week before the game, the media kept talking about us not being able to win the big games and saying I couldn't win a playoff game. They kept asking me about it over and over. "Why can't you win the big game," one reporter asked me and I shut him up. I said, "First of all, the question is why can't we win the big game, not why can't I win the big game." The quarterback gets all the publicity when his team wins and all the blame when his team loses. But that's not the way it is. Each and every guy on this team is responsible for us winning or losing. I told the media it was time they realized that Randall Cunningham doesn't carry this team alone. Buddy Ryan expected his "big name" players to carry the team and when Buddy was here we did what we had to do and came up with a lot of big plays. Now we realize that the "big name" players have to set the tone, but it's up to every guy to contribute and help us win. That's exactly what we did today. Freddie and Heath and Keith Byars all came up with some big plays, but if the offensive line hadn't played so well, we wouldn't have been able to do anything. On defense, Seth and Reggie and Eric came up with big plays, but everyone contributed and that's why the defense was able to shut out New Orleans in the second half.

Yeah, there was a lot of pressure to win after we lost the last three times we were in the playoffs. But we don't care about pressure or about what people write in the newspaper or say on television. We go out and play. Reggie, Seth and I go out and have fun and when we go out and have fun, that's when we win.

Earlier in the season, when people said I wasn't playing well (I was playing average), I think one of the reasons was that Richie was putting a lot of pressure on me and football wasn't as much fun as it used to be. For example, some people on the team were saying that I wasn't concentrating and I was calling plays wrong after Zeke signalled them in from the bench. Later, I found out that Richie had one of his assistants in the huddle during practices checking to make sure I called the plays right—the way they are written down on the list of plays we prepare for every game. The problem was, Zeke didn't always signal the play in exactly the way it was written on the script. Sometimes the play was written wrong and Zeke spotted it and changed it when he signalled it in. Or sometimes Zeke made little changes in the play to make it work better. The problem is, none of the coaches except Zeke know the signals. So if a play is called, the other coaches read it off the script and expect Zeke to signal it in exactly the way it's written. Because they don't understand the signals, they don't realize it's Zeke—not me—changing the plays when he signals them in.

One day in practice, Zeke signalled a Slot Ace Right Slip 19 Special Weak Hot Right. But on the script, it's written: Slot Ace Right Slip 19 Special Weak Hot Left. Zeke knew this, but he called it to the right—which means the motion man goes right, away from where we intended to throw the pass—because he realized the play was written down wrong on the script and would be more effective if we ran it hot right. Dick Wood was standing in the huddle when I called the play—just like Zeke signalled it in—and starts saying, "No, no, no, it's supposed to be hot left." That's when I began to realize that Dick's job was to stand in the huddle and make sure I was calling the plays right and he didn't even know the signals. Early in the season, we had a play where Herschel was supposed to run out to the right and the line shifts over and blocks the left side, so I don't have to worry about my blind side. If the blitz comes, I go to Herschel—the hot receiver—on the right side. At some point during the season, the play got changed so that the line was sliding over to the right side, which was where Herschel was heading. So I changed the play and ran it the way we used to run it. The coaches second-guessed me on that one too. I went to Richie and he told me I was right and he changed the play back to the way we had been running it.

I know that sometimes I make mistakes—I'm not perfect. But it adds a lot of pressure when you have someone hovering over you watching you and checking everything you do.

This book is about Randall Cunningham, not about Richie Kotite and I don't want it to sound like I'm picking on Richie—I'm not. Richie is a coach who likes to have total control of everything and that includes his quarterback. I have no problem with that. In 1990, when Buddy Ryan was the head coach and Richie was the offensive coordinator, I had more freedom with the offense because sometimes Buddy would just tell me to run the offense and make things happen. Now, people may think I have the same control of the offense, but I don't and I can't do some of the things I'd like to do. Richie runs this team and controls this offense. Nothing passes by Richie. If Buddy had been the coach when I got caught sneaking out of the hotel, he might have said, "I know you snuck out last night, you're not that slick. But since we won anyway, maybe you should sneak out before every game." With Richie, it was, "You're fined and that's that." I'm not saying one way is better than the other. Richie and Buddy are two completely different people and coaches and both of them are excellent coaches. But I did have more freedom in 1990.

The last four or five games of the season, I decided to go out and play the way I used to, which meant I was loose and relaxed and tried to have fun. Before the New Orleans game, Richie came up to me and said go out and play loose. He said he didn't want anyone being tight. That's what I needed to hear. Richie allowed me to play my game and that's when we get the best out of me.

C H A P T E R
16

The Eagles are in Dallas to face the Cowboys in the second round of the playoffs. The 13-3 Cowboys won the NFC East and are the NFL's up-and-coming team, but still many of the so-called experts are saying they are still a year away and that the San Francisco 49ers are the best team in the NFC and NFL. The Cowboys' defense is ranked number one in the NFC and their potent offense is led by Pro Bowlers Troy Aikman, Emmitt Smith, Michael Irvin and Jay Novacek and an improving offense line that is beginning to dominate games. The Eagles know they have a tough task ahead to beat the Cowboys in Dallas.

After the New Orleans win we were very pumped up and confident. We had momentum and were fired up and ready to play the Cowboys. Before the game, I felt great. I was pumped, but I was calm. We went out onto the field before the game and the Dallas fans started booing and that got us even more pumped up. We got the ball to start the game and started moving the ball down the field.

The Eagles take possession on their own 29 and begin moving. After a first down, the Cowboys appear to jump offsides on a third-and-four play, but the referee rules a false start on Alexander, saying he moved the ball before he snapped it to draw the defense offsides. Replays show that Alexander never moved the ball. On third-and-nine, the Cowboys blitz and, under pressure, Randall hits his safety valve out of the backfield—Herschel—but he is stopped after five yards and the Eagles line up to punt. On the punt, the Cowboys jump offsides again; this time it is called, and the Eagles have a first down at their own 41.

Randall hits Herschel in the flat for eight yards and Sherman runs for two more and a first down at the Dallas 49. Randall hits Barnett for seven and then Herschel reels off runs of nine, 14 and two yards to set up a second-and-eight at the 15. Off a play-action fake, Randall rolls left, but defensive end Charles Haley isn't fooled —or blocked—and has a clear shot at Randall. Randall tries to run around him and throw the ball to Byars, but Haley hits Randall's arm just as he releases, and the ball skids to the turf. On third down, Randall has to escape pressure again, rolls right, and thinks about running for an instant, then pulls up and tries to hit Williams in the end zone, but the pass is a little off target. Ruzek connects on a 32-yard field goal for a 3-0 Philadelphia lead.

On the second-down play, we ran a naked bootleg. On the play, Freddie comes in motion to the left and I faked to the right and then rolled left and looked to hit Freddie. But the defensive back was to the outside of Freddie and had him covered and Haley was coming right on me. I saw Byars starting to come clear in the end zone and I was trying to throw it to him, but Haley made a good play and grabbed my arm just as I threw it. On the next play, I was scrambling and was about to run, but I saw the linebacker coming and didn't think I could get the first down. I saw Calvin in the end zone and thought I had a chance to hit him, but I threw it a little wide and we had to settle for a field goal. When I got to the sideline, Richie

told me I should have just tucked the ball away and run on both of those plays. Trust me, I'm going to run when I have a chance to run, and I didn't on either of those plays. Before the game, Richie tells me to drop back, make my reads and throw the ball downfield, bing, bing, bing, and I'd cut them up like a surgeon. Then the game starts and I try to do that, but their rush is getting to me and Richie tells me to start running the ball. But I couldn't. For the most part, the Cowboys were rushing four guys and were able to get a lot of pressure on me. Behind those four, they had a linebacker or two dropped back waiting for me to run.

After the Eagles' field goal, Dallas comes right back, as Aikman comes out throwing and the Cowboys move the ball down the field. On second-and-goal from the one, Aikman fakes a handoff to Smith, steps back and hits wide-open tight end Derek Tennell for a 7-3 lead.

There is an interesting call on the Eagles' second possession, as two Cowboys on the left side of the defensive line jump into the neutral zone before the snap. Eagles' guard Eric Floyd stands up and the referee blows the whistle. It looks like an obvious encroachment penalty on the Cowboys. But the referee calls the Eagles for a false start and explains, "We had the defense jumping into the neutral zone [and] number 61 on the offense moved. This is a false start, a five-yard penalty (against the Eagles). If this happens hereafter in the ball game the penalty is on the defense."

We knew the penalty was on them, but then the referees turned around and called it on us and said the next time it would be on them. What does that mean? Are they going to take turns calling the penalties and the first one is on us? At that point, we began to believe that we were going to be cheated out of the game and some guys were even saying when teams play in Dallas the chances of winning are slim and none. I'm not going to go that far, but I do know that when you play the 49ers in San Francisco, you're not going to beat them that often. There were games we played this season where the opposing team's offense didn't get any holding penalties called on them. These guys are taught to hold and Reggie gets held on almost every play. All of this started in the mid-1980s when we became a very aggressive team and people started labelling us as dirty. That's when we started getting a lot of penalties called on us. So then they call this penalty on us and it was like, "Here we go again," and we started believing we had to beat not only the Cowboys and all their fans, but the referees too.

Both team's offenses struggle as the first half continues, as both defenses play aggressive, hard-hitting football. The Eagles' running attack isn't gaining many yards and the offensive line isn't having much luck stopping the Cowboys' defense line, which includes a rotation of eight players. "We came after them," Cowboys' defensive end Jim Jeffcoat said. "We used our depth to wear them down."

With just over three minutes to play in the first half, the Eagles face a third-and-11 from midfield. Randall lines up in the shotgun and while he's looking at his receivers and still calling signals, Alexander snaps the ball, which hits Randall in the shoulder and bounces to his left. A wild chase for the ball ensues before it finally rolls out of bounds and the Eagles are forced to punt.

That play was my fault. Up to that point in the game, I was under the center on every play and we had been using a silent snap count because of the crowd noise. When we use the silent snap count in the shotgun, I lift my foot to signal to Dave I'm ready. He waits two, three or four seconds and snaps the ball and everybody reacts to the ball. But, at this point, we went into the shotgun for the first time. The crowd noise wasn't too loud and I thought I could call the signals and the snap without using the silent snap count. But I didn't tell Dave, which was my mistake. When I call the signals verbally, when I lift my foot, this tells guys to go into motion. When I lifted my foot, Byars started to go into motion. But then I looked at the clock and time was running out, so I turned to Byars to tell him to stop and get set and that's when Dave snapped the ball and it hit me on the left shoulder and started rolling away from me. When we got to the sidelines I told Dave it was my fault and that was that. Earlier in the game, Dave made a mistake, snapping the ball on one instead of three. I'm not the type to holler at someone when they make a mistake, so I just held up three fingers and nodded at Dave and he knew what I meant. Everyone makes mistakes and I'm not going to holler at someone on the field and embarrass them. That's not my style.

After the Eagles' punt, Dallas takes over on its own 33 with 3:03 remaining in the half. Aikman goes deep to Alvin Harper for 41 yards and a first down at the Eagles' 14. After Aikman scrambles for eight yards, he hits tight end Jay Novacek for the touchdown and a 14-3 lead with 47 seconds remaining in the half.

Sikahema fumbles the ensuing kickoff and the Cowboys recover on the Eagles' 29. The clock runs out on the Cowboys and they settle for a 20-yard field goal and a 17-3 halftime lead.

The Cowboys receive the second half kickoff and promptly march 70 yards for another touchdown and a 24-7 lead and the game and season appear to be slipping away from the Eagles. The Cowboys up their lead to 34-3 in the fourth quarter before Randall hits Williams with an 18-yard scoring pass late in the game. On the play, Randall played tag with two Cowboys defenders—Russell Maryland and Chad Hennings, who each missed him twice—before he finds Williams in the end zone.

Randall, who is sacked five times, completes 17-of-30 passes for 160 yards and runs for 22 more in the game.

"It was one of those days," Randall tells the media after the game. "I feel bad, and I feel bad for everyone. We just never got anything going after the first drive. Give Dallas credit. They played a great game."

"We lose, we all lose together," Kotite says. "[Randall] didn't have a banner day, but also I do believe there were times when he

made some excellent throws. He did have a lot of pressure most of the game and it just didn't work."

We went into the game with a great game plan and a great blocking scheme to stop Dallas. But sometimes guys just get beat physically by the man across from them. All week, before the game, people were asking if Dallas having a week off to prepare and rest for the game would make a difference. I kept answering I didn't think it would. But in the end, it did make a difference. During the course of the year, we played five preseason games—which is too many—16 very tough regular season games and two playoff games. That wears on you by the end of the season, especially when you play in the NFC East—the toughest, most physical conference in the entire NFL. I don't want to make excuses, but we lost Jerome, Keith Jackson; we had injuries to both our starting safeties—Wes Hopkins and Andre Waters—and Ben Smith, our starting cornerback, never came back from his 1991 knee injury. Plus, everyone else on the team was nicked up. With about four or five weeks left in the season, I thought I broke my hand, but I wouldn't let them take any X-rays. I could still throw the ball without too much pain, so I figured there was no reason to take an X-ray just to find out it was broken and have the doctors and trainers tell me I couldn't play any more. Toward the end of the Dallas game, my hand swelled up pretty bad, but I could still throw the ball and wasn't about to come out.

Even though we lost to Dallas, we accomplished a lot this season. We fought through a lot of adversity and controversy. Last year, in week 15, we had to beat Dallas at home to make the playoffs but we lost. This year, in week 15, we beat the Redskins at home for a playoff berth. Richie said that when the pressure was on and we had to win big games against Minnesota and Washington, we stepped up and won. And then we went to New Orleans, got behind, came back and won. I'm not satisfied just because we made the playoffs and won one game; we weren't going to settle for anything less than a

Super Bowl win. But we got beat by a better team and I'll be the first to admit that. In the playoffs, what it comes down to is which team has the best players and coaching staff and great offensive and defensive lines.

One of the things I've learned this year is there are some things I can control and some things I can't. I control my own destiny by working as hard as I can in the off-season and in practice and by studying and preparing for games the way Doug Scovil taught me. But I can't control how this team is run. I can't control who gets paid what or what free agents we sign or how we run the offense. My job is to go out and do the best I can and when it's time for changes to be made, I want to know that I've done the best that I can do and I'll let the chips fall where they may. My first responsibility is to God to be the best person I can be, then to my family and then to my team and then the public. I try to be a nice guy all the time and the old saying goes that nice guys finish last. I don't mind finishing last as long as I know I'm doing the right thing. That's where my blessings come from, from doing the right thing and living my life as well as I can.

So when people ask me whether the offense should do this or that or be run this way or that way, or if we should re-sign Reggie White, my answer is: I have no control over any of that. Norman Braman owns this team and he hires the coaches he thinks will do the best job for the team. This is Rich Kotite's football team and I'm going to do things the way Richie wants me to do them. That's the bottom line. When it was Buddy's team I did things Buddy's way and now I do them Richie's way.

postscript

Everything you've read in this book is from my heart. In 1992 there was a big deal made about me coming back from my injury. In the beginning of the season we did well and there was a lot of praise. Then we lost a couple of tough games and the finger got pointed at me. Later I got benched and the criticism increased. But I wasn't about to give up. I'm not a quitter and I kept working as hard as I could and did everything I could to help the Eagles win.

Although there was a lot of pressure on the team as a whole, the bulk of the publicity was on two people: Richie Kotite and Randall Cunningham. So a lot of what you read in this book was the frustration that we both went through. Already, since the season has ended, my relationship with Richie has totally changed. All during the season, it seemed like once or twice a week he would call me into his office and tell me I couldn't do this or I couldn't do that. He was being like a protective father and I don't think either of us realized it at the time. He was looking out for my interests and when that happens, and somebody knows your potential and wants so much for you to do well, they can be overbearing and it can actually come off negatively. When we talked after the season, he was very upbeat and positive and said he wanted me to spend time with Zeke Bratkowski, who was our quarterbacks coach and was promoted to offensive coordinator after the 1992 season. I said no problem, I was anxious to get to work with Zeke. Richie and I are back on the same page.

When I first talked to Zeke I congratulated him and he told me how fired up he was. He said we're really going to put things together and make this offense work. I asked him what he had in mind and he said we were going to mix things up and throw the ball more on first down so teams wouldn't know what to expect, but at the same time utilize all of my talents. I was fired up by the time we finished talking.

Right now I feel so comfortable playing for Richie and working with Zeke. They both know I'm 100 percent committed to winning. I play best when I'm happy and right now I am. A few weeks ago, in Las Vegas, Mr. Braman and I sat down and talked for a long time. We're close friends and we respect each other and know better than to believe the things we read in the paper, like the stories saying the Eagles were trying to trade me. Mr. Braman wants to win a Super Bowl and he has a philosophy that he's going to use to try and help this team get there. He's going to do the best he can operating under the new agreement between the owners and the players and the new free agency and upcoming salary cap. We might lose a few players— we already lost Reggie White to the Green Bay Packers and Jim McMahon to the Vikings, and I'll miss them both very much—but we'll sign a few new players, get a lot of draft choices as compensation for losing star players and make this a younger and hopefully better football team. What it all comes down to is dollars and with the salary cap coming in 1994 it's impossible to keep too many high-priced players.

The way I look at it, I work for Norman Braman and play for Richie. But the main thing is I play for God and I will never lose sight of that. God will lead me in the right direction and hopefully to the Super Bowl.

My Aunt Nettie is a very good judge of character and at one point during the season, she sat me down and said, "Randall, stop being so hard on yourself." She told me to live my life and be happy and to stop dragging myself down by trying to do everything and be everything for everybody. She told me to take the time to do things for myself and enjoy my life. I tried to tell her I was already like that, but she broke me down and said, "Look, your mother would roll over in her grave if I didn't tell you this. I have to tell you. You're like a son to me and I want you to be happy." Next to my mother, Aunt Nettie is the strongest woman I have ever met and she knows me better than anyone. She told me not to get caught up in all the little stuff and to let myself be happy. Tears came to her eyes and she said my mother had asked her to look out for her babies before she died.

A week ago I was in Santa Barbara and went to visit my parents' gravesite. I told them I loved them and missed them and tears came to my eyes and I got all choked up and couldn't talk. I regained my composure and then told them about how I was getting married soon and how I wished they could be there with me on that day. I told them they would love Felicity. They never liked any of the girls I dated in high school. That's the way parents are—overly protective. But I know they would love Felicity like she was their own daughter. I told them that and started crying all over again. I tried to hold back my tears, but finally I just gave in and let them flow. I figured why hold back, these are tears of joy because I know I can come visit my parents and let them know how happy I am.

A week later, yesterday in fact, was the dedication of the youth center at St. John the Baptist Church in Camden. This was another big day for me. There were about 4,000 people gathered for the dedication ceremonies, including Governor James Florio, Mayor Aaron Thompson, and of course, Reverend Townsend. I had to deliver a speech and after I finished reading it, I felt so positive and upbeat and when I stepped away from the microphone I knew that this was what God wanted me to say and that this youth center was what he wanted me to build.

During my speech, I spotted Zeke in the crowd and introduced him to the audience as someone who is very important to me. I

didn't ask Zeke to come—he came on his own and it was a wonderful thing. His being there and supporting me meant more to me and my career than he could ever know.

While I was reading my speech, I could see a lot of people smiling and that showed me that now—in 1993—I'm happy and can achieve anything I put my mind to. The 1992 season is over. It was a hard struggle, but now it's behind me and it's time for Randall Cunningham to take his life to the next step. Right now I'm the happiest I've ever been in my life. I have a beautiful fiancée and on May 8, 1993, Felicity and I will be married. My faith in God will keep me strong and I'll always continue to push forward and strive to be the best person I can be. When I fall off course, I'll reach out to God and he'll help me get back on course. God is always there for you.

Randall Cunningham
April 1993